London's Hidden Walks 3

by Stephen Millar

Volume 3

London's Hidden Walks 3

Written by Stephen Millar
Photography by Stephen Millar, Chris Dorney & Tony Whyte
Cover Photograph by Chris Dorney
Edited by Abigail Willis
Additional research by Tony Whyte and Steven Magee
Book design by Lesley Gilmour and Susi Koch
Illustrations by Lesley Gilmour

All rights reserved. No part of this publication may be reproduced, stored in a retrieval system or transmitted in any form or by any means electronic, mechanical, photocopying, recording or otherwise without the prior consent of the publishers and copyright owners. Every effort has been made to ensure the accuracy of this book; however, due to the nature of the subject the publishers cannot accept responsibility for any errors which occur, or their consequences.

2nd edition published in 2024 by Metro Publications Ltd
www.metropublications.com

Metro® is a registered trade mark of Associated Newspapers Limited. The METRO mark is under licence from Associated Newspapers Limited.

Printed and bound in India.
This book is produced using
paper from registered sustainable
and managed sources.

MIX
Paper from responsible sources
FSC® C043100

© Stephen Millar
British Library Cataloguing in Publication Data. A catalogue record for this book is available from the British Library.

ISBN 978-1-902910-76-5

For the kids

Acknowledgements

As with the previous volume, both Chris Dorney (www.chrisdorney.com) and Tony Whyte contributed excellent photographs that really help to give a flavour of the walks. From reader responses to the last two books, I realise how important the photographs are in helping to imagine the route before setting off on the walk. I also greatly appreciated the feedback Tony and Chris gave as they literally followed in my footsteps, my draft walk (and sometimes umbrella) in hand. Thanks also to Steve Magee who kindly walked the routes for this new edition and provided updates.

Finally a big thank you to Metro for their continuing support and specialist local knowledge, in particular their contribution to the Hackney walk.

Contents

Introduction 1
Area Map 2-3
1. **Belgravia Walk** 4-33
2. **Islington Walk** 34-71
3. **Highgate Walk** 72-95
4. **Paddington & Marylebone Walk** 96-127
5. **Hammersmith & Chiswick Walk** 128-159
6. **Brixton & Brockwell Park Walk** 160-191
7. **Lambeth North & Borough Walk** 192-221
8. **Greenwich Walk** 222-261
9. **North Greenwich
    & Silvertown Walk** 262-289
10. **Whitechapel & Bow Walk** 290-335
11. **Bethnal Green
    & Hackney Wick Walk** 336-367
12. **Lee Valley & Olympic Park Walk** 368-383
Index 384-391

The Dove, Hammersmith to Chiswick Walk, see p.128-p.159

Introduction

After covering 25 hidden London walks in quick succession in volumes 1 and 2, I needed a break. Two years passed as I tried to rest my weary legs and recharge my batteries. It was with some hesitation that I began planning volume 3 – trying to piece together rewarding routes through parts of London I had not yet covered.

I began (of course) by opening up a large map of London and identifying those gaps. I also decided to tackle head on areas that I had previously shied away from: Greenwich, already covered so well in more mainstream guides; Walworth and Hackney – less well trodden for some perhaps but worthy of walking and Islington – well, how does anyone start a walk in a place with such a rich history?

Gradually however, I remembered what my past experience of researching London walks had taught me. Areas that I thought I knew well, invariably yielded something new and fascinating; areas I had prejudices about or thought potentially bland, would always prove rewarding and changed my view of that part of London forever.

My personal highlights include the mysteries of the Bow Back Rivers whose geography continues to both intrigue and baffle me; the surreal, other-worldliness of Silvertown; a windmill in Brixton and the Lambeth work house where a young Charlie Chaplin once wept for his mother.

London is a vibrant place – a world City, but one also haunted by memories, atmospheres and traces of the past. Everywhere, if you walk patiently and without haste, and look around enough, you too will notice things that so many others fail to see – a plaque on a wall recalling a long-forgotten society or a ghost advertisement announcing a by-gone product. I hope these walks give you the opportunity, perhaps even the excuse, to create the necessary space to see things slightly differently.

I would therefore encourage you to choose, sometimes, the walk that least appeals to you. It is often these walks and experiences that end up being the most memorable and you will nearly always view the district visited in a different light.

Once again, I look forward to readers' emails in response to this third collection of walks. Your feedback so far has been enormously useful. I hope you find some treasures that I have missed and make the routes your own. Let me know how you get on.

Stephen Millar   stephenwmillar@hotmail.com

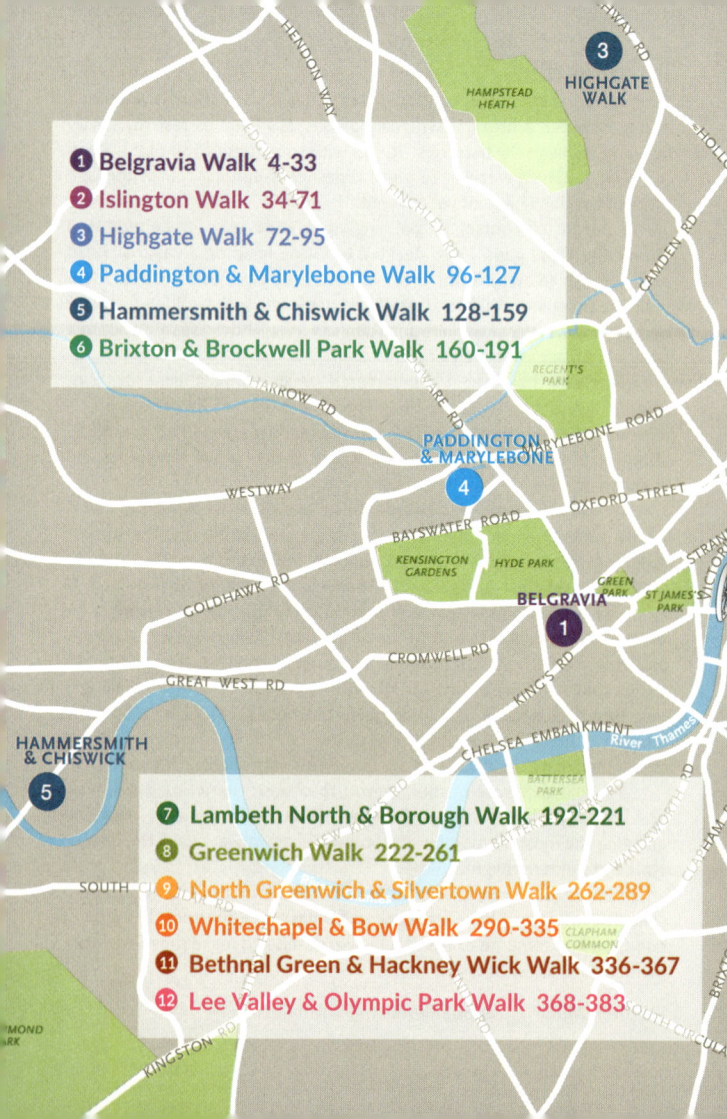

1. **Belgravia Walk** 4-33
2. **Islington Walk** 34-71
3. **Highgate Walk** 72-95
4. **Paddington & Marylebone Walk** 96-127
5. **Hammersmith & Chiswick Walk** 128-159
6. **Brixton & Brockwell Park Walk** 160-191
7. **Lambeth North & Borough Walk** 192-221
8. **Greenwich Walk** 222-261
9. **North Greenwich & Silvertown Walk** 262-289
10. **Whitechapel & Bow Walk** 290-335
11. **Bethnal Green & Hackney Wick Walk** 336-367
12. **Lee Valley & Olympic Park Walk** 368-383

AREA MAP

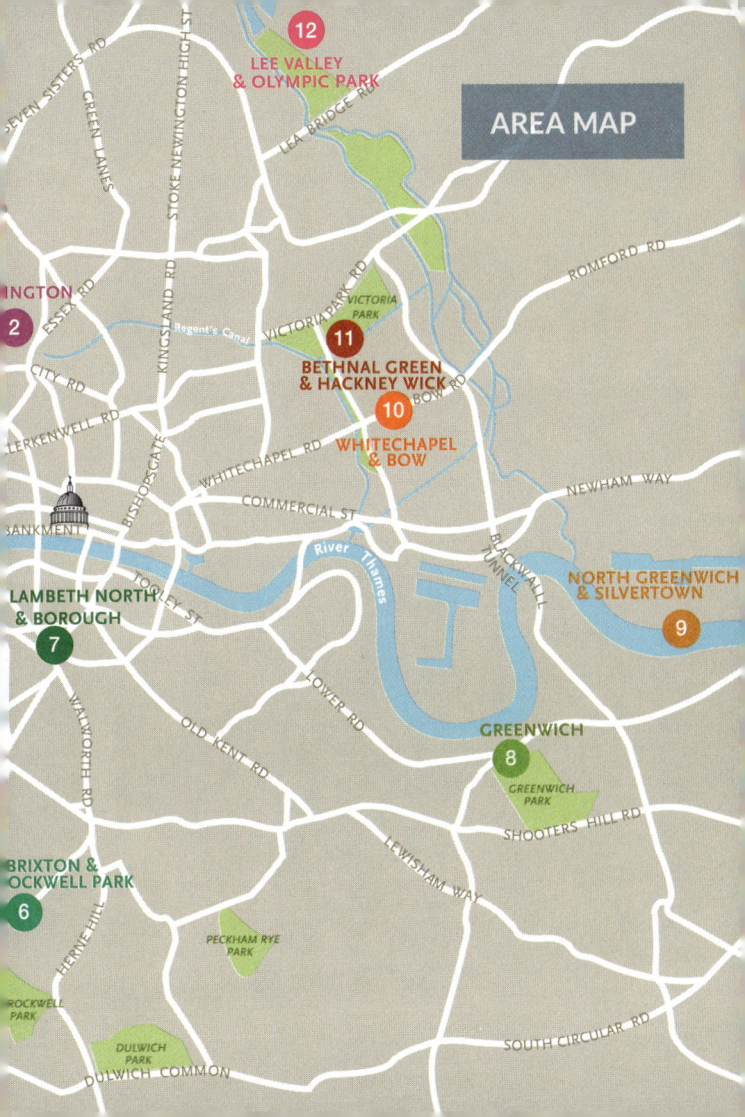

- **12** LEE VALLEY & OLYMPIC PARK
- **2** ISLINGTON
- **11** BETHNAL GREEN & HACKNEY WICK
- **10** WHITECHAPEL & BOW
- **7** LAMBETH NORTH & BOROUGH
- **9** NORTH GREENWICH & SILVERTOWN
- **8** GREENWICH
- **6** BRIXTON & ROCKWELL PARK

Grenadier public house, see p.30

1 Belgravia Walk

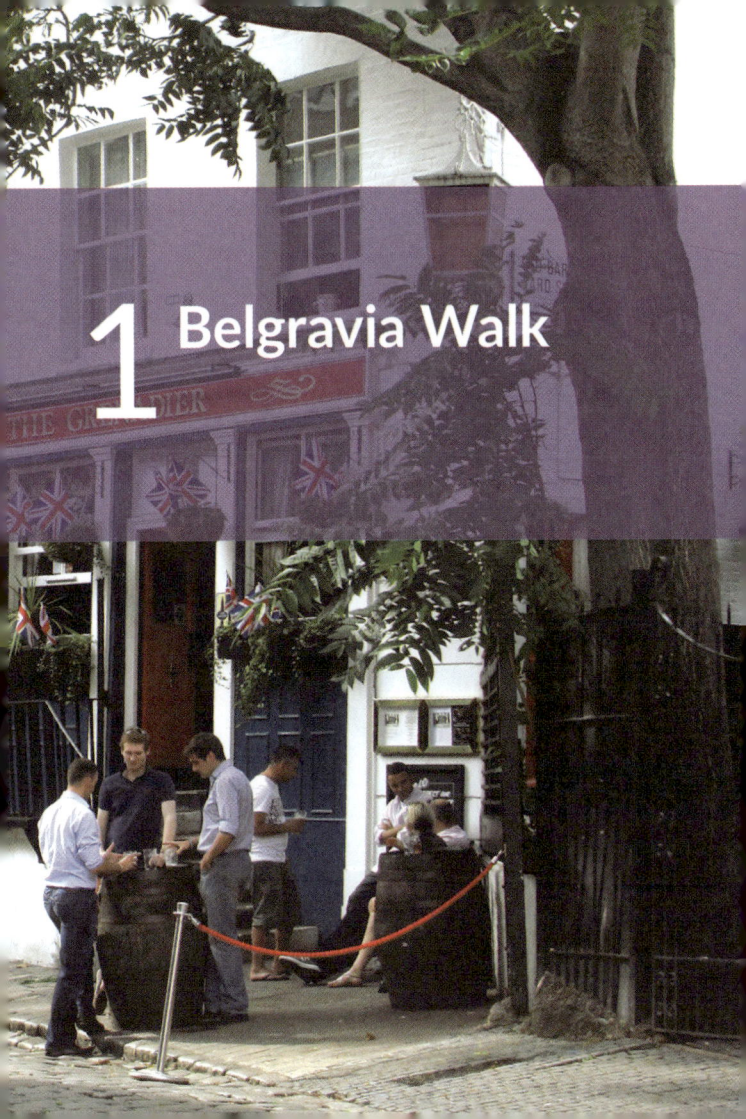

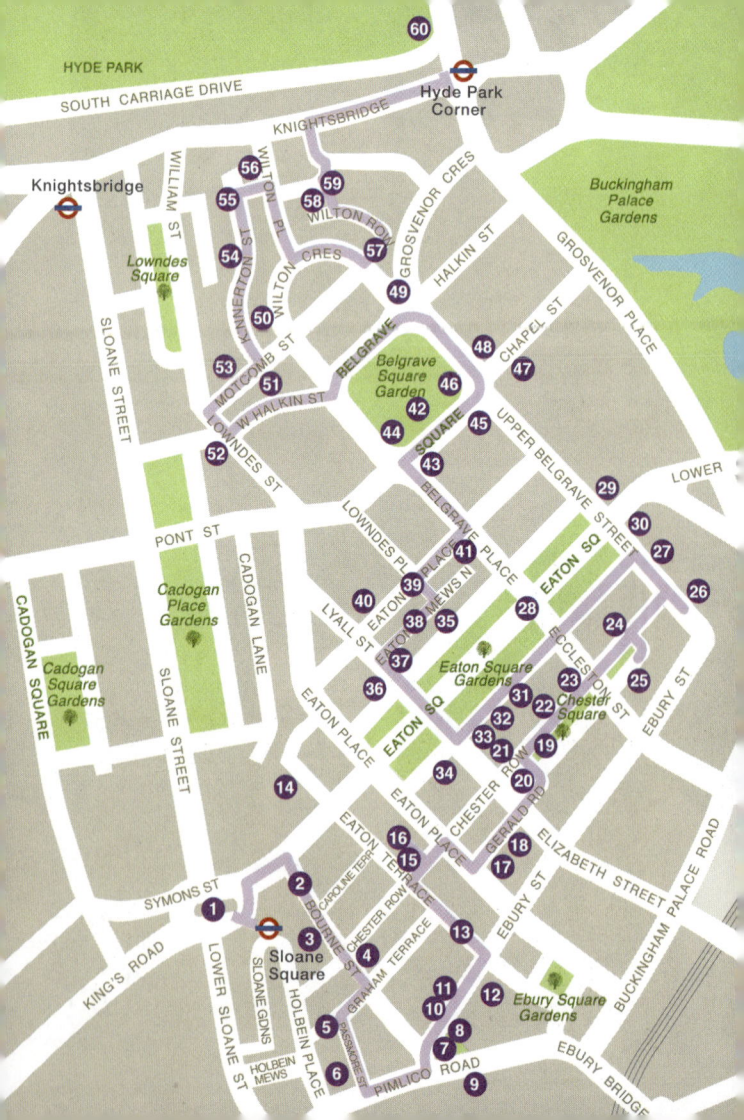

Map of Belgravia and Sloane Square area

Parks and Squares:
- Hyde Park
- Hyde Park Corner
- Knightsbridge
- Buckingham Palace Gardens
- Lowndes Square
- Belgrave Square Garden
- Cadogan Place Gardens
- Cadogan Square Gardens
- Eaton Square Gardens
- Sloane Square
- Ebury Square Gardens

Streets:
- South Carriage Drive
- Knightsbridge
- William St
- Wilton Pl
- Wilton Row
- Wilton Cres
- Grosvenor Cres
- Grosvenor Place
- Kinnerton St
- Halkin St
- Chapel St
- Motcomb St
- W. Halkin St
- Belgrave Square
- Upper Belgrave Street
- Lowndes St
- Sloane Street
- Pont St
- Cadogan Lane
- Lowndes Place
- Belgrave Place
- Eaton Mews N
- Eaton Sq
- Eaton Place
- Lyall St
- Eaton Mews S
- Chester Row
- Eccleston St
- Chester Square
- Ebury St
- Eaton Terrace
- Caroline Terrace
- Bourne St
- Chester Row
- Graham Terrace
- Gerald Rd
- Elizabeth Street
- Buckingham Palace Road
- Symons St
- King's Road
- Lower Sloane St
- Sloane Gdns
- Holbein Pl
- Holbein Mews
- Passmore St
- Pimlico Road
- Ebury Bridge
- Cadogan Square

Belgravia Walk

1. Sloane Square
2. Bourne Street
3. Tradesmens entrance
4. St Mary's Bourne Street
5. Fox & Hounds public house
6. Lumley Buildings
7. Wolfgang Amadeus Mozart
8. Coleshill Buildings
9. Orange public house
10. Harold Nicolson & Vita Sackville-West (plaque)
11. Young Mozart (plaque)
12. Cundy Street Flats
13. Eaton Terrace
14. Antelope public house
15. Duke of Wellington
16. Minera Mews
17. Noel Coward (plaque)
18. Former police station (plaque)
19. Chester Square
20. St Michael's Church
21. Guy Burgess (plaque)
22. Mary Shelley (plaque)
23. Harold Macmillan (plaque)
24. Matthew Arnold (plaque)
25. Margaret Thatcher (plaque)
26. Plumber's Arms public house
27. No 46 Lower Belgrave Street
28. Eaton Square
29. Church of St Peter
30. Lord Boothby (plaque)
31. Neville Chamberlain (plaque)
32. Prince Metternich (plaque)
33. Lord John Russell (plaque)
34. Vivien Leigh (plaque)
35. Stanley Baldwin (plaque)
36. George Peabody (plaque)
37. Heraldic wheatsheaf
38. Eaton Mews North
39. Eaton Place
40. No 65 Eaton Place
41. No 36 Eaton Place
42. Belgrave Square
43. Norwegian Embassy
44. Christopher Columbus
45. Viscount Gort (plaque)
46. Simon Bolivar
47. Brian Epstein (plaque)
48. Italian Cultural Institute
49. Sir Robert Grosvenor
50. Earl & Countess Mountbatten (plaque)
51. Spire of the Belfry
52. C Hoare & Co
53. Pantechnicon building
54. Nag's Head public house
55. Wilton Arms public house
56. Lillie Langtry (plaque)
57. Wilton Row
58. Grenadier public house
59. Old Barrack Yard
60. Achilles

Belgravia Walk

Start: Sloane Square underground station
Finish: Hyde Park underground station
Distance: 2.9 miles

The walk begins at Sloane Square tube station where you come out into ❶ **Sloane Square**. This marks the south-west corner of the district of Belgravia, named after the small village of Belgrave in the county of Cheshire. Belgrave is situated on the Eaton Estate whose principal residence – Eaton Hall – has long been the country seat of the Grosvenor family, currently headed by the seventh Duke of Westminster. There are few areas of London so associated with a single family, and Belgravia owes not just its name, but its very existence, to the patronage of the Grosvenors.

The Grosvenors came to England with William the Conqueror in 1066 and were just another aristocratic family until 1677, when the Cheshire baronet Sir Thomas Grosvenor married 12 year old Mary Davies. Mary brought with her a dowry that included several hundred acres of undeveloped fields that were part of Ebury Manor. These fields would later be developed into Mayfair, Pimlico and Belgravia. However in the 17th century the land here was mostly used for grazing and was intersected by rough roads that were plagued by thieves.

The Grosvenor family were not only fortunate but clever, holding onto their London acres just as the capital began to spread westwards. For many centuries London had centred around the City, but the Great Fire of 1666 and a surging population meant large-scale planned residential developments became common. These were primarily aimed at the wealthy who desired to live on well-planned new estates.

The Grosvenors began developing the fields around Mayfair for large, residential homes in the 1720s, but what became Belgravia

Belgravia Walk

remained rural until the 1820s. The district had previously been known as Five Fields because a number of paths divided the area into five parts, but in 1824 Richard Grosvenor, 2nd Marquess of Westminster (1795-1869) contracted Thomas Cubitt (1788-1855) to begin the development. Cubitt was a pioneering master builder who revolutionized the construction industry, developing a large-scale, well organized labour force capable of huge projects. He was responsible for transforming significant chunks of the capital during the 19th century, including parts of Bloomsbury and Buckingham Palace, Battersea Park and the Thames Embankment. Over the 30 years following his commission by the Grosvenors, Cubitt masterminded the development of the Belgravia estate so that it equalled the already prestigious district of Mayfair.

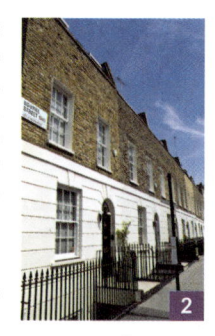

Follow the map out of the north-east corner of Sloane Square then turn almost immediately right down ❷ **Bourne Street**, named after the Westbourne River. Over the past few centuries, this 'lost' London river has been forced underground, but still flows from Hampstead, passing below Sloane Square, before reaching the Thames near Chelsea Bridge. You can see the large metal pipe which carries the river – above the platform at Sloane Square tube station. Along Bourne Street you will see the first of many expensive Belgravia properties.

Some of the cottages on this street were originally artisan dwellings however not many skilled workers could afford to live here now with properties on the street selling for upwards of £10 million. Evidence that Belgravia belongs to the upper classes can be seen just before number 93 on the right-hand side – the first of many signs you will see on this walk for ❸ **'Tradesmens Entrance'**.

Belgravia Walk

On the left-hand side look out for the elegant Catholic church of ❹ **St Mary's Bourne Street,** which dates from 1874 – it is deceptively small from the front but you can see more if you look down the road just after it. As Belgravia was developed, the Church of England, Catholic Church and other denominations became concerned about the potential spiritual vacuum that could exist in this new suburb. This led to a concerted drive to build new churches for use by the newly-arrived upper classes, as well as their domestic servants and the poor who still dominated some areas.

One clergyman who campaigned for new churches in the area was the Rev WJE Bennett, who wrote to his parishioners in 1844 appealing for construction funds. He described Ebury Street, Queen Street, Clifford's Row and New Grosvenor Place as being filled with a population of poor men, women and children, and urged 'Come with me into the lanes and streets of this great city. Come with me and visit the dens of infamy, and the haunts of vice, ignorance, filth and atheism with which it abounds'. It is hard to imagine the same streets being troubled by such poverty today.

Belgravia Walk

Carry on and a little further along turn right into Graham Terrace and then left into Passmore Street, with the ❺ **Fox and Hounds** pub on the corner – it dates from 1860 and claims the River Bourne, which runs beneath its cellar, helps the quality of its Guinness. Further down Passmore Street look out on the right for ❻ **Lumley Buildings**. This is an excellent example of 19th-century social housing in London. The flats were built in 1875 by the Improved Industrial Dwellings Company on land purchased from the Grosvenor Estate. The buildings were later acquired by the Peabody Trust (now branded Peabody) in 1984. The Trust was founded by the American banker and philanthropist George Peabody (1795-1869) in 1862 to provide social housing for those in need. Today it looks after 19,000 properties and we will see later on in the walk where George Peabody ended his days.

Continue on to reach Pimlico Road – full of chintzy boutiques, galleries and expensive coffee shops and restaurants. Turn left and shortly you reach a triangular area known as Orange Square. A farmer's market takes place here on Saturday mornings, and under the trees is a statue of ❼ **Wolfgang Amadeus Mozart** (1756-1791).

Mozart came with his family to London when he was eight years old, and was already a celebrated musical prodigy throughout much of Europe. He lived for a few weeks at number 180 Ebury Street during the summer of 1764. His father Leopold had brought his young son and daughter to play for the

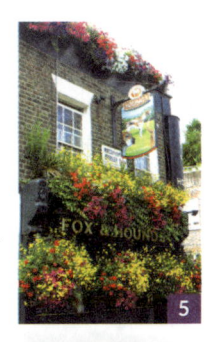

Court, and they also made numerous public performances as well as providing private lessons. Leopold fell dangerously ill and Wolfgang was forbidden to play the piano in the house to avoid disturbing his father. However, by the time the Mozart family were ready to return from Ebury Street to their original lodgings in Soho, the child prodigy had already completed his first symphony.

To the east of the statue look out for more evidence of 19th century social housing – the ❽ **Coleshill Buildings**. Built in 1871, by the Improved Industrial Dwellings Company and sponsored by the Grosvenor family, they originally housed 120 families and also incorporated ten shops at ground level.

Before Belgravia was developed, the area around here was a popular place for taverns, coffee shops and tea gardens as people travelled to Chelsea, particularly when the hugely popular Ranelagh Pleasure Gardens opened there in 1742. The name 'Orange Square' is probably derived from William of Orange who came to England in 1688 to depose the unloved James II. The famous Chelsea

Bun House also stood near here, its cakes and pastries (including the 'Chelsea Bun') ensuring that George II and George III were among its regular customers. It became a custom for Londoners to queue outside for 'cross buns' each Good Friday. On one occasion in the 1790s this resulted in 50,000 people gathering and the surrounding area came to a standstill.

Just south of Orange Square is ❾ **The Orange public house,** which provides a link to the area's 18th-century heyday. The archives of the Grosvenor Estate record a licence being given to the Orange Coffee House and Tavern in 1776, which stood approximately on the same site as today's public house.

Leave Orange Square and walk up Ebury Street, named after Ebury Farm that stood here before the street was developed in the 1820s. On the right you can see the elegant frontage of the Coleshill Buildings and on the left look out for two blue plaques that mark out neighbouring houses. These were once home to the writers ❿ **Harold Nicolson** and **Vita Sackville-West** (number 182) and the ⓫ **young Mozart** (number 180). As mentioned above, Mozart wrote his first symphony while at this address.

Opposite these houses look out for the ⓬ **Cundy Street Flats** – a classic, curvy construction that dates from 1952. They are named after Thomas Cundy (1790-1867) who succeeded his father as principal surveyor to the Grosvenor Estate and who worked closely with Cubitt during the development of Belgravia.

Belgravia Walk

Other notable people who have lived in Ebury Street include James Bond creator Ian Fleming who lived at number 22B. It was here in 1952 that he wrote the first Bond book, *Casino Royale*. It was also here that he entertained a string of young ladies, his rather aggressive tendencies resulting in the brother of one lady turning up at his flat with the purpose of horse-whipping the author, who was lucky enough to be out. Fleming had bought 22B in the 1930s from Fascist leader Sir Oswald Mosley who lived nearby with his family, and used the flat to conduct his many illicit affairs.

In 1963 Michael Caine and Terence Stamp shared a bachelor pad on Ebury Street, enjoying all the fun and opportunities that were available to world-famous young actors as the Swinging 60s went into full throttle.

Real-life spies also frequented Ebury Street and OSS, the forerunner of the CIA, had a safe house at number 18B during World War II for X-2 – a unit that liaised between the OSS and Britain's Secret Intelligence Service (SIS). As a young man Noel Coward lived at number 11 with his mother.

Head left down ⓭ **Eaton Terrace**, named after the Grosvenor family's country seat. The various titles used by the Grosvenor family can be confusing, but the senior title is the Duke of Westminster, as bestowed by Queen Victoria in 1874. The family also hold a number of subsidiary titles including Marquess of Westminster, Earl Grosvenor, Viscount Belgrave, Baron Grosvenor of Eaton, and Baronet of Eaton. The houses in this terrace largely date from the 1850s and normally sell for between £5-10 million.

The ⑭ **Antelope public house** (further north up the road at number 22) is mentioned in Dylan Thomas's unfinished novel *Adventures in the Skin Trade* (1955). You can visit it if you wish, although on this walk we turn right into Chester Row just by another fine pub – the ⑮ **Duke of Wellington**. The Duke of Wellington (or the 'Duke of Boots' to regulars) was originally a reading room and library for employees of the local aristocrats, but later became a pub. A Shepherd Neame establishment, it contains memorabilia relating the Duke.

Just a short way down Chester Row take a detour on the left down ⑯ **Minera Mews**, an excellent example of the many mews streets in Belgravia that originally housed the servants, horses and carriages that served the wealthy residents of the big houses facing the main streets. Chester, the county town of Cheshire, is where the Grosvenor family have significant landholdings in addition to their family seat at Eaton Hall.

Belgravia Walk

Follow the map right into South Eaton Place and then up Gerald Road. 'Gerald' is a commonly used first name within the Grosvenor family and another indication that the family like to make sure those walking Belgravia's streets are never too far from a reminder of who owns them. Number 17 has a blue plaque to ⓱ **Noel Coward** who lived here between 1930 and 1956. He wrote a number of his most famous works at the address including *Cavalcade* and *Brief Encounter*. Look out for the gas lamp brackets that predate electric lighting, and also for a ⓲ **plaque** further down the road on the right-hand side that recalls a building's previous role as a police station between 1846 and 1993. Beatles fans may be interested to know that George and Ringo paid a visit to the police station on 19 April 1964 to report the theft of various items from their flat in nearby William Mews.

Cross Elizabeth Street and into Chester Square, which has topped the list of Britain's most expensive addresses several times in recent years. ⓳ **Chester Square** was one of the three original squares designed when Belgravia was being laid out, although it is smaller than both Eaton and Belgrave Square. The smaller size of its houses probably saved it from being taken over by embassies or converted into flats – unlike the other two squares – and as a result Chester Square feels more impressive and is less blighted by traffic. Whilst the houses may be smaller, they are still expensive. A large house here will cost more than £30 million.

⑲ *Chester Square*

Belgravia Walk

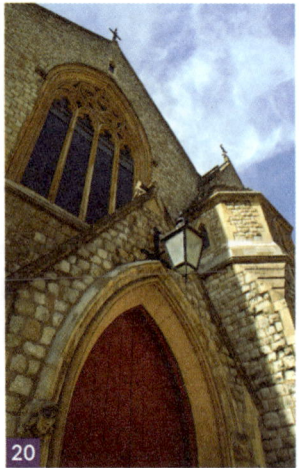

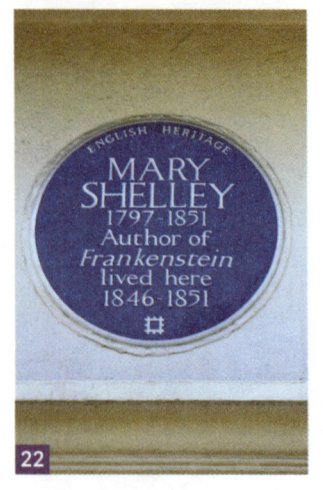

Belgravia Walk

Chester Square was laid out in 1840 by Thomas Cubitt. On the left just as you enter the square is ⑳ **St Michael's Church**, which was designed by Thomas Cundy and finished in 1844. As you walk through the square look down – you can still see the cast iron coal hole covers through which coal was once delivered.

Notable past residents include ㉑ spy **Guy Burgess** (no 38) and Sir Yehudi Menuhin; ㉒ **Mary Shelley**, author of *Frankenstein* and wife of the poet Percy Bysshe Shelley (no 24); ㉓ **Prime Minister Harold Macmillan** (no 14); and poet and critic ㉔ **Matthew Arnold** (no 2). ㉕ **Prime Minister Margaret Thatcher** lived at number 73 from 1991 before moving to The Ritz for health reasons a few months prior to her death.

One of the seminal meetings in London's counterculture history took place in a flat in Chester Square on 3 June 1965 when a party was thrown for the American Beat poet Allen Ginsberg. Ginsberg, most famous for his poem *Howl*, was vigorously celebrating his 39th birthday and became both very drunk and naked. Party guests John and Cynthia Lennon, George Harrison and his wife Pattie Boyd, arrived to find Ginsberg wearing nothing but a sign on his penis saying 'No Waiting'. Lennon – not yet the man who would feel comfortable posing naked for album covers after he left the Beatles – became very angry and stormed out after muttering at Ginsberg 'You don't do that in front of the birds!'. The poet and the former Beatle would later work closely together.

Continue on to exit on the far side of Chester Square. You reach Lower Belgrave Street and turn right, crossing over to reach the ㉖ **Plumber's Arms**. This pleasant pub dates from the 1820s, but is significant because of its role in a murder story.

28 *Eaton Square*

Belgravia Walk

On 7 November 1974 the bloodstained and injured Countess of Lucan burst into the bar and announced 'Help me, help me...I've just escaped from being murdered. He's in the house. He's murdered the nanny!'. The murderer she was referring to was her estranged husband and debonair professional gambler, Lord Lucan (b.1934). He had indeed killed the nanny – Sandra Rivett – at the Lucan family home at number 46 Lower Belgrave Street. Shortly before the murder Lucan had left his wife, and moved into a flat nearby. A bitter custody battle over his children, along with money problems, seems to have affected him badly, and may have triggered the attack. In any event he went on the run and became Britain's most famous fugitive. Over the years there have been reported sightings of 'Lucky' Lucan all over the world but his fate remains unknown. Walk back up Lower Belgrave Street, looking out for ㉗ **number 46** – where the murder took place – on the right-hand side.

Very shortly you reach ㉘ **Eaton Square**, considered by many to be the most prestigious address in London. I would suggest walking around the Square, heading right first and going anti-clockwise (passing number 1). The properties around the square are huge but most have been converted into flats (about five complete houses remain). Built by Cubitt between 1826 and 1855, the square employs the grand classical style that is typically Belgravian. In around 1890 it housed seventeen dukes, earls and viscounts; eight knights, nine titled ladies, six admirals and generals and nine MPs. In more recent years it has become known as Red Square on account of the number of Russian oligarchs who have bought properties here.

Today, the busy road going through the centre and the six rectangular gardens that

Belgravia Walk

are closed to non-residents (very common in Belgravia unfortunately), mean the square does not feel very welcoming and has a sterile, unlived in atmosphere. As you tour the square you will see the huge six-columned Ionic portico of the ㉙ **church of St Peter** on the eastern side, constructed in a Greek revivalist style to a design by John Henry Hakewill during the 1820s.

As you continue anti-clockwise around the square you will see a number of blue plaques recording famous past residents, beginning with ㉚ **Lord Boothby**, the controversial 20th-century politician who entertained his murderous friends the Krays at his home at number 1; ㉛ **Prime Minister Neville Chamberlain** (no 37), ㉜ **Prince Metternich** who stayed at no 44 while hiding in London as political and social upheavals erupted throughout Europe in 1848, ㉝ **Prime Minister Lord John Russell** (no 48) and ㉞ **Vivien Leigh**, star of *Gone with the Wind*, who lived for many years (and died) at number 54. Follow the map to find the former residences of ㉟ **Prime Minister Stanley Baldwin** (no 93) and ㊱ **George Peabody**,

American philanthropist and founder of the Peabody Trust (he died in 1869 while staying at no 80).

Other more recent famous residents include Bond actor Roger Moore and composer Andrew Lloyd Webber. It is estimated the handful of complete houses left in the square are worth over £50 million each, and so there is huge pressure on even the super-rich to maximise the space available in each property. In recent years this has led to disputes between residents as construction firms come up with ever more ingenious ways to develop space, including digging basements that threaten to undermine foundations.

Follow the map into Lyall Street. Turn right into Eaton Mews North on the right-hand side to see where the rich residents of the square once housed their servants and horses. Look out for the **37 heraldic wheatsheaf emblem** in the archway – one that you will see regularly throughout the Grosvenor Estate.

The wheatsheaf recalls a rare defeat experienced by the Grosvenor family when, in around 1390, they fought a bitter four year battle with the Scrope family as to who should be able to use a coat of arms. Under heraldic law there were restrictions on the design that could be used for a family's arms and the Grosvenor and Scrope versions, as emblazoned on their battle shields, were judged to be too similar. Each family tried to argue their use of the design came first in time, and hence should take precedence.

Hundreds of witnesses were called to the legal proceedings – known as Grosvenor vs Scrope – including Geoffrey Chaucer and John of Gaunt.

However Richard II finally ruled in favour of the Scropes and the Grosvenors were forced to adopt a new coat of arms. Known as the *Azure a Garb Or,* it was derived from the ancient arms of the Earls of Chester (in heraldic tradition a 'garb' is a wheatsheaf). The Grosvenors – the wealthiest landowners in Britain – have had the last laugh as the Scrope family has faded from national prominence.

❸❽ Eaton Mews North is typical of the many pretty, cobbled mews that are found throughout Belgravia. Walk down the mews and then left through an archway to reach **❸❾ Eaton Place**.

Thomas Cubitt based his headquarters at a number of addresses in Eaton Place, moving each time the property he was in was sold to the newly arriving residents. Eventually he had to move to Lyall Street. Frederic Chopin gave a concert at number 99 in 1848 after fleeing the revolution taking place in France. In the audience that night was author William Thackeray, just a week away from completing *Vanity Fair*. 165 Eaton Place is the home of the glamorous (but fictitious) Bellamy family who feature (along with their servants) in *Upstairs, Downstairs* – a hugely successful 1970s TV series that has recently been re-launched. The original series used **❹⓿ number 65** for the exterior shots of the Bellamy house, just painting on a number '1' during filming. Walk eastwards along Eaton Place until you reach the junction with Belgrave Place. In 1922 Field Marshal Sir Henry Wilson was assassinated by the IRA outside his house at **❹❶ number 36**.

Archway from 38 *Eaton Mews North through to Eaton Place*

Belgravia Walk

Turn left up Belgrave Place. Shortly you reach ㊷ **Belgrave Square** – a large site covering ten acres. Despite Eaton Square's current prestigious status, Belgrave Square was meant to be the focal point of Belgravia when construction began in the 1820s. Clay taken from the site to make bricks was replaced by soil and stone that was being excavated at the same time during the construction of St Katherine's Dock (just beside Tower Bridge). This means much of Belgrave Square actually rests on what was originally part of the East End of London.

Much of the square was designed by George Basevi (1794-1845), a distinguished architect commissioned by Cubitt. By 1840 many of the properties were occupied and in the following years aristocrats continued to flock here. Queen Victoria rented number 36 for her mother, and by 1860, 3 dukes, 13 MPs and 13 other nobles had lived here. However, after World War II the sheer size of the properties proved too large for normal residential living, and the square became dominated by embassies and other institutions.

As you head anti-clockwise around the square, look out on the right-hand side for the ㊸ **Norwegian Embassy** (at the junction with

Belgrave Place). The exterior wall contains Coade Stone carved figures that were part of the Norwegian-Danish embassy in Wellclose Square in Stepney and date from 1796.

Opposite on the corner of Belgrave Square Garden is a statue of ㊹ **Christopher Columbus**, a gift from Spain on the 500th anniversary of his discovery of America.

As you continue around the square – look out for number 34 which has a blue plaque remembering ㊺ **Field Marshal Viscount Gort** (1886-1946). An outstanding solider, he won a Victoria Cross during World War I, and in World War II masterminded both the evacuation of the British Expeditionary Force from Dunkirk and later the defence of Malta. Gort lived here in the 1920s, but left upon discovering that his wife was having an affair with an official at the Spanish Embassy nearby.

On the corner of Belgrave Square Garden is a bronze statue of ㊻ **Simon Bolivar**, liberator of South America. It was erected in the 1970s to commemorate Bolivar's connections to London.

Beatles fans may wish to take a short detour down Chapel Street and stop outside number 24 on the right-hand side. This was home to ㊼ **Brian Epstein**, manager of the Beatles, from 1964 until his death (at the house) on 27 August 1967. Epstein was crucial to the band's breakthrough and they visited the house many times, perhaps most notably when they hosted a press launch here for their seminal album *Sgt Pepper's Lonely Hearts Club Band*.

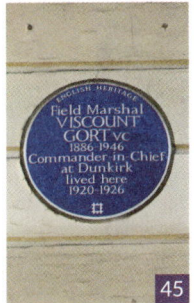

Belgravia Walk

In February 1966 Paul McCartney attended an electronic musical evening given by the Italian avant garde composer Luciano Berio at the ㊽ **Italian Cultural Institute** at 39 Belgrave Square. Unfortunately the press found out and the Beatle had to endure their attention, but it was experiences like this that encouraged McCartney's leanings towards greater experimentation within the band.

Continue anti-clockwise around the square, looking out for a statue commemorating ㊾ **Sir Robert Grosvenor** (1767-1845), First Marquess of Westminster. He initiated much of the development of the Grosvenor family property holdings, including Belgravia, that his son, Richard Grosvenor, the Second Marquess (of Westminster), brought to fruition. His foot rests on a distance stone indicating it is 197 miles to Chester, near the Grosvenor family seat. The statue was commissioned by Gerald Grosvenor, the 6th Duke of Westminster, and the back panel contains some family history which is worth a read. The current Duke was recently estimated to be worth over 10 billion pounds, making him the richest Briton although there are residents of Belgravia who are even wealthier.

Belgravia Walk

Continue past the statue along the edge of the square and turn right into Wilton Terrace that becomes Wilton Crescent. On the left-hand side at number 2 is a blue plaque remembering this was home of the **50 Earl and Countess Mountbatten** for many decades. They first came here in 1950 shortly after the Earl – in his role as the last Viceroy of India – had overseen its move to independence. Next door, 5 Belgrave Square was owned by Russian billionaire Oleg Deripaska. In 2022 police removed squatters protesting against Putin and Russian oligarchs.

Follow the map along West Halkin Street looking out on the right for the **51 spire of the Belfry**. Dating from 1830, it was originally a Presbyterian church, but is today the up-market Mosimann's restaurant. You soon reach Lowndes Street, named after William Lowndes, Secretary to the Treasury, who purchased the surrounding land in the 1720s. Straight ahead at 32 Lowndes Street is a branch of **52 C Hoare & Co**, England's oldest privately-owned bank that has served the upper classes since the 1670s. The bank's only other London branch is on Fleet Street.

Turn right on Lowndes Street and then right up Motcomb Street, full of North Belgravia's high-end shops. On the left is the imposing **53 Pantechnicon building**, built in 1830 and originally a warehouse. If you're in need of a coffee pick-me-up – enter this to reach the Halkin Arcade where you'll find lots of independent eateries. The name 'Halkin' derived from the Grosvenors' Halkyn Castle in Flintshire.

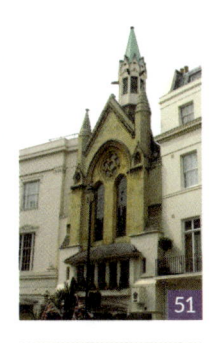

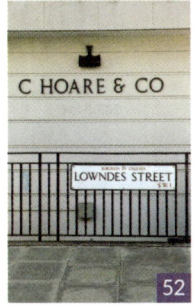

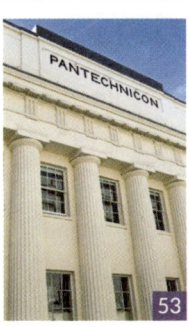

Turn left and walk down Kinnerton Street, a very agreeable and quiet Belgravia street that almost has a village feel to it. Shortly you will see ❺❹ **The Nag's Head public house,** which has a pleasant atmosphere and originally catered for the footmen and stable-men who looked after the horses kept in the mews nearby. Continue on to reach the ❺❺ **Wilton Arms** on the left – a public house dating from 1826, and another fine place to stop for a break.

Opposite the Wilton Arms, walk down Kinnerton Street a short way to reach Wilton Place. The 'Wilton' connection with Belgravia began in 1794 when the first Marquess of Westminster married Lady Eleanor Edgington, daughter of the first Earl of Wilton. Look out for the blue plaque outside number 8 that commemorates where the actress and Royal mistress ❺❻ **Lillie Langtry** (1853-1929) once lived. Turn right on Wilton Place and bear left along Wilton Crescent and then left down **Wilton Row** – the latter is very easy to miss so walk carefully. If you reach the rear of the Grosvenor statue again, you've gone too far.

Continue down ❺❼ **Wilton Row** (bearing left round a bend) to reach ❺❽ **The Grenadier public house**. One of the most charming (and hidden) posh pubs in London – it has also long enjoyed a reputation as being one of the most haunted! Wilton Row was built in the late 1820s as a service road for grander neighbouring streets, and the Grenadier dates from the same time although the legend that it began its life as

58 *Grenadier public house*

Belgravia Walk

an officers' mess for the nearby barracks is probably not true – it was meant to be a public house all along. Legend has it that the Duke of Wellington played cards here and that the pub is also haunted each September by the ghost of an army officer who was caught cheating and flogged to death.

Just beside the Grenadier – again very easy to miss – is a door that you go through into 59 **Old Barrack Yard**, near to where a barracks for the Foot Guards was built in 1758. The streets and houses in this vicinity were developed from the 1830s and some are exceptionally pretty and quiet. It is hard to imagine in these tranquil surrounds, but walk down Old Barrack Yard, bear left then right and you will soon be standing amid the noise and traffic of Knightsbridge.

From here take a right and walk along Knightsbridge. As you ascend the incline towards Hyde Park Corner the vast bronze figure of 60 **Achilles** will be visible to the left. A plaque at the statues' base states that it was built through public subscription by 'the women of England to Arthur Duke of

Wellington and his brave companions'. It was the first of many public monuments erected in honour of the 'Iron Duke' and was the first public monument to depict a naked man. The Christian anti-slavery campaigner, William Wilberforce, campaigned against the corrupting influence of public male nudity and a fig leaf was latter added to protect the young warrior's modesty from public gaze. There are many more monuments on Hyde Park Corner to explore if you should have the energy, but our walk concludes here, by the entrance to the underground station.

VISIT...

Apsley House
Hyde Park Corner, W1J 7NT
www.english-heritage.org.uk

EAT, DRINK...

The Antelope (see p.15)
22 Eaton Terrace, SW1W 8EZ

The Duke of Wellington
(see p.15)
63 Eaton Terrace, SW1W 8TR

The Fox & Hounds (see p.11)
29 Passmore Street,
SW1W 8HR

The Grenadier (see p.30)
18 Wilton Row, SW1X 7NR

Halkin Arcade
Motcomb St, SW1X 8LB

The Nag's Head (see p.30)
53 Kinnerton Street, SW1X 8ED

The Orange (see p.13)
37-39 Pimlico Rd, SW1W 8NE
www.theorange.co.uk

Plumber's Arms (see p.19)
14 Lower Belgrave St, SW1W 8LN

The Wilton Arms (see p.30)
71 Kinnerton St, SW1X 8ED
www.thewiltonarms.co.uk

CANONBURY
GROVE

2 Islington Walk

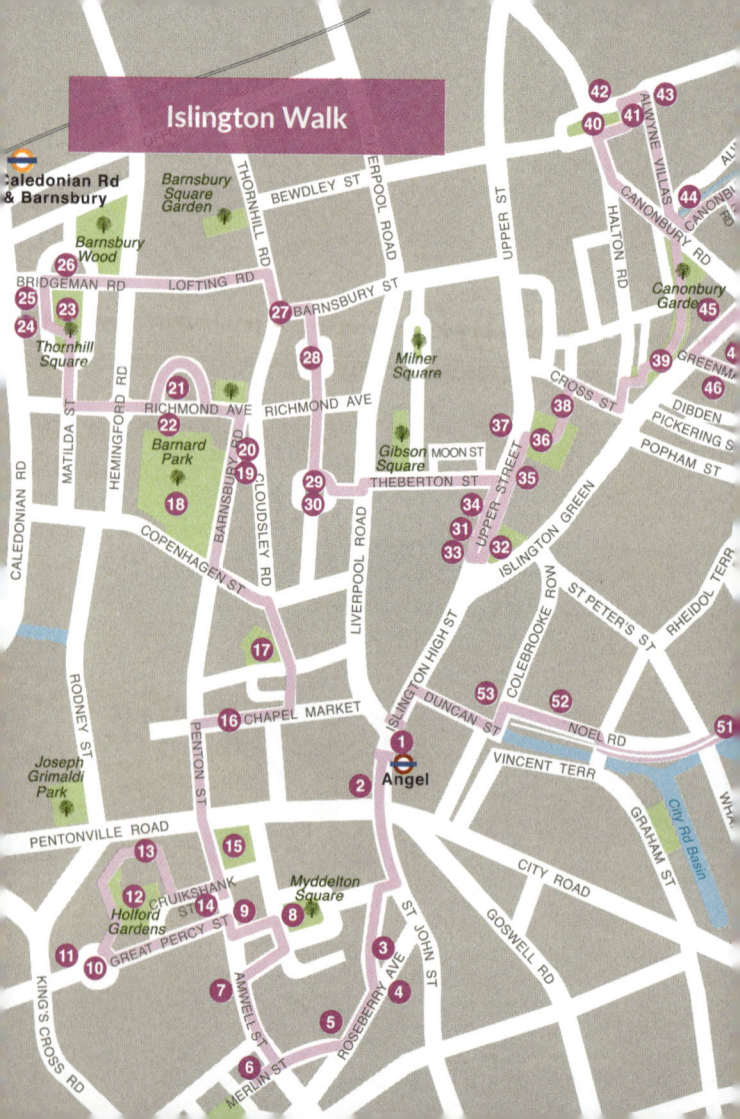

Islington Walk

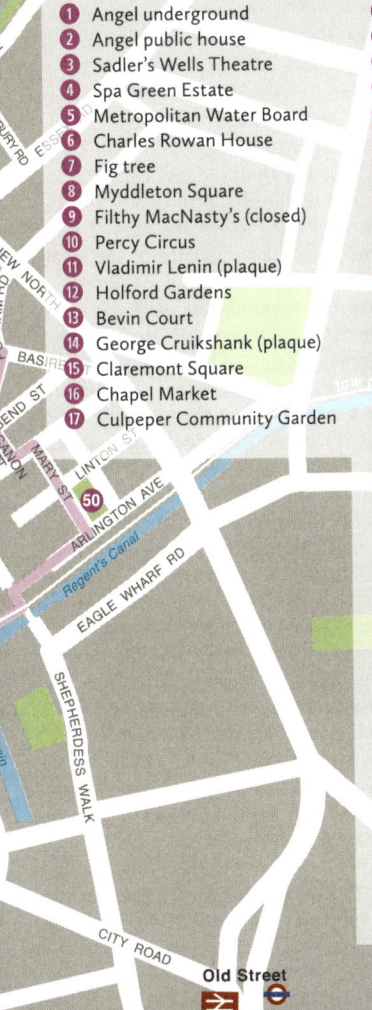

1. Angel underground
2. Angel public house
3. Sadler's Wells Theatre
4. Spa Green Estate
5. Metropolitan Water Board
6. Charles Rowan House
7. Fig tree
8. Myddleton Square
9. Filthy MacNasty's (closed)
10. Percy Circus
11. Vladimir Lenin (plaque)
12. Holford Gardens
13. Bevin Court
14. George Cruikshank (plaque)
15. Claremont Square
16. Chapel Market
17. Culpeper Community Garden
18. Barnard Park
19. No 164 Barnsbury Road
20. No 176 Barnsbury Road
21. Richmond Crescent
22. Egyptian sphinxes
23. Thornhill Square
24. Edith Margaret Garrud (plaque)
25. West Library
26. St Andrew's Church
27. Barnsbury Street
28. Lonsdale Square
29. Cloudesley Square
30. Holy Trinity Church
31. Electric Cinema
32. Islington Green
33. Gracie Fields (plaque)
34. Screen on the Green cinema
35. Angel Studios
36. St Mary's Church
37. King's Head public house
38. Little Angel Theatre
39. Astey's Row Rock Gardens
40. Canonbury Square
41. George Orwell (plaque)
42. Estorick Collection
43. Canonbury Tower
44. New River Walk
45. Carlton Cinema
46. Peabody Estate
47. Tibberton Baths
48. City of London Academy
49. St James's Church
50. Arlington Square
51. Narrow Boat public house
52. No 25 Noel Road (plaque)
53. Church of St John the Evangelist

Islington Walk

Start/Finish: Angel underground station
Distance: 6 miles

The walk begins from ❶ **Angel tube**, which was opened in 1901 and (at nearly 200 feet) has the third longest escalator in Europe. This feature attracted a Norwegian daredevil who skied down the escalator in 2007 – much to the annoyance of the local police (particularly as he was not caught).

Leave the tube station onto Islington High Street. About 500 meters to your right Upper Street begins, which most people regard as the heart of Islington. However, it was only as recently as 1965 that the new London Borough of Islington was created incorporating districts such as Holloway, Tufnell Park, Highbury, Canonbury, Barnsbury, Pentonville, Clerkenwell and St Luke's as well as the old borough of Finsbury. You will walk through many of these districts on the walk as well as the heart of the original Islington parish.

Turn left down Islington High Street and cross over, passing a branch of the Co-operative Bank on the corner with Pentonville Road. Beside it is a Wetherspoon pub called ❷ **the Angel**. The bank occupies the site of the old Angel tavern that gave this area its name. The inn had medieval origins and was later rebuilt as a coaching inn. It became an important overnight stopping point for travellers who did not want to risk running into the robbers who plagued the fields between Islington and central London after dusk.

In Charles Dickens's *Oliver Twist*, John Dawkins (otherwise known as the Artful Dodger) adopted a different strategy while guiding Oliver into the city – in the book he

Islington Walk

Chadwell Street

'objected to their entering London before nightfall, it was nearly eleven o'clock when they reached the turnpike at Islington. They crossed from the Angel into St. John's Road'.

The Angel was rebuilt twice during the 19th century, and the current building – occupied by the bank – dates from 1903. After it stopped being used as an inn it became a Lyons' Corner House (a smarter, larger version of a tea house) from 1921 to 1959.

Cross over the junction and follow the map south along St John Street then head right along Chadwell Street and then left along Arlington Way to reach ❸ **Sadler's Wells Theatre**. If the theatre is open you might want to go inside and spend some time reading about the theatre, and the history of Islington before you carry on.

The name 'Islington' is probably a corruption of the original Anglo-Saxon settlement known as Gislandune (or 'Gisla's Hill'). The original village of Islington was based around St Mary's church on Upper Street, which we will visit later. For many centuries Islington was known as the dairy of London, its cows producing milk sold throughout the capital.

It also became a stopping point for cattle and sheep that were being brought to London from the countryside – the last chance for the animals to be rested and fattened up before they were sold and slaughtered at Smithfield meat market.

Many of the cattle and sheep drovers needed somewhere to stay and this fuelled the growth of inns and various entertainments along the main roads through Islington village, principally Upper and Lower Streets – the latter now known as Essex Road – and Liverpool Road (formerly Back Road).

The current Sadler's Wells Theatre is thought to be the sixth on the site, and dates from 1998. In medieval times a religious order occupied the land here, and used a well whose spring water apparently had miraculous healing properties. During the Dissolution of the Monasteries in the 1530s, Henry VIII is supposed to have ordered that the well be covered over, regarding it as an unwelcome relic of superstitious practices. By 1683 a surveyor named Thomas Sadler owned a property here and while he was doing some construction work the old well was uncovered.

Sadler decided to exploit the well, given that spa resorts were at the time very fashionable in England. He marketed the waters as being effective against 'dropsy, jaundice, scurvy, green sickness and other distempers to which females are liable – ulcers, fits of the mother, virgin's fever and hypochondriacal distemper.' He also founded a theatre beside the well to attract more visitors, and at its peak Sadler's Wells was attracting several hundred people a day. Ironically, over the following decades the theatre thrived while spring water fell out of fashion.

By the beginning of the 18th century the theatre was staging shows full of jugglers, tumblers, rope-dancers, ballad-singers, wrestlers, stage-fighters and dancers. The famous clown Joseph Grimaldi was a favourite here. By the mid-19th century, changes in the law allowed a much larger number of theatres to put on serious plays and Sadler's Wells became known for its performances of Shakespeare.

Later it was used as a music hall, featuring stars such as Marie Lloyd and Harry Champion, and during the mid-20th century it became famous for its ballet and opera companies. After the Second World War the ballet company took up residence at the Royal Opera House in Covent Garden, and in the 1960s the opera company decamped from Islington to form the core of the English National Opera at the Coliseum. Today Sadler's Wells remains a prominent centre for dance in this country, with many leading companies performing here.

If you enter the lobby and bear right you can see the original well discovered by Sadler, which is now sunk into the floor of the new theatre.

Directly opposite the theatre is the ❹ **Spa Green Estate**, a Grade II* listed development. Cross over Rosebery Avenue to take a look. Rosebery Avenue is named after Archibald Primrose, the 5th Earl of Rosebery (1847-1929), who was the first chairman of the London County Council and who served as Prime Minister for a brief period in the mid-1890s. You will start to notice that many parts of Islington are named after politicians.

Spa Green Estate was planned in the 1930s by Finsbury Borough Council, then the most radical political body in London, and willing to employ equally far-thinking architects. The war interrupted construction, and the estate received its first tenants in the late 1940s.

The estate is noted for its Modernist architecture, and was designed by Berthold Lubetkin (1901-1990). A Russian émigré, he was the leading force in the Tecton architectural practice, and was also responsible for other historically important architectural creations such as the Highpoint housing complex in Highgate (see p.78), the Finsbury Health Centre (located further to the west of here along Rosebery Avenue) and the penguin pool at London Zoo. At the time Finsbury was known for its many slums and the local council employed Lubetkin to produce well-constructed homes that would improve the health and social conditions of local residents.

This resulted in what was regarded as the most innovative public housing development of its time. The Minister of Health, Aneurin Bevan, laid the foundation stone in July 1946 and Princess Margaret planted a plane tree during the ceremonial opening three years later.

The estate was built on the site of Islington Spa (a rival to Sadler's wells) which was founded in the 1680s. During the 19th century the spa went into decline and the gardens were eventually built over in the 1840s. The remaining buildings – now part of a sprawling slum area – were cleared when the estate was laid out.

Islington Walk

When finished on the estate walk down Rosebery Avenue (with the theatre on your right) for 2-3 minutes before turning right on Hardwick Street. On the right hand side is the former location of New River Head. For many centuries the reservoir here was the final destination of fresh water that was brought to London from Hertfordshire along the New River.

The story of the New River began in the early 17th century when a now largely forgotten man named Edmund Colthurst came up with a daring plan to cut a canal over 30 miles long to bring fresh water from Hertfordshire to London. He obtained a charter from James I to begin the work but encountered financial difficulties. It was left to a man with deeper pockets, City Goldsmith Hugh Myddelton (c 1560-1631) to step in and accomplish the project, in the process becoming one of the most influential men in the history of Islington's development.

Myddelton was a determined character, overcoming resistance from landowners who opposed the cutting of the canal through their lands, and having to deal with a constant shortage of funds. Eventually James I stepped in to save the project with a substantial investment, taking a share of future profits at the same time. The grand opening of the New River took place in 1613.

The New River began between Ware and Hertford in Hertfordshire and used water from the River Lea as well as the Chadwell and Amwell Springs. Originally its course was above ground but in the second half of the 19th century some sections were put underground enabling the course to be straightened. When the water reached New River Head it was held in a reservoir and then distributed via wooden pipes throughout North London using only gravity to help the flow. In 1946 the water supply to New River Head was truncated north of here at Stoke Newington. However the New River still supplies some water to London, and is today controlled by Thames Water.

Islington Walk

Continue south down Roseberry Avenue. At the juncion with Hardwick Road you will see the ❺ **former headquarters of the Metropolitan Water Board**, which took over the New River Company in 1904. The Board was itself incorporated into Thames Water – responsible for London's water supply – in 1973. This part of the complex dates from 1920, while the Laboratory Building on the eastern part of the site dates from 1938. Thames Water stayed here until 1987, and the buildings were then converted into luxury flats.

The New River Company was influential in the development of Islington from a semi-rural area in the late 18th century to a thoroughly urban centre just 100 years later. The Company owned a great deal of land in the area and as London grew in the 19th century, it was able to develop the fields around New River Head.

As a result, many of the surrounding streets and squares have names that relate to the Company – for example, Amwell Street and Chadwell Street are named after the Hertfordshire springs, Mylne Street after the Company's surveyor William Mylne, and Myddelton Square is of course named after the Company's founding father.

Islington Walk

William Chadwell Mylne (1781-1863) was an engineer and architect, and became the main assistant to his father Robert who also worked for the New River Company. When his father retired in 1810 William became chief engineer – a post he retained until 1861. During this time he was responsible for laying out many residential streets and squares such as Myddelton Square, Amwell Street, Inglebert Street, and River Street. He also designed the Neo-Gothic St Mark's Church in Myddelton Square, which you will see shortly.

Continue up Hardwick Street, crossing Amwell Street to reach Merlin Street. Its name recalls Merlin's Cave and Merlin's Place, both of which were to be found here in the 18th century and which appear on old maps of London. Merlin's Cave was in fact a public tea-garden, although some have suggested it had some kind of mystical significance connected to Arthurian legend.

Continue down Merlin Street and on the right-hand side you will find ❻ **Charles Rowan House** – enter through the gate to look inside the main courtyard. Like the Spa Green Estate, this is another example of a well-built, publicly-owned housing development. Grade II listed, it dates from around 1930 and was originally intended for married policemen. It is named after Sir Charles Rowan (c 1782-1852), an army officer who served in the Peninsular War and fought at Waterloo before becoming the founding senior Commissioner of the Metropolitan Police in 1829.

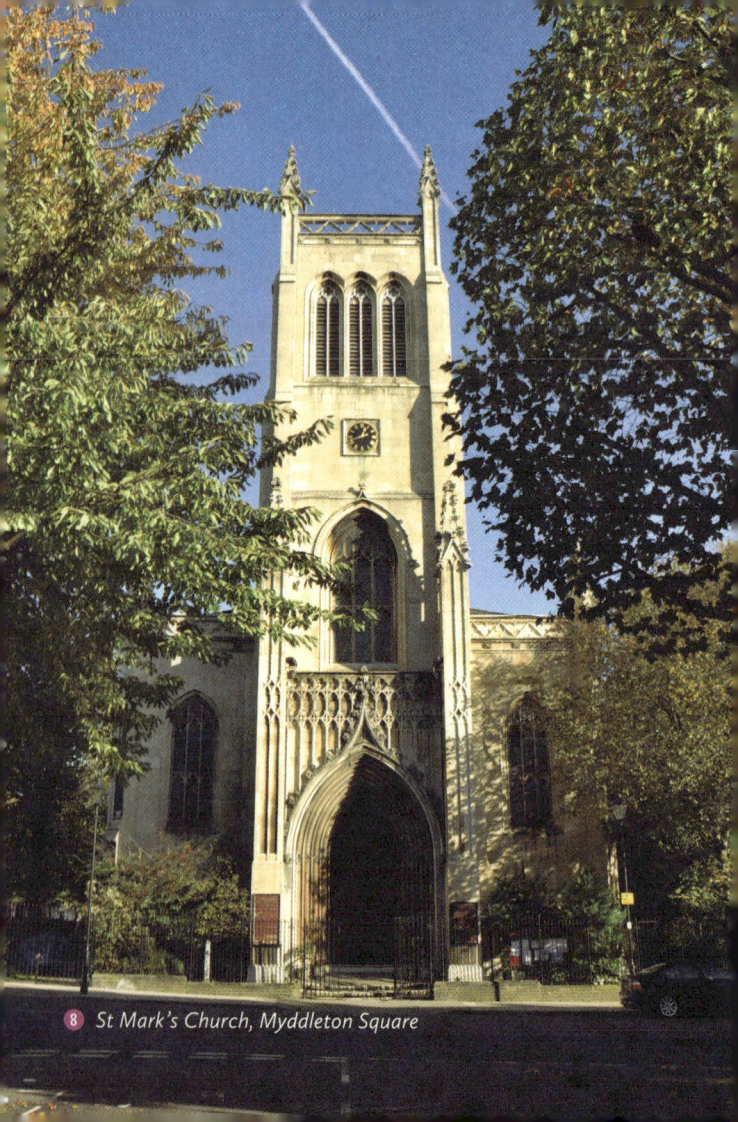

8 *St Mark's Church, Myddleton Square*

Retrace your steps to turn left (north) up Amwell Street. You will soon see on the left (just after Margery Street) the ❼ **Fig tree** which has been here for over 200 years and in fact comprises three trees which have become intertwined. The vast branches have grown horizontally over the years and are now supported by a series of wooden frames. Cross over the road and take a right into River Street to reach ❽ **Myddleton Square**, which was laid out in the 1820s. The square and **St Mark's Church** were also designed by William Mylne, and this is the first of many elegant squares you will see along this walk, making parts of Islington among the most desirable in London. However, it is also a place of huge contrasts with some estates in the borough among the most deprived in the country.

Walk up the west side of the square, passing Mylne's lovely St Mark's Church that was consecrated in 1828. Turn left along Inglelbert Street to reach Amwell Street once more. On the right hand corner is the former site of ❾ **Filthy MacNasty's** which was one of London's quirkiest pubs, known for its literary and musical events. The Pogues front man, Shane MacGowan, was a regular and once had a bed permanently prepared for him upstairs. Other well-known patrons include Johnny Depp, Pete Doherty, Irvine Welsh, Will Self, Helen Fielding, Nick Hornby and Allen Ginsberg. Sadly, MacNasty's closed its doors for the last time in 2013 and the site is now an upmarket wallpaper shop.

Turn right up Amwell Street and then left along Great Percy Street, named after Robert Percy Smith, a director of the New River Company in the 19th century. On the left you pass Lloyd Street which leads down to Lloyd Square (although do not go down here unless you have time). This was laid out in the early 1830s by father and son John and William Booth for the Lloyd Baker family, who owned the estate until the mid-20th century.

Continue along Great Percy Street to reach the unusual, polygonal shaped ⑩ **Percy Circus**. The houses here may be relatively cheap by Islington square standards, but still typically sell for over a million pounds. It was laid out in the early 1840s by William Mylne and named for Robert Percy Smith, a governor of the new River Company. Its most famous resident was ⑪ **Vladimir Lenin** (1870-1924) who lived at number 16 with his wife in 1905. Lenin stayed in London several times before the Russian Revolution in 1917, largely to avoid persecution in Russia and to attend secret congresses of the socialist and Bolshevik movements.

Islington Walk

When Lenin first came to stay in London in 1902 he lived with his wife around the corner from here at 30 Holford Square – during the day editing the *Iskra* newspaper from his office on Clerkenwell Green. In 1905 he returned to attend the first Bolshevik congress in London, and stayed with his wife at number 16 (there is a plaque outside). A number of other people attending the congress stayed at other addresses in Percy Circus, so for a brief period this was arguably the most radical street in the world.

On the north-east side of the circus walk down a narrow path (half-way between Vernon Rise and Great Percy Street) that leads off Percy Circus and into ⓬ **Holford Gardens**. These stand on the site of the former Holford Square, which was laid out in the 1840s. The square – and Lenin's home of 1902 – were destroyed during the Blitz.

Walk through the gardens on the left-hand side and through the exit on the other side. Then bear right (with Bevin Court on your right) to reach Cruikshank Street. ⓭ **Bevin Court** now stands behind you, its distinctive design another example of the Soviet inspired style of Berthold Lubetkin.

In 1942 Lubetkin had designed a bust of Lenin that stood on the site of the revolutionary's house in Holford Square. The bust was unveiled when the USSR was a war-time ally. The monument proved to be controversial, attracting communists, but also those who tried to vandalise it. At one time the bust received a police guard.

Islington Walk

By the time Lubetkin began to build new council housing on the World War II bomb-site, the Cold War had begun and USSR was now Britain's enemy. The original plan had been to call the new complex Lenin Court but – to Lubetkin's disgust – this was rejected. It was instead named Bevin Court – after the Labour minister Ernest Bevin – and was completed in 1954. Lubetkin had his revenge by placing the bust of Lenin inside the foundation of the stairwell at Bevin Court, where it remains to this day. Its presence there did not prevent the authorities awarding Bevin Court Grade II* listed status in 1998.

Continue along Cruikshank Street looking out for the two remarkable modern houses on the right hand side. At the end you reach Amwell Street again. The illustrator George Cruikshank (1792-1878) lived at various addresses around here, and a ⑭ **plaque** between numbers 69 and 71 Amwell Street commemorates his last two residences. Cruickshank was known as the 'modern Hogarth' and famously illustrated several books by Charles Dickens. Dickens visited his illustrator several times in Islington and they became friends. However they later fell out and after the author died Cruikshank wrote a controversial letter to *The Times* claiming that he had provided Dickens with the Oliver Twist story.

Cross over Amwell Street to enter ⑮ **Claremont Square**, one of the most unique in London. The square was developed in the 1820s around the old Upper Pond

Bevin Court

Islington Walk

reservoir of the New River Company. The Upper Pond was built in 1709 in order to boost water supplies from the New River. It was originally open to the elements, but after a cholera epidemic in 1846 new laws were passed that prohibited open areas of standing water and the reservoir here was covered over in 1852. This explains the unusual mound in the middle of the square the reservoir beneath is still in use today. It is supplied with treated water from the Thames Water Ring Main (completed in 1994 and extended in 2010) and was Grade II listed in June 2000.

From Claremont Square head north to reach Pentonville Road, named after Henry Penton who developed a number of residential streets in this area in the 1770s. It was also once part of the New Road – London's first bypass that was built from the mid-18th century and was designed to ease congestion in central London. Modern roads such as Marylebone Road, Euston Road, Pentonville Road, City Road, and Moorgate now follow the route of the New Road. The New Road diverted cattle and sheep heading for Smithfield from the crowded streets of central London and in so doing helped the growth of Islington, as the village benefited from the increased passing traffic.

Cross Pentonville Road, walking up Penton Street for a few minutes before turning right into ⑯ **Chapel Market**. This is home to one of London's longest running street markets having been founded in the 1860s and is open every day except Monday.

Islington Walk

In it's heyday the market extended all the way to Penton Street, but these days the stalls seldom extend much beyond Baron Street. The market as a location in the popular comedy series 'Only Fools and Horses'.

Head north up White Conduit Street. Under your feet is the tunnel of the Islington Canal, so you may have a canal boat floating by below you. Keep going straight through the Sainsbury's car park, then cross over Tolpuddle Street to reach the pleasant ⓱ **Culpeper Community Garden**, which is open to the public. It is named after the 17th-century herbalist Nicholas Culpeper.

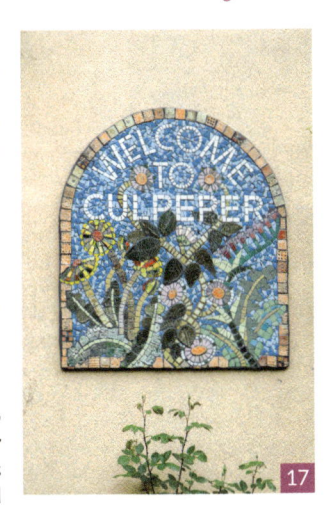

Walk along the east side (Cloudesley Road) and at the top bear left into Copenhagen Street. Shortly on the right head north up Barnsbury Road, with the ten-acre ⓲ **Barnard Park** on your left. You may wish to walk through the park, which is open to the public and contains a great kids' adventure area.

Barnsbury lies to the west of central Islington. Its name is derived from the de Berners family, who owned much of the land around here until the early 16th century. Before 1800,

Islington Walk

Barnsbury was mostly covered by dairy pastures and pleasure gardens, and a tavern just to the south of here named the White Conduit House was particularly popular with Londoners visiting the countryside on day trips. The sport of cricket was born in the 1780s on White Conduit Field, which extended over part of the present Barnard Park.

The field became the venue for a pioneering gentleman's cricket club known as the White Conduit Club – or 'WCC'. The WCC became fed up playing so near to the local taverns and increasingly encroaching residential streets, so they decided to move. In the early 1790s – under the leadership of professional bowler Thomas Lord (1755-1832) – the WCC relocated to Dorset Square in Marylebone. The club was re-named the Marylebone Cricket Club or 'MCC' – the now world-famous body that codified the rules of the game. Under Lord's organization the MCC later moved to Lord's Cricket Ground in St John's Wood where it remains to this day.

Barnard Park was opened in 1975 and laid out over former streets that had been destroyed during the Blitz. The park is named after a local councillor named George Barnard in recognition of his promotion of sport in Islington.

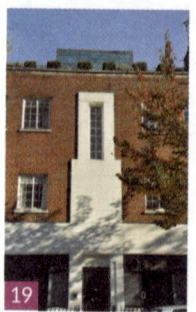

Follow Barnsbury Road, which contains several fine terrace properties dating from the 1820s, until you come to numbers 164-176 on your right. These properties are now residential but still bear signs of their commercial past. The art deco building at ⑲ **number 164** was formerly a public house known as The Eclipse, while just a few doors down ⑳ **number 176** still carries the name of a former proprietor, Henry Licht, carved above the entrance façade. On the corner of Richmond Avenue and Cloudsley Road

Islington Walk

are the remains of a 'Dispensing Chemist' ghost sign. Similar converted shop fronts on this road indicate that this was once a thriving shopping area.

At the northern end of Barnard Park turn left along Richmond Avenue and then take a right into ㉑ **Richmond Crescent**. This is one of Islington's most prestigious residential streets. Number 1 was where Tony Blair lived for four years prior to winning the 1997 General Election.

During the 1990s Islington became closely associated with Blair and many of his New Labour colleagues who lived around here. During much of the 20th century Islington declined as the middle classes moved away and many of the houses built for them were sub-divided into flats and a number of slums developed. However, from the 1970s a creeping gentrification began and Islington became popular with those in the media, advertising and politics.

Retrace your steps and continue along Richmond Avenue looking out on the left-hand side for houses dating from the 1840s that feature ㉒ **Egyptian sphinxes** and mini obelisks outside.

After a few minutes take a right into Matilda Street and continue north to reach ㉓ **Thornhill Square**. This is one of the most picturesque Islington squares, and particularly attractive for walkers as it has an open public garden at its centre. The square is named after the Thornhill family who for many years owned the land around here, leasing it to developers in the 19th century.

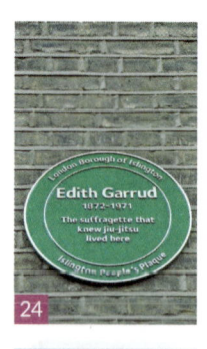

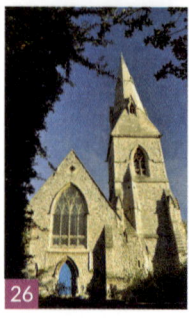

Number 60 was the home of an extraordinary woman named **Edith Margaret Garrud** (1872-1971). She was both a suffragette and a pioneering teacher of Jiu Jitsu who learnt her skills from the earliest practitioners of this Japanese martial art to arrive in Europe. She went on to run her own Jiu Jitsu classes and teach her fellow suffragettes how to defend themselves against police harassment during the most militant phase of the movement's struggle. Garrud also founded and trained a group of 30 women who were known as the Bodyguard – their fighting skills regularly employed against the police. After the First World War broke out the Suffragette's leader Emmeline Pankhurst decided to suspend militant suffrage actions and the Bodyguard was disbanded. Edith inspired Helena Bonham Carter's character in the film 'Suffragette' (2015).

On the north-west side at the junction with Bridgeman Road look out for the ornate **West Library** dating from 1906. It has a highly unusual frontage described in one architectural guide as 'Byzantine striped pink and yellow' – an example of how London's local authorities in the past were surprisingly daring in their architectural commissions.

Thornhill Square was designed by the Thornhill Estate surveyor Joseph Kay and dates from around 1850. It is the largest square in Islington and in 1946 was given to the council for public use by Captain Noel Thornhill. **St Andrew's Church** on the north side was built around 1854.

Islington Walk

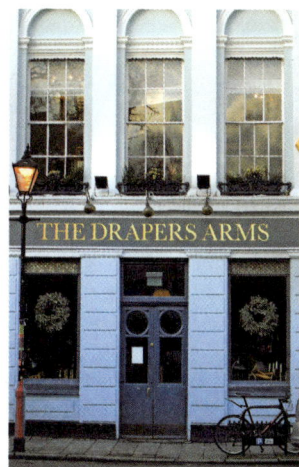

The square regularly features in television and film productions, including *Four Weddings and a Funeral* (1993). In recent years the world famous conductor Simon Rattle lived here.

Exit the square on the eastern side along Bridgeman Road and cross over Hemingford Road to continue along Lofting Road on the other side. Walk for a few minutes and then head right down Thornhill Road before turning left into ㉗ **Barnsbury Street**. The Islington Workhouse once stood further along this road from 1777 to 1867 (at the junction with Liverpool Road). On this walk we continue down the road and turn right (opposite the Drapers Arms pub) into Lonsdale Square.

㉘ **Lonsdale Square** was laid out around 1840 and its unusual Tudor-style features are courtesy of Richard Cromwell Carpenter – an architect known for his neo-Gothic designs. As a result the square feels very different to the others you will see along this walk. Carpenter's father, Richard, was surveyor to the Drapers' Company Estate and was also responsible for laying out the square. The Drapers had owned the land here from 1690 and remain one

28 Lonsdale Square

of the great City Livery companies. These medieval guilds were established to regulate and protect various professions, and in recent years have increasingly become involved in charitable enterprises. In a map of 1830 the area where the square stands was marked as a cattle yard.

Exit the square to the south and walk along Stonefield Street, crossing over Richmond Avenue to reach ㉙ **Cloudesley Square**. In 1973 Stonefield Street was at the centre of a campaign by local residents against property developers who were buying up old houses and letting them rot so as to make it easier to demolish them and build new flats. The success of the residents' campaign proved a turning point in the area, starting the gentrification that you see today.

Cloudesley Square itself dates from the 1820s and is most notable for containing architect Sir Charles Barry's ㉚ **Holy Trinity Church**, the third of his Islington churches. Barry (1795-1860) is best known for the Palace of Westminster – otherwise known as the Houses of Parliament. The square is named after a 16th-century landowner called Richard Cloudesley who bequeathed his estate in 1518 for the benefit of churches and medical services in the area. Today a charity administers this bequest, which still provides around £600,000 per year to good causes in the local area.

Exit on the east side to cross Liverpool Road – known as the 'Back Road' for many years as it runs parallel to the busier Upper Street, and was often used to drive cattle and sheep down towards Smithfield. Enter Therberton Street, passing Gibson Square and Gibson Square Gardens on the left. This and Milner Square (lying directly to the north) were part of the estate laid out from 1823 for Thomas Milner Gibson – whose

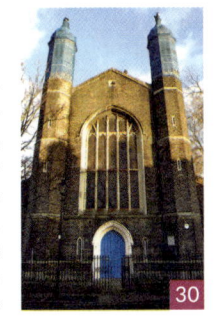

Islington Walk

family had made their money from sugar plantations in Trinidad. During the Second World War the gardens were dug up for air raid shelters and later replanted.

Continue on to reach Upper Street, the heartland of Islington. Head right (south) down Upper Street for a few minutes. At number 75, is the site of the former **31 Electric Cinema,** now a Caffè Nero. The small entrance dome is original to the cinema, which was opened in 1909 by Electric Theatres Ltd, the first enterprise to open a chain of cinemas in London.

Opposite is **32 Islington Green** – a surviving triangle of common land that sits in the apex between Upper Street and Essex Road. At the south end is a statue of the New River's creator **Sir Hugh Myddelton** dating from 1862. Upper Street is now very fashionable with some of the best restaurants in London and a number of well known theatres that rival the West End. However, in the 19th century, as urbanisation continued, it was given the nickname of 'the Devil's mile' because of the number of pubs, peep-shows and brothels that existed here.

In the pamphlet *London at Midnight* published in 1885 by Henry Vigar-Harris, the social commentator mentions the statue of Myddelton and how 'behind it is a huge drinking saloon, which is now emptying its human contents in the road. It's an interesting fact that within a radius of a mile and a half from this spot there are 1,030 public houses and beer shops'.

Vigar-Harris goes on to describe Islington as 'one of the most debauched [districts] the city contains... the devil's imps seem to perambulate through it, both day and night. It's past midnight, and look at these young girls with their besotted countenances. They have been torn from all that is pure and bright; swept, as by an irrepressible torrent, into the sea of vice... young men who walk with unsteady gait, and with their heads bent low'.

If you walk around here at midnight on any given Friday or Saturday there is a fair chance you will see a few drunks stumbling around as they exit one of Upper Street's many pubs and bars, so perhaps things have not really changed that much since Vigar-Harris's time.

Just a few doors further along (south), look up to see the ❸❸ **Gracie Fields blue plaque.** Fields began her career in the north of England and always kept her strong Rochdale accent. However her great success came in the music halls of London and she spent three years (1926-29) living above a sweet shop on Islington Green while making her fortune. In the 1930s Gracie became a major movie star playing plucky working-class girls fighting against the odds and managing to sing about it. This plaque was unveiled in 2011 in recognition of her brief but important time in Islington.

Retrace your steps up Upper Street. Just on the left is the ❸❹ **Screen on the Green cinema**, originally the Empress Picture Theatre when it opened in 1913. You can still see its distinctive original lines from the outside. The Clash made their London debut here in August 1976, sharing the bill with the Buzzcocks and the Sex Pistols.

Pass Therberton Street again on the left and cross over to continue north up

Islington Walk

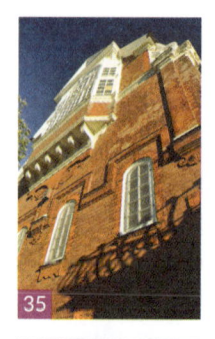

Upper Street, looking out for the spire of St Mary's Church. Just before St Mary's there is a substantial red-brick building that dates from 1888, which was originally the United Reform Church. In 1980 it was converted into ㉟ **Angel Studios** where numerous famous artists, bands and orchestras have recorded including Adele, Eric Clapton and James Morrison. Following the death of the studio's founder (the fabulously named James de Wolfe), it closed in 2019. There are now plans to reopen under a new name.

Right nextdoor is the imposing ㊱ **St Mary's**, Islington's original village church. The first recorded church on this site dates from the 12th century and the current building was consecrated in 1754. In the early 19th century St Mary's was the only church in Islington parish; however, as the population of the area increased dramatically as new residential streets were laid out, several other churches were founded nearby.

Opposite the church is the ㊲ **King's Head pub and theatre**. There has been a pub on this site for centuries, however it has become known nationally since 1970 for the theatre here and since then it has attracted some of the nation's best actors and playwrights. In 2023 the theatre moved to a purpose built space and the King's Head returned to being nothing more than a good pub without the drama.

Just a few doors down from the King's Head (at number 127) is the former site of the Granita restaurant. According to political lore, it was at Granita one night in 1994 that Tony

Blair and Gordon Brown met to thrash out the leadership of the Labour party. Blair apparently won Brown's support in return for the promise that Brown would later succeed him. Both men deny the deal took place; however, many have suggested that it was Blair's refusal to keep his word that helped sour the relations between the two men in the later years of the Blair administration.

Walk through the grounds of St Mary's – it has pleasant gardens at the rear if you want to sit down and have a break. Otherwise, head into Dagmar Passage to the north-east of the church, and pass the ㊳ **Little Angel Theatre** on the corner. Described as the 'home of British puppetry', it opened in 1961 and is one of the very few dedicated puppet theatres in the country.

Walk down Cross Street and before you reach busy Essex Road turn left and walk a short distance up Halton Road. Turn right at Halton Cross Street and ahead you will see Pleasant Place. This was once part of the waterway of the New River – an inscription in the pavement marks the New River's route.

Islington Walk

Continue through the gate into ❹ **Astey's Row Rock Gardens** – one of a series of linear parks forming part of the New River Walk. A garden since the 1860's, the rock gardens were installed in the 1950's and re-landscaped in the late 1990's.

Continue north through the gardens until you reach Canonbury Road. The district of Canonbury covers the area between Essex Road, Upper Street and Cross Street and either side of St Paul's Road. Its name is derived from Canon's Burgh, itself the result of the de Berners family (mentioned earlier) granting land here to the Canons of St Bartholomew's Priory, Smithfield, in 1253.

Turn left and walk along Canonbury Road until you reach ❹ **Canonbury Square** – one of the most prestigious addresses in the area, despite the often heavy traffic passing through. It was laid out in 1800, one of the very earliest of Islington's squares, on land owned by the Marquess of Northampton. The 4th Marquess later opened the pretty square gardens to the public in 1884. Famous former residents include writers Evelyn Waugh (number 17), ❹ **George Orwell** (number 27), and the artists Duncan Grant and Vanessa Bell (number 26). They all lived here when the square was unfashionable, and Orwell wrote much of his novel *1984* in his cold, dank flat. In the book Victory Mansions, the run-down home of the novel's main character, Winston Smith, is based on Orwell's Canonbury Square flat.

Islington Walk

Just across the square is the ㊷ **Estorick Collection**, which houses the collection of early 20th century Italian art acquired by the American sociologist Eric Estorick (1913-93). Estorick left his collection to a foundation on his death and the Heritage Lottery Fund bought this imposing property and garden on Cannonbury Square in 1994 to provide it with a public home. It's a great place to visit and has the added appeal of a wonderful café.

Bear right (on the north-east side of the square) down Alywne Villas. On the corner is Islington's oldest building, ㊸ **Canonbury Tower,** with foundations that may be pre-Roman. The main structure was built in the early 1500s by William Bolton, the last Prior of St Bartholomew's before the Dissolution enforced by Henry VIII. In later years notable residents included Sir Francis Bacon and Ephraim Chambers, founder of the famous encyclopedia. Just beside the tower, off Alywne Villas, is Canonbury Place. This is where Weedon Grossmith, author of *The Diary of a Nobody*, lived at number 5 in the 1890s.

Continue down Alywne Villas and at the bottom turn left into Canonbury Grove. You will see on the left some railings and a gate which will return you to the ㊹ **New River Walk**. As described earlier, the New River was long ago truncated further north at Stoke Newington, however in recent years a pleasant walk has opened alongside the remains of the original water channel that passed through Islington. It is a great place to get a sense of what the New River must have looked like as it wound its watery way through Islington before ending at the New River Head.

When finished exit New River Walk and head down Northampton Street to join the busy Essex Road. Head right (westwards) and walk along the right-hand side. You pass

Islington Walk

Essex Road station, which opened in 1904, and just after this on the next corner is the fantastically ornate Egyptian style façade of the former ㊺ **Carlton Cinema**. It opened in 1930 with Harold Lloyd's first talkie, *Welcome Danger*. You will see the building is far bigger than the older Electric Cinema seen earlier on Upper Street, evidence of how by the 1930s cinema architecture had entered a golden age of construction that would never be repeated. In recent years the building was used for a bingo hall and also as a conference centre.

Pass the old cinema and cross over to the south side of Essex Road and then take a left down Greenman Street and continue down the hill. On the right you see the distinctive ㊻ **Peabody Estate**, which opened in 1865. This was only the second such estate to be constructed by the Peabody Trust, the first having opened in Spitalfields the year before. The Peabody Trust was founded in 1862 by the American banker and philanthropist George Peabody (1795-1869). The pre-1900 Peabody estates all look very similar because they had the same architect – Henry Darbishire. During the late 19th century Islington's rapid urbanisation resulted in a number of slums in the area, and the size of the problem was evidenced by the fact that Peabody chose to build his second estate here.

Darbishire's design spread out the blocks of flats to provide for good ventilation, with a central space that permitted a safe playing area for children. The Peabody Trust today looks after nearly 19,000 properties and houses almost 50,000 people.

On the left as you go down the hill look out for Tibby Place. This public park houses the remains of ㊼ **Tibberton Baths** which were built in 1897 and closed in the 1980s.

Islington Walk

Today all that remains is the ghostly, painted ironwork of the baths roof structure.

At the end turn right into Popham Road and stop on the corner to look at the modern ㊽ **City of London Academy**. Popham Street is a world away from the monied environment of Richmond Crescent and the immediate area around here was used for some scenes in *Cathy Come Home* – the controversial and gritty TV drama directed by Ken Loach in 1966.

The Academy was built on the site of the Islington Green School – a comprehensive school that was controversially shut down then demolished in 2008 after receiving poor Ofsted reports. It was also the school that in 1979 supplied the kids who sang the chorus on Pink Floyd's hit record *Another Brick in the Wall*. Pink Floyd had their studio at Britannia Row nearby (seen later) and their producer Bob Ezrin hit upon the idea of using local school children to sing (or shout), 'We don't need no education...'. The school received £1,000 at the time, but in the mid-90s some of the children – now adults – tried to claim royalties for their part in the famous record.

Continue down Popham Road. At the end turn left and first right and walk down Bishop Street. At the end is ㊾ **St James's Church**, built by the Clothworkers' Company in the 1870s on the site of an earlier medieval City church. The Clothworkers are another City livery company that – like the Drapers – was once a major landowner in Islington and laid out many new residential streets here during the 19th century.

Islington Walk

In medieval times the land in this vicinity was owned by the canons of St Paul's Cathedral, but the Clothworkers acquired some of it during the reign of Henry VIII as the Dissolution forced many religious institutions to close, or at least sell off, much of their property. However, the historical connections with St Paul's can still be seen in the names of surrounding streets – Prebend Street, St Paul's Street, Canon Street, Rectory Street and Bishop Street. Britannia Row lies behind the church – Pink Floyd's old studio is found at number 35 where artists such as Joy Division and Kate Bush have recorded.

Cross over Prebend Street and walk down Canon Street (opposite the church). Turn left into St Paul Street then right into Mary Street and head down into ⑤⓪ **Arlington Square**, which was laid out in the 1850s. Before this, from the reign of Henry VII to 1791, the area was used as part of the exercise ground of the Archers' Division of the Artillery Company. Today it boasts an excellent public garden at its heart, looked after by an active local residents' association.

On the south-west side head out of the square and right along Arlington Avenue. On the right of Arlington Avenue is the old Packington Estate, which is being redeveloped after suffering from a bad reputation as a sink estate. The name Packington refers to Dame Ann Packington, who bequeathed around 60 acres of land to the Clothworkers' Company in 1563. The Clothworkers sold their last holding in the area in the 1940s.

Continue on until you reach an opening on the left that provides access to the Islington stretch of the Regent's Canal. Before you cross under the bridge and head right, look over to the left to the other side of the canal to see the former site of Gainsborough Studios. Previously an old power plant in Poole Street, in 1919 the site became the centre of British filmmaking. Classics such as Hitchcock's *The Lodger* and *The Lady Vanishes* were filmed here. The studio closed in 1951 and the building was

Regent's Canal

Islington Walk

eventually demolished in 2002, making way for the luxury flats which you see today.

Continue west along the Regent's Canal towpath. The canal was built to connect the Paddington arm of the Grand Union Canal (north-west of Paddington Basin) to Limehouse Basin and the Thames in east London. This allowed access to and from the Port of London to the national canal network. The canal is nearly nine miles long and the Islington section opened in 1820.

You pass the excellent 51 **Narrow Boat public house** which – unusually – opens out onto the tow path and is worth a visit. Continue on for a few minutes and exit the canal at the Danbury Street exit, which should be marked.

At the top turn right then left into Noel Road. Walk up this road stopping outside 52 **number 25**. The playwright Joe Orton (1933-67) lived here from 1960 with his lover, Kenneth Halliwell. Before Orton became famous, the two men spent most of their time here avoiding paid work, and playing pranks. They were eventually convicted for defacing books borrowed from the local library on Essex Road and spent several months in prison. Orton soon found success with his subversive and darkly comic plays *Loot* and *What the Butler Saw*. Halliwell's failure as a writer and Orton's promiscuity soon began to cause tension in the relationship. Halliwell became increasingly unbalanced and in August 1967 battered Orton to death with a hammer before committing suicide. A plaque can be seen on the second floor.

Continue on up Noel Road and at the end you enter Colebrooke Row (with Duncan Terrace on the other side). Former Prime Minister Boris Johnson lived in a five-storey house on this street from 2009-18 with his barrister wife, despite at the same time railing against 'lefty Islington lawyers'. On the Duncan Terrace side is the ⓱ **Church of St John the Evangelist** established in 1839, just 10 years after Catholic Emancipation. Duncan Terrance is named after Admiral Duncan (1731-1804), who defeated the Dutch navy at Camperdown in 1797. It was a popular victory and several streets and pubs continue to be named after the Admiral to this day.

Continue up Duncan Street (beside the church) to reach Upper Street. Turn left to return to Angel tube station and the end of this walk. ●

VISIT...

Estorick Collection (see p.65)
39a Canonbury Square, N1 2AN
www.estorickcollection.com

King's Head Theatre (see p.62)
115 Upper Street, N1 1QN
www.kingsheadtheatre.com

The Little Angel Theatre
(see p.63)
14 Dagmar Passage, N1 2DN
www.littleangeltheatre.com

Sadler's Wells Theatre
(see p.39)
Rosebery Ave, EC1R 4TN
www.sadlerswells.com

SHOP...

Chapel Market
N1 9EX (see p.52)

Camden Passage Antique's Market
Camden Passage, N1 8EA
www.camdenpassageislington.co.uk

EAT, DRINK...

Drapers Arms (see p.57)
44 Barnsbury Street, N1 1ER
www.thedrapersarms.com

Ground Control
61 Amwell Street, EC1R 1UR

Narrow Boat (see p.70)
119 St Peter's Street, N1 8PZ
www.thenarrowboatpub.com

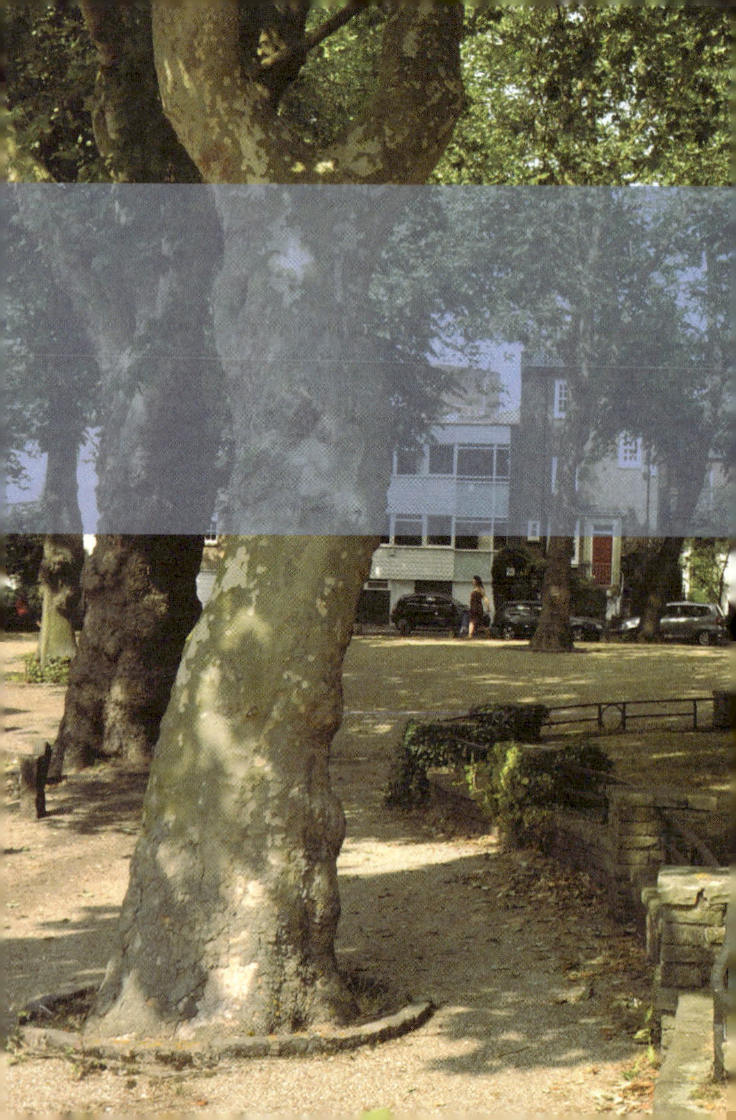

3 Highgate Walk

Pond Square, see p.81

Highgate Walk

1. Abandoned station
2. No 26 Priory Gardens
3. Peter Sellers (plaque)
4. Highgate Wood
5. Boogaloo pub house
6. Lubetkin Highpoint Apartments
7. Charles Dickens (plaque)
8. AE Houseman (plaque)
9. Chapel of Highgate School
10. The Gatehouse public house
11. No 44 Highgate High Street
12. Pond Square
13. Highgate Literary & Scientific Institution
14. Church House
15. Moreton House
16. No 16 The Lawns
17. The Old Hall
18. St Michael's church
19. The Flask
20. Samuel Coleridge (plaque)
21. Witanhurst
22. No 40 Highgate West Hill
23. Sir John Betjeman (plaque)
24. Holly Lodge Estate
25. Holly Village
26. Highgate Cemetery
27. Waterlow Park
28. Lauderdale House
29. Whittington Stone

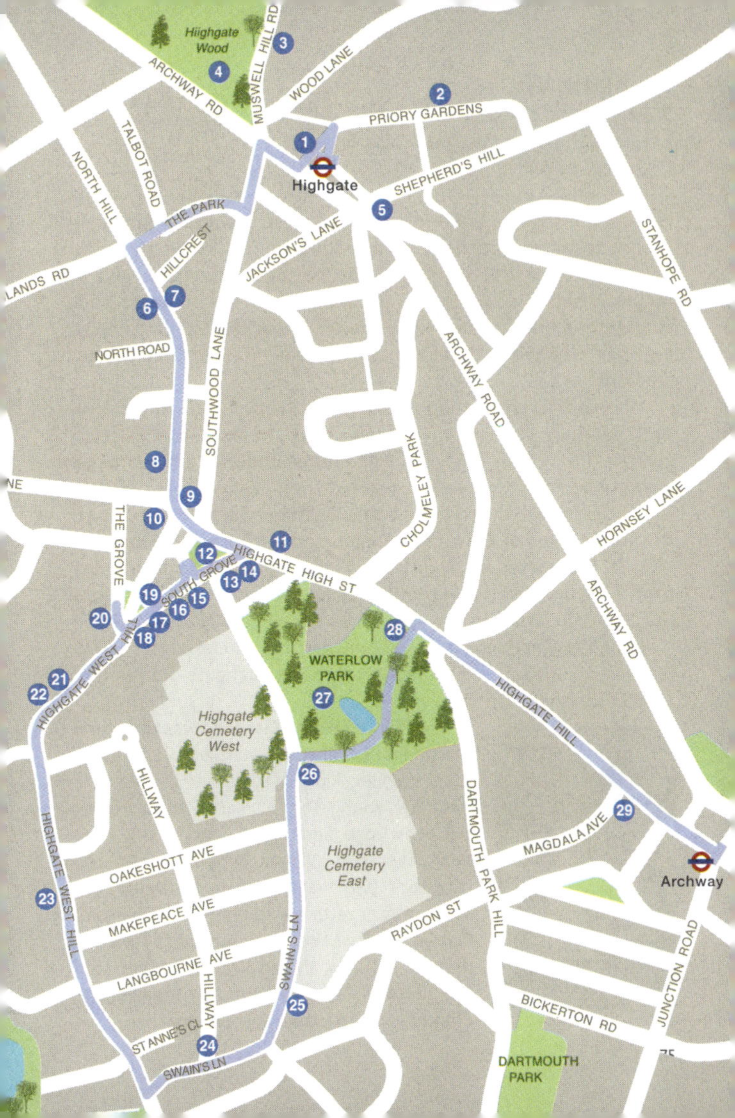

Hiighgate Wood
ARCHWAY RD
MUSWELL HILL RD
WOOD LANE
PRIORY GARDENS
Highgate
SHEPHERD'S HILL
NORTH HILL
TALBOT ROAD
THE PARK
HILLCREST
JACKSON'S LANE
LANDS RD
STANHOPE RD
NORTH ROAD
SOUTHWOOD LANE
ARCHWAY ROAD
CHOLMELEY PARK
NE
THE GROVE
HIGHGATE HIGH ST
HORNSEY LANE
SOUTH GROVE
ARCHWAY RD
HIGHGATE WEST HILL
WATERLOW PARK
HIGHGATE HILL
Highgate Cemetery West
HILLWAY
DARTMOUTH PARK HILL
MAGDALA AVE
Archway
Highgate Cemetery East
OAKESHOTT AVE
MAKEPEACE AVE
RAYDON ST
LANGBOURNE AVE
SWAIN'S LN
JUNCTION ROAD
BICKERTON RD
ST ANNE'S CL
DARTMOUTH PARK

Highgate Walk

Start: Highgate underground station
Finish: Archway underground station
Distance: 3.1 miles

Highgate is one of London's most affluent suburbs, with ready access to parks and benefiting from stunning views over the capital. It was once owned by the bishops of London, and in medieval times a road running north out of the city was built through the bishops' hunting grounds. It was the toll gate in this high part of London that gave, what was once an isolated village, its name.

Leave the tube station via the Priory Gardens exit. If you look back carefully towards the underground station you may get a glimpse through the foliage of a ❶ **long-abandoned station** on an overground line operated by Great Northern Railway that ran from King's Cross (via Potters Bar) to the North between 1867 and 1941. It was later part of a Northern Line extension known as Northern Heights that closed in 1954. The 4.5 mile course of the railway line from Finsbury Park to Alexandra Palace has been converted into the Parkland Walk, which was declared a Local Nature Reserve (London's longest) in 1990. The only part that is closed (for safety reasons) to walkers is the section through Highgate station and adjacent tunnels.

❷ **No.26 Priory Gardens** was the home of Bridget Dowling who married Adolf Hitler's older brother, Alois, in 1910. She settled here with her young son, William Patrick Hitler, between 1930 and 1939. During this time both Alois and William benefited from the dictator's patronage back in Germany, but William later returned to his mother in Priory Gardens before they both moved to America in 1939. During World War II Bridget sold her 'inside' story on life on the fringes of the Hitler family to many newspapers.

Another World War II connection to this area concerns the controversial politician and entertainer Jerry Springer. He was born at the tube station in 1944 while his mother was sheltering from a German bomb attack.

Return to the station and exit on the other side to reach the Archway Road exit. There are a couple of optional detours here.

The first is a few hundred yards up Muswell Hill Road where you will find, at No.10, a blue plaque commemorating ❸ **Peter Sellers**, who lived here between 1936 and 1940. It was the first plaque placed by the Dead Comics Society, as a reaction to English Heritage's Blue Plaque Panel's perceived neglect of comedians. Also on this detour you can see ❹ **Highgate Wood** on your left and Queen's Wood on your right, both of which comprise rare ancient woodland (some of the nearest to central London).

The second detour leads you left down the hill of Archway Road. Shortly on the left, you come across the ❺ **Boogaloo pub** at number 312, a legendary music venue where Pete Doherty and Carl Barat reunited (as the Libertines) and Doherty sang with his then-girlfriend Kate Moss (whose former house you will see later). This has also been a favourite haunt of The Pogues front-man, Shane MacGowan, who used to live upstairs.

If you do not want to follow these detours, cross Archway Road at the crossing just to the right of the station exit and continue south along Southwood Lane. There is a passageway on the right called Park Walk – take this to reach North Hill.

When you reach North Hill, on the other side you will see the ❻ **Highpoint apartment block complex**. This comprises Highpoint I and II, a renowned example of Modernist architecture designed by the Russian emigré Berthold Lubetkin (1901-90). Highpoint I was completed in 1935, with II following in 1938. Le Corbusier was a fan of Lubetkin's innovative design, particularly its use of reinforced concrete, and he described it as 'the seed of the vertical garden city'. Lubetkin was also responsible for other important London landmarks such as the Penguin Pool at London Zoo, the Spa Green Estate and the Finsbury Health Centre.

From the Highpoint complex continue southwards down North Hill. On the opposite side, at number 92 (just a few doors down from The Wrestler Public House) there is a plaque remembering the brief stay of ❼ **Charles Dickens** (1812-1870) here in 1832. At this time his father John was moving his family around to avoid his many creditors and the young Charles wrote to his friend Henry Kolle that his new address was 'Mrs Goodman's next door to the old Red Lion.... I am sorry I cannot offer you a bed because we are so pressed for room that I myself hang out at the Red Lion'.

Dickens came back to Highgate many times during his life, and David Copperfield – thought to be his most autobiographical character – also stayed here (see later in the walk). Several members of the writer's family, including his mother, father and daughter Dora, are buried in Highgate West Cemetery.

Highgate Walk

The Red Lion that Dickens knew was demolished in 1900, and was one of 19 inns that once served what was still a fairly small village in the 19th century. The inns were famous for the ancient ceremony of Swearing on the Horns, which involved initiates having to kiss a pair of stag antlers, swearing an oath to only drink strong ale and various other amusing rites. Those who completed the initiation were granted the Freedom of Highgate and given the right to kiss the most beautiful girl in the room.

As you continue down look for number 17 (on the right-hand side) – there is another plaque that recalls that ❽ **AE Houseman** (1859-1936), the poet and scholar, wrote *A Shropshire Lad* (1896) whilst living here. The poem begins by remembering the names of Shropshire men who died fighting for their queen, and its nostalgic tone and theme of death made it the most popular poem amongst the British troops during World War II.

You soon reach Highgate High Street, at which point cross over the road. Look out for ❾ **the Chapel of Highgate School** on the left-hand side, part of the main entrance to the senior school. This served as the main place of worship in the village until the 1820s when the authorities decided that villagers should not be worshipping in a school chapel. This led to the building of St Michael's parish church seen later on during the walk. The original free school in Highgate was founded by Sir Richard Cholmeley in 1565 under the patronage of Elizabeth I (old boys are still called Old Cholmeleians). This was an era when aristocrats were beginning to build mansions in the village, attracted by the clean country air and space. Today it costs around £24,000 a year to send a senior pupil to Highgate School.

Past pupils include the poet Sir John Betjeman (1906-1984). As a child he lived nearby (the house is seen later) and was taught at the school during 1916 by another famous poet – TS Eliot. Other former pupils include film critic Barry Norman, cricketer Phil Tufnell, footballer Joe Cole, inventor Sir Clive Sinclair, composer Sir John Tavener, and a fair number of pop stars including Crispian Mills of Kula Shaker, Ringo Starr's son Zac (who has been the drummer with Oasis and The Who), Johnny Borrell of Razorlight, and John Moss of Culture Club.

Just over the roundabout opposite the school you will see **The Gatehouse public house**. This is located near the site of the original toll gate that was demolished in 1892, having collected road tolls since 1318. The pub is an excellent place for an early refreshment break before tackling Highgate's many hills, and is reputedly haunted by the ghost of Mother Marnes who was robbed and murdered inside the old gate. Charles Dickens is said to have visited the previous pub on the site (the current building dates from the early 20th century) and the first cartoon to appear in Punch magazine was sketched at the pub.

In medieval times a hermit lived on the site and his job for the Bishop was to maintain the road that served as the main exit route north out of London. As part of his road building duties he dug gravel from the ground nearby which in turn became a pond, now the heart of Pond Square (seen later on). Highgate's development was linked to the increasingly heavy traffic on the road and drovers would stop in the village's many public houses to drink and rest before heading into London's Smithfield Market to sell their animals.

Follow the map down Highgate High Street, full of elegant shops and Georgian buildings. ⓫ **Number 44** (by Townshend Yard) was once a chemist's where poet Samuel Taylor Coleridge (1772-1834) would enter by a secret door in order to take delivery of laudanum. Coleridge, best known for the poems *The Rime of the Ancient Mariner* and *Kubla Khan*, and whose house we visit later in the walk, was addicted to this opium derivative. He lived in Highgate with his protector Dr James Gillman and his family for many years until his death in 1834. Gillman did his best to cure Coleridge of his terrible addiction but was unsuccessful. Somewhat incongruously, the Sharon Stone film *Basic Instinct 2* featured scenes shot in and around these streets in 2005.

Follow the map along South Grove. You very soon reach ⓬ **Pond Square**. This is the location of the original village green although the pond was drained in 1844. Francis Bacon (1561-1626), the great philosopher, lawyer and – according to conspiracy theorists – the true author of the plays attributed to

Shakespeare – caught a fatal chill here after experimentally using snow that had fallen to freeze a chicken. Bacon died in 1626 in Arundel House which stood on the site of the current Old Hall (seen slightly further along the walk).

Highgate is fond of its ghosts and it is even said the square is haunted by the ghost of Bacon's frozen chicken. The Square is also the site of the Highgate Festival normally held every June, and which in the past had been partly funded by the late George Michael when he was a Highgate resident.

Continue along, looking on the left for ⓭ **The Highgate Literary and Scientific Institution** at number 11 South Grove. It was founded in 1839 to encourage intellectual pursuits and today houses a library and special collections on Coleridge and Betjeman. It also holds regular lectures on a variety of topics, many presented by well-known media figures and academics. An individual membership costs around £60 a year if you want to rub shoulders with Highgate's intelligentsia and enjoy the institution's extensive library.

Beside the Institution at number 10 South Grove is ⓮ **Church House**. This is thought to be the 'old brick house at Highgate on the very summit of the hill', where the Steerforths live in *David Copperfield*. Copperfield is invited to stay and describes it as '... a genteel old-fashioned house, very quiet and orderly. From the windows of my room I saw all London lying in the distance like a great vapour, with here and there some lights twinkling through it.'

⓯ **Moreton House** at number 14 South Grove is nearby. It was here that Coleridge first came to live in Highgate with the Gillman family in 1816. Originally he came to have tea with Gillman, and discuss a way he might overcome his opium addiction.

14 Church House

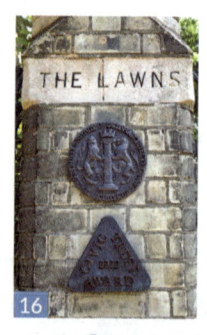

Gillman suggested the poet stay with him and his family just for a few weeks, but Coleridge never left. Many of the great literary and intellectual figures of the day would visit Coleridge in Highgate, including Dante Gabriel Rossetti, John Stuart Mill, William Wordsworth, William Hazlitt, Robert Southey and Charles Lamb. According to Thomas Carlyle, 'Coleridge sat on the brow of Highgate Hill in those years looking down on London and its smoke-tumult, like a sage escaped from the inanity of life's battle'.

At ⓰ **number 16** is **The Lawns**, a sleek steel and glass house that was shortlisted for the 2001 Stirling Prize for Architecture (Britain's premier architecture award) and was described by the Guardian as 'the most important house built in Britain for years'. Perhaps ironically, the owner at the time, John Sorrell – a former chairman of the Design Council – objected to his next-door neighbour's plans to build a futuristic roof extension on his house. Sadly, The Lawns lies discreetly behind a wall and very little can be seen from the road.

The target of the complaint – film director Terry Gilliam – had a little dig at the 'relative newcomers' in a public statement, having lived in the next house up (The Old Hall) since the 1980s. In 2009 Gilliam was interviewed by the *Evening Standard* and when asked about what advice would he give to a tourist visiting London, answered 'Get the f*** out of this town, we can't move for you. We get a lot of tourists in Highgate looking for Marx's grave'. Don't take it personally.

Continuing west, you pass ⓱ **The Old Hall** – the largest residence on South Grove and the core of which dates from the 1690s. As mentioned earlier, it stands on part of the site of the long-demolished Arundel House where Sir Francis Bacon died after his frozen chicken experiment. Elizabeth I visited

Arundel House, and James I was entertained there with Ben Jonson's play *Penates*.

Next door is ⑱ **St Michael's church**, opened for worship in 1832 and said to be the highest church in London (the entrance is level with the cross on the top of St Paul's Cathedral). Coleridge was originally buried in the little graveyard at the top of the High Street by the school chapel but his remains were brought to St Michael's in 1961 and the Poet Laureate, John Masefield, gave the address at the unveiling of the stone memorial (found in the central isle). Coleridge almost certainly worshipped at the church, as it was consecrated 18 months before he died. In *David Copperfield*, Dickens described St Michael's as 'The church with the slender spire, that stands on top of the hill'.

Opposite is ⑲ **The Flask,** the most famous pub in Highgate. It dates from at least the 1660s although the main structure is roughly 100 years older. The pub took its name from the flasks of Hampstead spring water that were once sold here when Hampstead was still a popular spa resort (Hampstead has its own pub of the same name). The Flask is well-known for the 'Swearing of the Horns' ceremony mentioned earlier. The poet Lord Byron swore the oath and referred to it in his poem *Childe Harold's Pilgrimage*. The Flask can count highwayman Dick Turpin, Coleridge, Karl Marx and artist William Hogarth among its former customers, and is also said to be haunted by a female ghost whose presence is announced by a sudden drop in temperature.

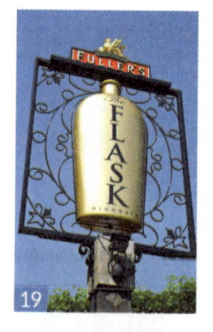

Follow the map to enter The Grove. This contains the finest houses in the village, many dating from the late 17th century and costing on average more than £13 million. It is also home to perhaps the highest concentration of famous pop stars and actors in London.

However, its first famous resident was **20 Samuel Coleridge** who lived on the top floor of number 3 for the last 11 years of his life after moving with the Gillman family from Moreton House. The house was later occupied by JB Priestley, making this a rare property that can boast two commemorative plaques. The model Kate Moss lived here for many years but moved in 2022.

Other local residents have included (no.2) Yehudi Menuhin and Sting, Jamie Oliver (no.4), George Michael (no.5), Annie Lennox (no.6), Robert Donat (no.7) and spy Antony Blunt (no.9). It was at Sting's house that Madonna met her second husband Guy Ritchie.

Follow the map down Highgate West Hill looking out for the gates of **21 Witanhurst** on the right-hand side. This is said to be the second largest private residence in London after Buckingham Palace. The original house was built in 1774, but was later torn down and rebuilt by the soap magnate Sir Arthur Crosfield in 1913. The Crosfield family owned the house until the early 1970s.

The house was bought for £50 million in 2009 and work has undergone years of redevelopment. It has been reported that the house now boasts 65 rooms including 25 bedrooms, 12 bathrooms and a walnut-panelled Grand Ballroom, together with a huge two-storey subterranean extension intended to house a 70ft swimming pool and a cinema. Over the years the property has served as a location for a number of costume dramas, including *Tipping the Velvet* and *Nicholas Nicklebly*.

At ❷❷ **number 40 Highgate West Hill** is a building that was formerly the Fox and Crown public house. In 1837 its landlord James Turner saved Queen Victoria from a potential disaster when a wheel from her carriage fell off. She rewarded him with a Royal Coat of Arms for his pub.

Continue down Highgate West Hill looking out for the childhood home of ❷❸ **Sir John Betjeman** at number 31. He later remembered his days here in his blank verse autobiography *Summoned by Bells* (1960):

> *Safe, in a world of trains and buttered toast*
> *Where things inanimate could feel and think,*
> *Deeply I loved thee, 31 West Hill!*
> *At that hill's foot did London then begin*
> *With yellow horse-trams clopping past the planes.*

From here follow the map to descend Highgate West Hill before turning left into Swain's Lane and continue eastwards. The lane dates from the 15th century at least, one of four old parallel pathways leading up to Highgate village. It was also once known as Swines Lane, and allowed access to the farms – presumably populated with pigs (or swine) – on either side.

On your left after a few minutes you will see the entrance to the amazingly neat and ordered ㉔ **Holly Lodge Estate**. The origins of Holly Lodge date back to 1798 when Sir Henry Tempest built a villa here. The land he developed included Traitor's Hill, said to be where members of the gunpowder plot met to watch the Palace of Westminster blow up in 1605. The villa was named The Holly Lodge and in 1809 was leased by an actress named Harriot Mellon. She later married the banker Thomas Coutts in 1815 and enlarged the estate.

When she died in 1837 she left her estate to Mr Coutts' granddaughter, Angela Burdett-Coutts (1814-1906). Burdett-Coutts was widely regarded as one of the most remarkable women of her age, using her enormous wealth to help fund a vast number of philanthropic causes. She entertained the great and good of Victorian society at her villa here, including Queen Victoria and Charles Dickens (who dedicated his novel *Martin Chuzzlewit* to her). She was also close friends with the Duke of Wellington. After her death, her husband put the estate on the market and in the 1920s it was developed into the residential estate seen today. The villa was demolished and the meadows where Burdett-Coutts had once entertained her famous visitors were built over. Part of the new estate was acquired by The Lady Workers' Homes Co. Limited who built accommodation for single women moving to London in order to work as secretaries and clerks in the City.

Continue along and on the right-hand side you will see (just before Chester Road) ㉕ **Holly Village**. This dates from the 1860s and was designed by the architect Henry Astley Darbishire for Burdett-Coutts. It consists of a group of eight buildings built around a green. The houses may have been intended for senior or retired workers on the estate.

25 Holly Village

Highgate Walk

What is not in doubt is that this neo-Gothic fantasy is one of the very few developments of its type in London to survive. The diamond-shaped Coutts coat-of-arms appears prominently in Portland stone on each building, and over the entrance archway is inscribed, 'Holly Village Erected By A.G.B. Coutts A.D. 1865.' The sculptures on either side of the archway are of Burdett-Coutts herself and her governess and long-time companion, Hannah Brown. Darbishire later designed some of the first flats built by another great Victorian philanthropist, George Peabody.

Today Holly Village is a private residence, so please respect their privacy. Coutts Bank – whose profits helped build the village – continues to this day and is still the bank used by the Royal Family.

Continue north up Swain's Lane (the Holly Lodge Estate is on your left). You soon reach the main entrance to the western and eastern sections of ㉖ **Highgate Cemetery**. This is considered to be one of the most important cemeteries in Europe, covering a total of 37 acres. The original cemetery (now called the West Cemetery) was founded in 1839 and an extension (the East Cemetery) opened in 1854. About 170,000 people are buried here in 52,000 graves, and the two sides were once linked by a tunnel under Swain's Lane.

The West Cemetery (see p.95 for opening times) is the most impressive, crammed full of gothic tombs covered in ivy. It is here that the poet Christina Rossettie was buried in 1894. The plot served the illustrious Rossetti family and in 1862 was the resting place for the wife of the poet and painter Dante Gabriel Rossetti, Elizabeth Siddal. The grieving poet placed some manuscript poems in the grave but seven years later, and evidently short of cash, he arranged to have the tomb opened so he could retrieve the poems and get them published.

Unfortunately given the delicate state of many of the tombs you can only visit the West Cemetery via a guided tour organised by the Friends of Highgate Cemetery, who set up a trust in 1975 to take control of both cemeteries and acquire the freehold. Not normally on the tour, but possible to visit by special request, are the graves of Dickens's parents John and Elizabeth, his daughter Dora Annie Dickens (1850-51) and his elder sister, Fanny (1810-48).

Highgate Walk

If you cannot take the tour of the West Cemetery you can still visit the East Cemetery. It contains the tomb of Karl Marx, who was buried in a section of unconsecrated ground on account of being a Jew. The Marx Memorial Library in Clerkenwell holds a memorial service for Marx at his tomb every year on March 12, the date he died. The Communist clearly stirs emotions even after his death – his tomb has been lucky to survive several attacks over the years.

Other notable people buried here are Douglas Adams, author of *The Hitchhiker's Guide to the Galaxy*; the author Beryl Bainbridge; Charles Cruft, founder of Crufts dog show; George Eliot (Mary Ann Evans); Michael Faraday, chemist and physicist; Paul Foot, campaigning journalist; Claudia Jones, black political activist and the 'mother' of the Notting Hill Carnival; Alexander Litvinenko, Russian dissident, murdered by poisoning in London; Malcolm McLaren, punk impresario; Ralph Miliband, left wing political theorist, father of David and Ed Miliband; actor Sir Ralph Richardson; 19th-century boxer Tom Sayers; Max Wall, comedian and entertainer; and Adam Worth, criminal and possible inspiration for Sherlock Holmes's nemesis, Professor Moriarty.

Close to Karl Marx is the more recent grave of the young *Observer* journalist Farzad Bazoft, who was arrested on false charges of spying and executed under the orders of Saddam Hussain in 1990. The execution was one of the key turning points in relations between the West and Iraq that led to harsh sanctions and two wars.

In the 1970s the derelict cemetery became the haunt of Satanists and other strange groups, and a media frenzy erupted over stories about a vampire stalking the residents of Highgate. However when the Friends of Highgate Cemetery took over in 1975 they made the cemetery a sensible, well-ordered place to visit without fear of being vampirised.

When finished at Highgate Cemetery follow the map to enter ㉗ **Waterlow Park,** a good spot for a picnic if the weather is fine. The park was given to the public in 1889 as a 'garden for the gardenless' by the businessman, MP and philanthropist Sir Sydney Waterlow (1822-1906).

27 Waterlow Park

Highgate Walk

Head for ㉘ **Lauderdale House** on the eastern side, built during the reign of Elizabeth I. Charles I let his mistress Nell Gwyn live here and, according to legend, when he refused to acknowledge their illegitimate son she threatened to drop the child from a window, to which the King reputedly responded with some dash 'save the Earl of Burford!'. The house now hosts cultural and other activities, including many music concerts – it is worth checking what is happening on their website in case you want to plan your walk around an event (www.lauderdalehouse.co.uk). The house also has a very good café which has outdoor seating looking out over the park.

When finished leave through the main entrance of Lauderdale House to reach Highgate Hill. Head down the hill. Soon you will see the ㉙ **Whittington Stone** at the corner with Magdala Avenue. Erected in 1821, it commemorates Sir Richard (or 'Dick') Whittington who, so the story goes, was sulking his way north out of London when the Bow Bells called him to 'turn again'. He returned to London and went on to become its Mayor four times between 1397 and 1420. In reality Whittington was not the poor boy of pantomime lore but the son of a wealthy Gloucestershire family. In Dickens' *Oliver Twist*, Bill Sikes passed this stone after the murder of Nancy.

From here continue down the hill through an area the estate agents refer to as 'Highgate Slopes', to reach Archway Station and the end of this walk. If you look back up Highgate Hill, try to picture the first cable car in Europe, which ran from here to Highgate Village between 1884 and 1909, carrying people up the notorious 1 in 11 (9%) climb. ●

28 *Lauderdale House*

VISIT...

Highgate Cemetery (see p.91)
Swain's Lane, N6 6PJ
Tel: 020 8340 1834
www.highgatecemetery.org

Highgate Literary & Scientific Institution (see p.82)
11 South Grove, N6 6BS
www.hlsi.net

Lauderdale House
Waterlow Park, N6 5AT
www.lauderdalehouse.org.uk

EAT, DRINK...

Boogaloo Pub (see p.77)
312 Archway Road, N6 5AT
www.theboogaloo.co.uk

The Flask (see p.85)
77 Highgate West Hill, N6 6BU
www.theflaskhighgate.com

The Gatehouse (see p.80)
1 North Road, N6 4BD
www.thegatehousen6.com

Lauderdale House Café
Waterlow Park, N6 5AT
www.lauderdalehouse.co.uk

Queens Wood Café
42 Muswell Hill Road, N10 3JP
www.queenswoodcafe.co.uk

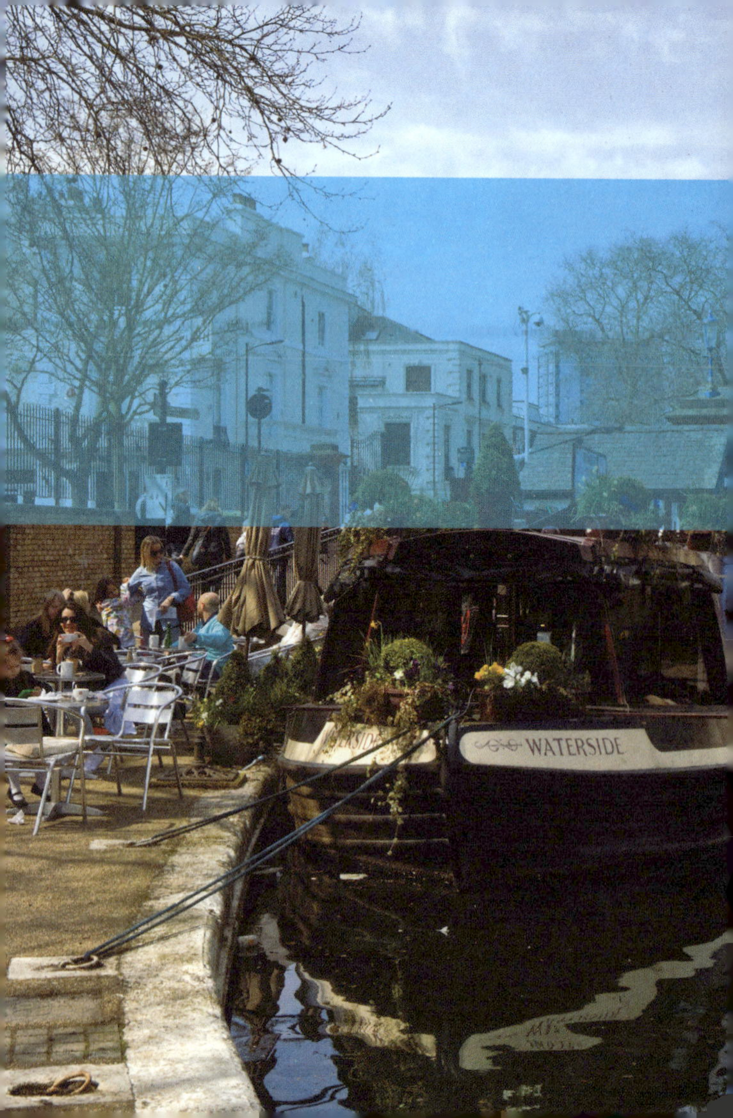
WATERSIDE

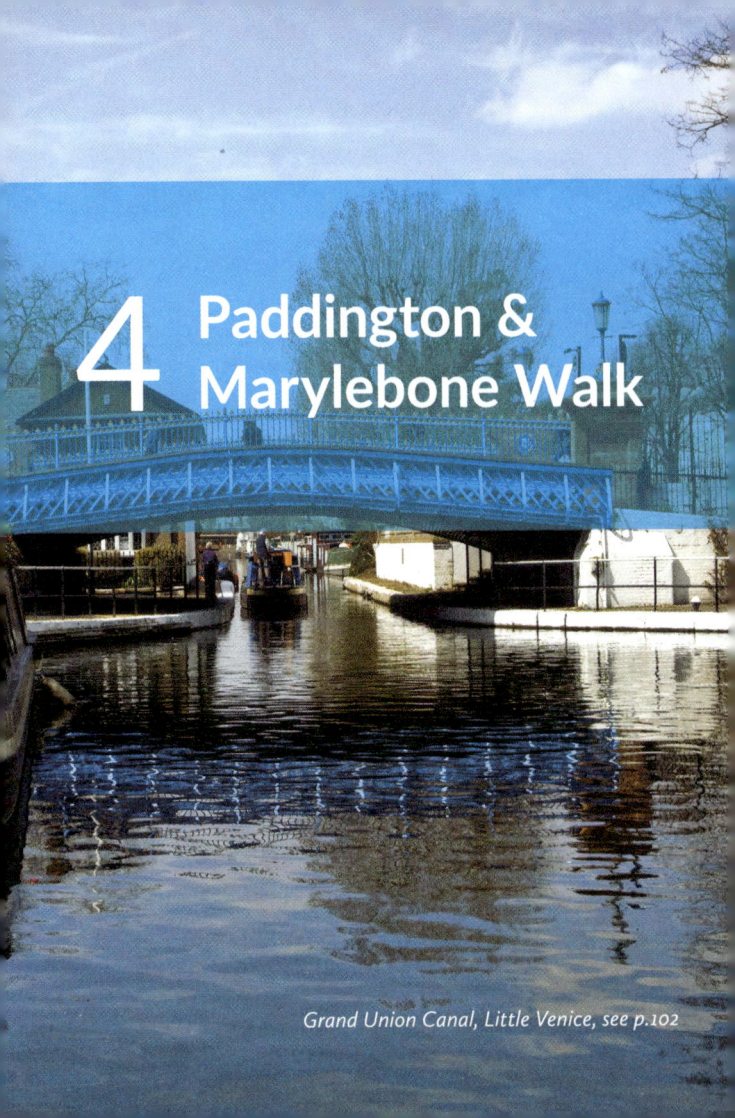

4 Paddington & Marylebone Walk

Grand Union Canal, Little Venice, see p.102

Paddington & Marylebone Walk

1. Cabmen's Shelter
2. Grand Union Canal
3. Bridge
4. Little Venice
5. Browning's Pool
6. Puppet Theatre Barge
7. Westway
8. Walking Man & Standing Man
9. St David's Welsh church
10. St Mary's Paddington
11. Fleming Court
12. Public garden
13. Sarah Siddons
14. Paddington Green
15. City of Westminster College
16. Paddington Green Hospital
17. Former Paddington Green Station
18. Edgware Road
19. Edgware Road tube station
20. Joe Strummer Subway
21. Robertsons
22. Coade stone keystones
23. Christian Union Almshouses
24. Cato Street Conspiracy
25. Seymour Leisure Centre
26. St Mary's Church
27. St Mary Le Bone Western National School
28. Maltese Cross
29. York Street Ladies Residential Chambers of 1892
30. Parish Hall of St Mary's
31. Meacher Higgins & Thomas
32. John Lennon (blue plaque)
33. Marble Arch
34. Connaught Square
35. Frederick Close
36. St George's graveyard
37. Lord Randolph Churchill (blue plaque)
38. Tyburn gallows

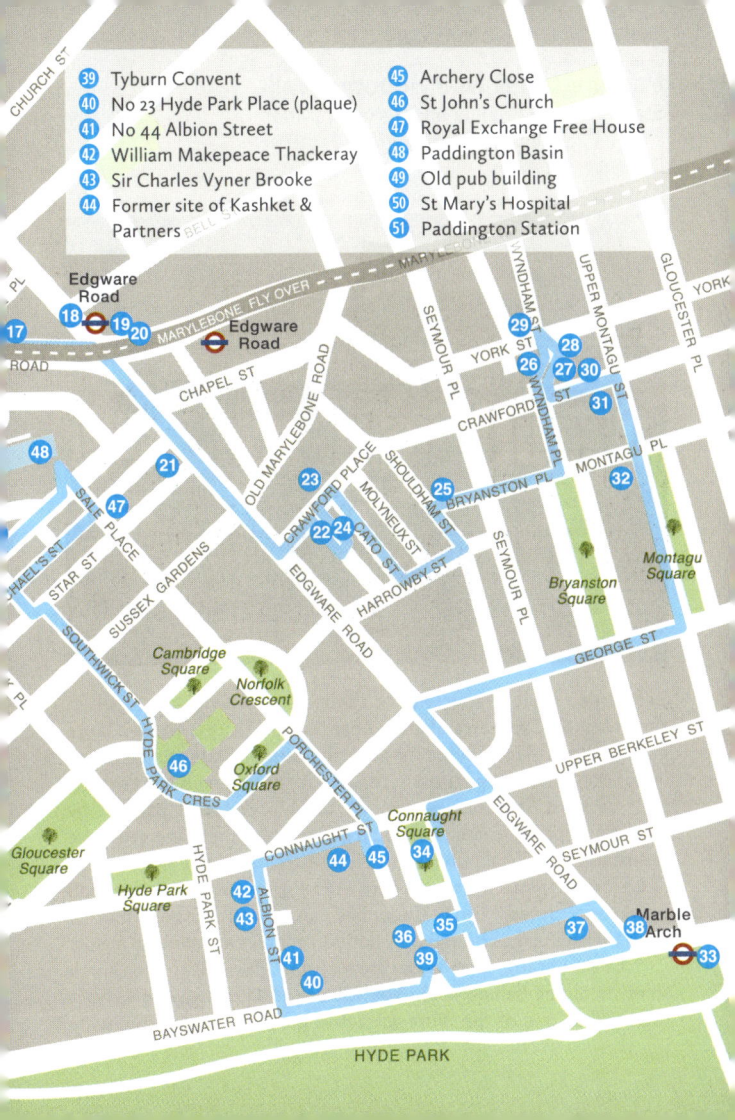

- 39 Tyburn Convent
- 40 No 23 Hyde Park Place (plaque)
- 41 No 44 Albion Street
- 42 William Makepeace Thackeray
- 43 Sir Charles Vyner Brooke
- 44 Former site of Kashket & Partners
- 45 Archery Close
- 46 St John's Church
- 47 Royal Exchange Free House
- 48 Paddington Basin
- 49 Old pub building
- 50 St Mary's Hospital
- 51 Paddington Station

Paddington & Marylebone Walk

Paddington & Marylebone Walk
Start: Warwick Avenue underground station
Finish: Paddington rail/underground station
Distance: 6.4 miles

Before you leave the vicinity of the station, walk over to look at the green ❶ **Cabmen's Shelter** near the exit (it resembles a large garden shed). This is one of 13 such shelters that can still be found in London. They originated in the mid 1870s when philanthropists such as Lord Shaftesbury decided to help London's cabbies by providing a place where they could get a decent meal and avoid the temptations of local public houses. The shelters were not allowed to be longer than a horse and cart and by 1914 over 60 shelters had been constructed. Today the public can purchase food and drink from the shelters although only London cabbies are allowed inside.

Exit the station and follow the map up Clifton Villas (the church spire should be behind you). You will see straight away why this is regarded as one of the more attractive parts of London, the wide streets flanked by elegant stuccoed 19th-century villas. Warwick Avenue itself is named after Jane Warwick of Warwick Hall in Cumbria who, in 1778, married into a family that once owned much of the land around here. As late as 1830 maps of London show the area north of the canal still covered by open fields as far as Kilburn.

You soon reach Blomfield Road, which runs alongside the Paddington Branch of the ❷ **Grand Union Canal**. This canal stretches for 137 miles between London and Birmingham. It was built between 1793 and 1805 and initially connected the Midlands with London west of here at Brentford. It was then decided to bring the canal even further into the capital, and in 1801 this section – the Paddington Branch – was completed. It leads to Paddington Basin, seen later on in the walk.

However, Paddington Basin is still several miles from the Thames and the docks and wharves that made up the Pool of London – the greatest port in the world during the 19th and first half of the 20th century. The need to connect up inland trade with the Port of London more effectively led to the creation of the Regent's Canal, built between 1812 and 1820. This cuts eastwards through St John's Wood, around Regent's Park and then through Camden, King's Cross and Islington until it reaches the Thames at Limehouse and connecting with the Grand Union Canal on the way.

From Blomfield Road look out onto the canal boats below. Delamere Terrace faces Blomfield Road on the other side. The painter Lucian Freud (1922-2011) moved into 4 Delamere Terrace (on the other side of the canal) in 1944 and he lived and worked there for over 30 years. In 1945 the painter caught a teenager burgling the studio and instead of calling the police, persuaded the local boy to model for him.

One of Britain's greatest living entrepreneurs, Richard Branson (b.1950), was driving down Blomfield Road in 1971 when his car broke down. He was already keen to live on a canal boat,

Paddington & Marylebone Walk

and began a conversation with an Irishman standing on the pavement who, upon hearing about Branson's interest, directed him to a narrow boat the Irishman had recently sold to a young woman. Branson ended up moving in and later stayed for many years on a large canal boat beside Blomfield Road. His canal boat features in his autobiography, and many key moments in his life were played out there. A few years ago it was reported in the press that the billionaire had renovated the vessel after complaints from local residents about its dilapidated appearance.

Head left down Blomfield Road and cross over ❸ **the bridge** (Westbourne Terrace Road Bridge) to join the tow path on the other side. Continue to walk eastwards. You are now entering ❹ **Little Venice** – London's modest, yet pretty answer to the great Italian city. Little Venice is essentially the junction of the Grand Union Canal (Paddington Branch) as it leads down to Paddington Basin, and the entrance to the Regent's Canal that leads to Limehouse.

❹ Little Venice

Paddington & Marylebone Walk

The origin of the name Little Venice is unlikely ever to be fully known, although the best explanation is that it was first coined by the poet Lord Byron. He was possibly, tongue firmly in cheek, comparing the area with the canals of the Venice that he knew so well. The origin has also been attributed to another poet, Robert Browning (1812-1889), who lived in Warwick Crescent for many years after his wife, and fellow poet, Elizabeth Barrett Browning died in 1861 (they had lived together in Italy). However, the area was not commonly known as Little Venice until the second half of the 20th century.

As you continue along the tow path you will see a small island lying in a large triangle of water. This is known as ❺ **Browning's Pool** and is the heart of Little Venice. Originally known as 'The Broadwater', it formerly served as a holding area for the barges making their way down to Paddington Basin or the Regent's Canal.

Paddington & Marylebone Walk

If you have time you can take a canal boat trip from Little Venice (see the London Waterbus Company p.127). The ❻ **Puppet Theatre Barge** (on the north side) is also worth a visit if you have children with you. Visitors in May should look out for the canal boat festival that takes place here – a great jamboree as dozens of canal boats congregate and various entertainments are put on. The festival helps make this area feel unlike any other part of London.

Continue along the right-hand tow path of the canal that leads down to Paddington Basin. You soon pass under the ❼ **Westway**, with hundreds of vehicles thundering overhead. This elevated section of the A40 runs for 3.5 miles and was built between 1965 and 1970. It was a controversial development, forcing hundreds of people to be moved out of their homes that were demolished along its route. The looming Westway has always attracted strong views and inspired JG Ballard's book *Concrete Island* (1974) which saw a middle class man stranded in a no-man's land under the road.

Walking under the Westway you will encounter two men who are permanent features of the landscape. These disturbingly life-like figures are called ❽ ***Walking Man*** and ***Standing Man*** and are the work of artist Sean Henry.

The Clash also referred to the Westway in their song *London's Burning*. Countless bands have had their photographs taken under its dramatic urban lines (see the cover of The Jam's *This is a Modern World*).

Just after you pass under the Westway cross over the footbridge and walk through the bright orange underpass on the other side of the canal. This leads you under the roaring Westway again and once on the other side turn right, following the map up Porteus Road and then bear right into St Mary's Terrace.

On the left-hand side look out for an ornate gothic entrance that leads down to **❾ St David's Welsh church**. This dates from 1890 and replaced London's last thatched house. It is a rare example of a church offering Welsh language services in London.

Continue along St Mary's Terrace, and very soon you see another church – **❿ St Mary's Paddington**. This was the original parish church and stands at the very heart of the old Paddington district.

However, before visiting St Mary's, stop on the left-hand side at **⓫ Fleming Court**. This is an excellent example of post World War II social housing, though its real point of interest can be seen under the entrance on the right. Here you will find a memorial plaque that commemorates the opening of this building by Sir Alexander Fleming (1881-1955), most famous for his discovery of penicillin at St Mary's hospital in Paddington in 1928. By the time Fleming opened the building named after him in 1948 he was a world famous scientist, and had recently been awarded the Nobel Prize. Since its discovery, penicillin has helped eradicate or control many diseases such as syphilis and tuberculosis and so saved millions of lives.

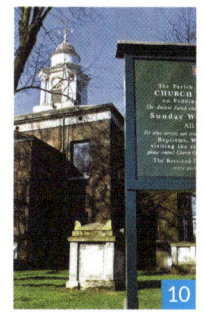

Part of Fleming's drive came from his years of service during World War I when he realised more soldiers were dying of infected wounds than in battle. He returned from the war to begin his research at St Mary's Hospital – seen later on in the walk.

Continue along to visit St Mary's church. The first church here was recorded in the 13th century and this building dates from 1791. The great poet John Donne preached at an earlier incarnation of St Mary's and the painter William Hogarth was married here.

Next to the church is a ⑫ **public garden** which was originally the churchyard of St Mary's – you can still see hundreds of gravestones that were moved beside the wall when the park was created in the 1890s. Look out for the grisly skull and crossbones carved onto one of the gravestones on the north-west wall of the park (near to the rear of St Mary's).

South of the church and within the park is a striking statue of the 18th-century actor ⑬ **Sarah Siddons** (1755-1831) – now gazing out over a brutally busy road instead of the fields and canal that would have dominated the landscape during her lifetime. She was the leading tragic actress of her day giving performances that were legendary for their emotional intensity, provoking fainting and hysteria from her adoring public. Siddons was particularly famous for her portrayal of Lady Macbeth. She was also the subject of portraits by Reynolds, Gainsborough and Lawrence, engravings of which further added to her fame.

When finished continue past the church to reach ⑭ **Paddington Green** to the east. Paddington is named after 'Padda's tun' (or farm) – Padda being possibly a Saxon landowner or a 7th century King of Mercia whose followers took control of London. In medieval times the district was just fields surrounding a small village under the control of the Abbott of Westminster until his lands were seized by Henry VIII. It was later returned to the control of the church. The development of the canal and growing suburbs surrounding this area means Paddington Green remains the only real remnant of the old parish of Paddington.

Between 1998 and 2001, the BBC broadcast *Paddington Green* – exploring over six series the colourful lives of several residents in the area. This perhaps reinforced the perception that Paddington had more than its fair share of hard luck stories, with many residents keen to escape the area.

George Shillibeer ran the first omnibus service in London from Paddington Green to Bank in 1829, and number 13 housed the office of England's first famous private detective – Ignatius Paul Pollaky (1828-1918). Known as 'Paddington Pollaky', he came to England from Hungary and had a colourful career, serving as a special with the Metropolitan Police and at one point keeping track of Confederate agents who were buying arms in London during the American Civil War. It has been suggested he helped inspire Arthur Conan Doyle's fictional detective Sherlock Holmes.

The famous English song *Pretty Polly Perkins of Paddington Green* also brought this area into the public consciousness. It was composed for the music hall by Harry Clifton in the 1860s and the lyrics include the lines: '*She was as beautiful as a butterfly and proud as a Queen, Was pretty little Polly Perkins of Paddington Green*'.

On the east side is the striking ⓯ **City of Westminster College**. It was designed by Danish architects schmidt hammer lassen and has won several architectural awards since its opening in 2011. You can visit the foyer to get some idea of the interior and the college also participates in the Open House weekends.

On the north-east side look out for a red-brick building that was once the ⓰ **Paddington Green Children's Hospital**. It was

Paddington & Marylebone Walk

founded in 1883 and is today a Grade II listed residential complex. You can see figures of a woman surrounded by children above the main entrance. The neighbouring houses (numbers 17 and 18) date from the 18th century.

Follow the map to leave Paddington Green on the south-east side and walk east along Harrow Road. On your left, just before Edgware Road, once stood the grim looking former ⑰ **Paddington Green Police Station**. It was built in 1971 was used for holding high profile terrorist suspects. The high security did not prevent the IRA exploding a bomb outside the building in 1992. The station closed in 2018 and was redeveloped in 2023.

Continue on to reach ⑱ **Edgware Road**, which follows the course of Watling Street, the Roman road that ran north to St Albans. If you follow the road northwards you come to Edgware itself, a town in North London. The name is derived from a Saxon name – Ecgi – and refers to his pond or weir (hence 'ware').

This is one of the most cosmopolitan roads in Britain, and the centre of Arabic London. Men sit outside cafés using a hookah – or water pipe – and on a hot day you can understand why many Londoners refer to the area as Little Beirut or Little Cairo. Arab immigrants first came to London in the 19th century, mainly because of trade with the Ottoman Empire. In recent decades political unrest in parts of the Middle East have encouraged more people from that region to come and settle in this part of London.

Head south down Edgware Road, ideally crossing over so you are on the left (eastern side). You pass by ⑲ **Edgware Road tube station**. This was opened in 1863 and was part of the Metropolitan Railway, which ran between Paddington and Farringdon – the world's very first underground railway. On 7 July 2005 six passengers were killed here when Mohammad Sidique Khan detonated a bomb on a train leaving the station at about 8:50 am. Other attacks in London that day killed in total 52 people.

Continue south down Edgware Road, crossing under the Westway again (at this point called the Marylebone Flyover). Look out on the left for ⑳ **Joe Strummer Subway** which remembers the rock legend who busked here in his early days before The Clash. Over the years the underpasses below the road have fallen out of favour, some having been bricked up, giving rise to urban myths about people living in the recesses.

Continue southwards, looking out on the right for a neon sign at no.199 advertising ㉑ **Robertsons** – a famous London pawnbroker that was established in 1797 and is still going strong.

Head left down Crawford Place and follow the map just a few yards down Brendon Street. Look out for the intriguing ㉒ **Coade stone keystones** above the front doors of the late 18th century houses (just past the Lord Wargrave public house).

Coade Stone was a famous ceramic artificial stone produced by Eleanor Coade (1733-1821). It became legendary for its ability to resist London's pollution, and many examples around the capital can still be seen today. After it came out of a mould, it was easy to manipulate for a while until it became too hard. This made it the perfect material for the makers of these fabulous keystone faces.

The reason for these unique keystones is connected to the London Building Act of 1774. In an attempt to reduce the risk of fires, the Act prohibited any unnecessary exterior woodwork. This created a new risk – that the

Paddington & Marylebone Walk

exteriors of the new brick buildings being thrown up by developers all around central and west London would look very bland. These keystones were an attempt to bring some character to the entrances of the new houses and Mrs Coade was commissioned by architects all over London to produce the faces.

Mrs Coade actually called her product Lithodipyra – meaning stone fired twice in Greek. She produced it from the 1770s at her Artificial Stone Manufactory in Lambeth, London. When she died in 1821 her business partner carried on the business until 1833. The stone is extremely difficult to make, requiring high temperatures although it could still be made today – despite the London myth that when Coade died her secret formula was lost forever. Today Coade Stone keystones can sell at auction for many thousands of pounds.

At this point we have entered Marylebone – named after the parish church of St Mary's that stood by the Tyburn river or bourne. St Mary at the Bourne was shortened over time to Marylebone.

Continue along Crawford Place looking out on the left for ㉓ **The Christian Union Almshouses**, run by a charity dedicated to providing housing for local poor people of the Christian faith. The almshouses were founded in 1832, and the property here was purchased with contributions raised by local parishes with the stated aim of providing an 'asylum for poor and aged believers in full communion with some Protestant church'. Many of the original guests were retired female servants or seamstresses, and were chosen by elections held every six months.

Opposite the almshouses, walk through a narrow passageway into Cato Street, then stop outside the house immediately on your right (there is a blue plaque). This was the site one of the most notorious episodes in British history – the ㉔ **Cato Street Conspiracy** – took place in 1820. At this time in Britain, radicalism was on the rise as people struggled to cope with the social upheaval caused by the Industrial Revolution and the aftermath of the Napoleonic Wars. A group of men, many of whom had met at a local Marylebone reading club and were influenced by the radical Thomas Spence, decided to assassinate the whole Cabinet.

The plan was to attack the home of Lord Harrowby (on nearby Grosvenor Square) when the Cabinet were due to meet there. By killing the government, the group hoped to trigger a revolution. However, they were infiltrated by a government agent who controversially encouraged their plans. The radicals stayed in this house and on February 23 they were themselves attacked by members of the Bow Street Runners, backed up by the Coldstream Guards.

The conspirators were arrested for treason. Five were later hanged and decapitated in front of a large crowd outside Newgate Prison, while the remaining five were deported for life.

Continue down Cato Street as it leads out into Harrowby Street, and turn left. Follow the map north up Shouldham Street and then right at the ㉕ **Seymour Leisure Centre** and along Bryanston Place, which becomes Montagu Place.

The leisure centre is an excellent example of municipal architecture from the 1930s – look out for the foundation stone from 1935 that recalls William C Cole's role as chairman of the Baths and Wash-House Committee. The Bishop of London was the first President of the original Committee formed in the 1840s, and more committees were established around the country over the next few decades. The aim of the movement was to encourage greater health and hygiene among the poorer classes in crowded urban districts.

Paddington & Marylebone Walk

These were the decades when cholera was still a huge problem in London and most of the less well off had no access to fresh running water at home. Several bathhouses were established in central London, drawing thousands of users who would get their only regular bath there. Things have certainly changed around here since 1935 – today you visit the Seymour Leisure Centre to tackle the climbing wall or try a Zumba class.

Follow the map along Bryanston Place and then Montagu Place, taking a left northwards up Wyndham Place with the spire of 26 **St Mary's**, Bryanston Square, ahead. The street and square names in this part of Marylebone often derive from the country estate's main landowner – the Portman Estate. Sir William Portman of Somerset first acquired 270 acres here in 1532, and development began in the 1750s. At that time the Portman family owned Bryanston – a village in North Dorset – hence the name of the square.

Today the estate covers about 110 acres and is ultimately owned by Christopher Portman, 10th Viscount Portman (b. 1958). His wealth has been estimated at over £1.2 billion.

Paddington & Marylebone Walk

Walk towards St Mary's, one of the prettiest and most distinctive churches in the capital. It was built in the early 1820s as one of the 'Waterloo Churches'. These were funded by Parliament under the Church Building Acts of 1818 and 1824 – a period after the end of the Napoleonic Wars when the authorities were concerned about the scarcity of churches in the increasingly crowded districts of central London. The architect of St Mary's was Sir Robert Smirke.

Unfortunately the church is not open very often. Walk around the right-hand side of the church building. On the right look out for the old signage for the former ㉗ **St Mary Le Bone Western National School**, which was completed in 1825 and restored after damage caused by a German bomb in 1944. This is an early public building in this area and stopped being used a school in 1969.

Today part of the building is occupied by St John Ambulance, and you can see their emblem – ㉘ **the Maltese Cross** – on the wall. The organisation has an odd link with the past as the medieval Knights of St. John of Jerusalem – also known as the Hospitallers – used to own the land here. A religious-military order similar to the famous Knights Templar, the Hospitallers were forced out of the Middle East as the Crusades finished, eventually being ousted from their final great base on Malta by Napoleon. The strongly Catholic Order then splintered into different organisations, although the headquarters are today in Rome. The St John Ambulance service was born out of a revivalist movement that sprung up in England in the 1870s and adopted the Maltese Cross emblem that the knights had used on their shields and tunics.

Walk towards York Street on the north side of the church and look towards the junction with Wyndham Street. There is evidence up high of old Marylebone – a sign reading ㉙ **York Street Ladies Residential Chambers of 1892** – built as accommodation for professional women.

Retrace your steps past St Mary's, back to Crawford Street, where you turn left. On the left-hand side look out for the red brick building that was the ㉚ **Parish Hall of St Mary's**. The foundation stone recalls it was laid by HRH The Princess Christian on 20th October 1897. Largely forgotten now, Princess Christian born Princess Helena (1846-1923), was the fifth child of Queen Victoria and Prince Albert, and caused a minor controversy after falling in love with Albert's German librarian. Victoria quickly dismissed the librarian and her daughter dutifully went on to marry Prince Christian of Schleswig-Holstein. She became well-known for her public appearances and involvement in worthy causes. We shall see other evidence of her work later on.

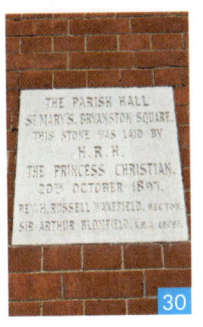

Continue eastwards and stop on the south side at the junction with Upper Montagu Street. On this corner (number 105A) is a distinctive pharmacy ③① **Meacher Higgins and Thomas**, which was established in 1814. The ornate and historic shop front includes signage to the effect that 'toilet requisites' and 'photographic chemicals' are on offer. Jutting out over the street is a rare example of a huge iron lamp.

Walk down Upper Montagu Street to reach Montagu Place. Cross over into Montagu Square and stop on the right-hand side outside number 34. There is a ③② **blue plaque** outside recalling that **John Lennon** once lived here. In fact this is probably the most rock and roll address in the country as Ringo Starr first moved here in 1965. When he moved out, Paul McCartney used number 34 as an experimental recording studio and made demos of songs such as *Eleanor Rigby* here. He also allowed members of London's underground scene to record spoken word productions here, including readings by the writer William Burroughs, of *Naked Lunch* fame. Ringo still had the lease in 1967 when Jimi Hendrix moved in with his manager Chas Chandler. In 1968 John Lennon and Yoko Ono moved in, the Beatle having left his home in Surrey after splitting up with his wife Cynthia.

John and Yoko were photographed naked in the flat – the shot being used for their album *Two Virgins*. A police raid on the flat on 18 October 1968 resulted in Lennon being convicted for possessing cannabis. The media furore that followed the raid enabled the landlords to force Ringo to sell the lease and number 34's connection with rock and roll history was at end until 2010, when Yoko returned one last time to unveil the blue plaque remembering her late husband.

Head south along the side of Montagu Square to reach George Street and turn right, heading back towards Edgware Road. Keep an eye on the left-hand side as you will be able to see ❸❸ **Marble Arch** in the distance at one point. This was designed by John Nash in 1825 and originally stood outside Buckingham Palace. It now stands near the site of the Tyburn Tree – originally a tree, and later a set of gallows, that became the largest and most notorious public execution site in London from the 12th century until the 1780s.

The name Tyburn (burn or bourne meaning stream) comes from the now hidden stream that flows from north London right through central London into the Thames.

After a few minutes you reach Edgware Road again. Continue southwards, cross over, and then walk along Connaught Street. If you are up early you may see the horses of the Royal Artillery who come down here on their early morning rides.

Turn left into ❸❹ **Connaught Square**. The Square was laid out in 1820s and was the first to be built in Bayswater – the area you are now in. The Square was named after the Duke of Gloucester, also known as the Earl of Connaught, who had a large house nearby. If you look over to the west side you will see number 29 which for a while was Tony Blair's main residence. The Blairs bought the house in 2004 for £3.5 million, with some press coverage at the time about whether local Middle Eastern residents would welcome a new neighbour who had recently made the decision to invade Iraq. The Blairs also bought the mews house behind number 29. They then commissioned extensive building works to merge the two properties together – the resulting disruption testing the patience of their neighbours.

Other notable past and present residents of the square include the music producers Paul Oakenfold and William Orbit, politicians Jonathan Aitken and Michael Heseltine and television personality Claudia Winklemen.

Richard Branson began what became the origin of his Virgin empire from a basement flat on the square in 1967. The flat was owned by the parents of his friend Jonny Gems, and Branson later recalled it was 'dark, dank... we slept on mattresses on the floor'. From the flat Branson ran his publication *Student*. He began it while still a pupil at Stowe School, and it quickly became a huge success. From Connaught Square the teenage Branson would venture out to interview famous figures such as John Lennon and Vanessa Redgrave, and secure contributions from the likes of David Hockney and Jean-Paul Sartre. *Student* caught the mood of the radical late 60s, but did not go down so well with the Church Commissioners, who owned the freehold to the flat. They did not like commercial activities taking place there and Branson was forced to move. You will shortly see where he went next.

35

Paddington & Marylebone Walk

On the south side of the square continue straight ahead and take a right down ㉟ **Frederick Close**. There are some pleasant smaller mews houses down here, and it feels beautifully secluded despite being just a stone's throw from the busy Bayswater Road.

If you look through the gate at the end of Frederick Close you can see gardens on the other side. This is the site of ㊱ **St George's graveyard**, Hanover Square, used between 1763 and 1852. Those buried here included the Rev. Laurence Sterne, author of *Tristram Shandy*, and Lt. General Sir Thomas Picton, who was killed at Waterloo.

Follow the map (nearly opposite Frederick Place) to walk down Connaught Place. At the end, at the junction with Edgware Road, look out for a ㊲ **blue plaque** that marks the house where **Lord Randolph Churchill**, father of Winston Churchill, lived between 1883 and 1892.

Continue south down Edgware Road and stop at the junction. To your left you can see Marble Arch and in the pavement at the junction a marker identifying the likely spot of the ㊳ **Tyburn gallows**. It has also been suggested there were gallows where Connaught Square now stands.

Walk down Bayswater Road. This was called Uxbridge Road until around 1890, and London's first horse-drawn tramway service used to run along here in the early 1860s. It was run by George Train who lived on Bayswater Road, near the corner with Porchester Terrace. He was said to have been the inspiration for the character

119

Phileas Fogg in Jules Verne's novel *Around the World in Eighty Days*.

The name Bayswater is most likely derived from 'Baynard's Watering Hole' – the owner being Ralph Baynardus, who came over with William the Conqueror in 1066. A fresh water spring would have been a valuable possession in medieval times.

On the right-hand side as you walk along Bayswater Road, look out for the ㊴ **Tyburn Convent** which is home to The Adorers of the Sacred Heart of Montmartre. This Catholic order of Benedictine nuns was founded by a Frenchwoman named Marie Adele Garnier in Montmartre in Paris in 1901. At that time the French authorities were making things difficult for monasteries and convents, and Mother Marie re-located to London in 1903. The order is dedicated to the memory of Catholic martyrs, and in particular the 105 people who were executed for their faith on Tyburn Tree including Saint Oliver Plunkett and Saint Edmund Campion. It is possible to visit the convent and see the Shrine of the Martyrs at Tyburn – a sister is available for guided tours of the shrine daily at 10.30am, 3.30pm and 5.30pm.

Continue past the convent and on the right look out for a ㊵ **plaque (number 23 Hyde Park Place)** with the word 'Oranjehaven'. This commemorates the site of a World War II club that was used by Dutch people who had fled the German occupation of their country and joined the Allied forces.

Follow the map up Albion Street. Richard Branson lived at ㊶ **number 44** – in 1969 after he was forced out of Connaught Square. He ran *Student* from here, and also from the crypt of St John the Evangelist (seen shortly).

The author of *Vanity Fair*, ㊷ **William Makepeace Thackeray**, also lived on Albion

Street at **number 18** (there is a blue plaque) in the 1830s when studying to be a barrister. ㊸ **The last Rajah of Sarawak, Sir Charles Vyner Brooke**, lived at number 13 until his death in 1963. Largely forgotten now, the Brooke family ruled the Kingdom of Sarawak on the Island of Borneo from 1841 to 1946. It became part of Malaysia in 1963.

The first Brooke in charge was James Brooke, who was granted a 40,000 square mile tract of land on Borneo by the Sultan of Brunei. He created a dynasty known as the White Rajahs, and Sir Charles was the third and last of those in charge. His *Who's Who* entry recorded that he had 'led several expeditions into the far interior of the country to punish head-hunters; understands the management of natives; rules over a population of 500,000 souls and a country'.

At the end of Albion Street turn right into Connaught Street. On the right-hand side (number 35) is the former site of old military and ceremonial outfitters, ㊹ **Kashket & Partners**, which incorporated Firmin & Sons. Firmin & Sons began in 1655, and its publicity boasts that its 'products were present at the Battles of The Nile, Trafalgar, Waterloo and Gettysburg'. The company still produces many of the buttons, regalia and uniforms worn by army officers and the Royal Family at State ceremonies but closed this branch in 2015. Visitors to the National Maritime Museum in Greenwich can see the famous Firmin uniform that was worn by Admiral Lord Nelson at Trafalgar and in which he died.

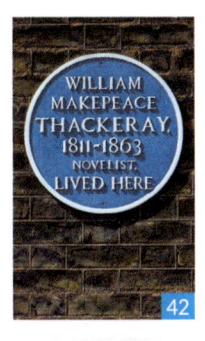

Continue along, passing pleasant shops and cafés that are popular with the wealthy international residents that live around here. On the right, look out for the small entrance into ㊺ **Archery Close** – the house that forms the rear of the Blair residence is down here. The name recalls the popularity of the sport of archery in Regency times. A dedicated practice area was used by the Royal Toxophilite Society on the old burial ground of St George's that you glimpsed through the gates along Frederick Close earlier on.

This area is known as Tyburnia – a planned development of fine streets and squares that began in the 1820s. By then the area east of Edgware Road was already developed but London's growing middle

㊺ Archery Close

Paddington & Marylebone Walk

and upper classes needed ever more houses and the empty fields of Paddington were ripe for development. The close proximity of Hyde Park just to the south made this a very attractive area, although unlike Belgravia, the name Tyburnia never caught on.

In the Ambulator guide of 1800 the Bayswater area is still described as 'a small hamlet in the Parish of Paddington a mile from London'. The fact that Bayswater was largely developed by 1850 suggests the level of building activity in the intervening decades must have been astonishing and the only comparison in the modern era for London is probably the development of the Docklands from the 1980s.

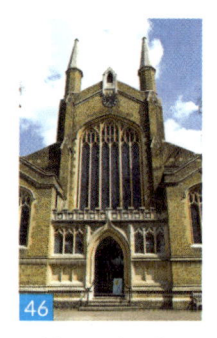

Walk up Porchester Place to reach a large oval with Norfolk Crescent to the east and Oxford and Cambridge Squares to the south and north respectively. Walk along Oxford Square and then north along Hyde Park Crescent to reach ㊻ **St John's Church**. It was consecrated in 1832 and is the second oldest church in the area. Richard Branson ran *Student* from the crypt here after moving into Albion Street.

It was also here that he was visited by police in 1969 and warned that the publication's advertisements for venereal disease treatment were violating the Indecent Advertisements Act and Venereal Disease Act. He ignored them and was arrested and charged. His barrister John Mortimer, best known for his creation *Rumpole of the Bailey*, helped Branson escape prison but the entrepreneur was convicted and fined £7. Later the law was changed and Branson received an apology from the then Home Secretary, Reginald Maudling.

Continue north up Southwick Street, crossing Sussex Gardens, to reach Star Street. Cross the street, then up Bouverie Place and turn right along St Michael's Street, passing by pleasant but slightly run-down houses that are different in character to the grandeur of Connaught Square. At the end is the ㊷ **Royal Exchange Free House** – the exterior a good example of a classic Victorian pub and the interior worth exploring if you fancy a pint.

Turn left, and head north up Sale Place to reach Praed Street, one of the main roads in Paddington. Cross over and head along a pedestrian section of ㊸ **Paddington Basin**, the terminus of the Paddington arm of the Grand Junction Canal. This area has been transformed in recent years with a great deal of property redeveloped, although it is fairly soulless. It is hard to

48 Paddington Basin

Paddington & Marylebone Walk

imagine how it must have appeared in its early 19th century heyday when hundreds of workers would have milled around here loading and offloading goods onto the barges, while the bargemen looked after their horses. The construction of Paddington Basin was a huge boost to the development of this area.

Return to Praed Street and head westwards, passing the ㊾ **old pub building** on the junction with South Wharf Road. Now a restaurant, the ornate signage for Truman Hanbury Buxton & Co. is still evident. The Truman's brewery had its origins on Brick Lane in East London in the 1660 and it went on to become the biggest brewer in the world by the end of the 19th century. However, it declined during the 20th century and eventually closed in 1989.

Continue along Praed Street, which was laid out in the early 19th century and named after William Praed, the chairman of the company that built the canal basin. Today it is a bit tatty, and has a fairly seedy reputation. On the right you pass ㊿ **St Mary's Hospital**, which was founded in the mid 19th century. As mentioned earlier, Alexander Fleming discovered penicillin here in 1928. Diacetylmorphine was also first synthesized here in 1874 by CR Alder Wright. Ironically given its reputation today, diacetylmorphine – marketed by Bayer under the trademark Heroin – was promoted as a non-addictive morphine substitute. You can visit the Alexander Fleming Museum at the hospital Monday – Thursday 10am-1pm (see below for more details). St Mary's maternity hospital with where many members of the Royal Family have been born, including Prince George in 2013.

Continue along Praed Street, 113-115 was The Paddington Kitchen in the 1970s, where The Clash held their first rehersals. Shortly on the right is **51** **Paddington Station**. The first station in this area opened in 1838 at the very start of the railway age. Most of the current complex dates from 1854, and was designed by Isambard Kingdom Brunel (1806-1859). He was also responsible for the Great Western Railway that had its terminus here, as does this walk. ●

VISIT...

Alexander Fleming Museum
St Mary's Hospital,
Praed Street, W2 1NY

London Waterbus Company
Trips from Little Venice to
London Zoo & Camden Lock
www.londonwaterbus.com

Puppet Theatre Barge
(see p.105)
Little Venice, W9 2PF
www.puppetbarge.com

SHOP

Meacher Higgins & Thomas
105A Crawford St, W1H 2HU

EAT, DRINK...

The Royal Exchange (see p.124)
26 Sale Place, W2 1PU

Waterside Café
Little Venice, W2 6NE

THE CITY

The City Barge, see p.155

5 Hammersmith & Chiswick Walk

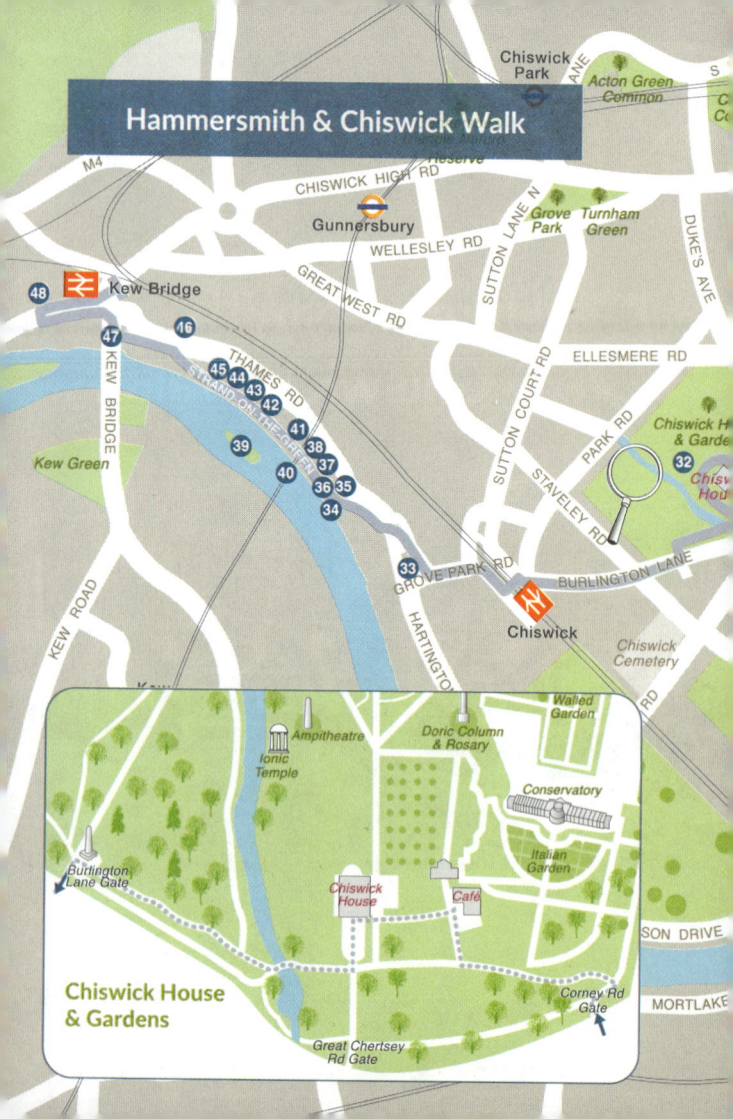

Hammersmith & Chiswick Walk

1. Hammersmith Bridge
2. Lower Mall
3. British Rowing sign
4. The Blue Anchor public house
5. Furnivall Sculling Club
6. Furnivall Gardens
7. The Dove public house
8. Kelmscott House
9. Laytmer Preparatory School
10. Andy Holmes (blue plaque)
11. Eric Ravilious (blue plaque)
12. Linden House
13. Old Ship public house
14. The Black Lion public house
15. Hammersmith Terrace
16. Calligrapher Edward Johnston
17. Sir Emery Walker
18. Boot scraper
19. Chiswick Mall
20. Chiswick Eyot
21. Walpole House
22. Fuller's Griffin Brewery
23. Said House
24. Bedford House
25. Church Street Causeway
26. St Nicholas Chiswick
27. William Hogarth
28. Philip James de Loutherbourg
29. Old Burlington
30. Lamb Brewery
31. Hogarth House
32. Chiswick House
33. St Paul's Church
34. Small fountain
35. Almhouses
36. Strand-on-the-Green
37. Miniature doors
38. The Bull's Head public house
39. Oliver's Island
40. Kew Railway Bridge
41. The City Barge public house
42. Ship House
43. Dutch House
44. Zachary House
45. The Bell & Crown public house
46. Steam Packet Pub
47. Kew Bridge
48. Kew Bridge Steam Museum

Hammersmith & Chiswick Walk

Start: Hammersmith Bridge, a ten minute walk from Hammersmith underground station
Finish: Kew Bridge rail station
Distance: 4.2 miles

The name Hammersmith was first recorded in 1294 and is probably derived from the Saxon words for hammer and smithy – the trade with which the area was long ago associated. In recent decades the district, at least away from the river bank, has become dominated by busy roads with the most gruesome offender being the Hammersmith Flyover (dating from 1961).

The original bridge here was built in the 1820s by William Tierney Clarke and was the first suspension bridge in London. Tierney Clarke is best known for his design of the spectacular Széchenyi Chain Bridge across the Danube in Budapest that still stands today. Sadly his efforts in Hammersmith have been relegated to the history books as the bridge he built was unable to cope with the demands later placed upon it and was replaced 60 years later.

These demands were largely due to the huge increase in road traffic in London during the 19th century, however additional strain was placed on the bridge by the thousands of spectators who would congregate to watch the annual Oxford v Cambridge University boat race. The bridge is located almost half way along the 4 mile course between Putney and Mortlake.

The second, and current **Hammersmith Bridge**, was designed by Sir Joseph Bazalgette (1819-1891) and opened by the Prince of Wales in 1887. Bazalgette is best known for designing London's first modern sewerage system that helped save the Thames from chronic pollution and so eradicated the scourge of cholera from the capital. The central span of the bridge

Hammersmith & Chiswick Walk

is 129 metres long (423ft). It has been targeted by the IRA three times – the first in 1939 when a local hairdresser named Maurice Childs was passing by and saw the bomb, bravely picking it up and throwing it into the river. More recent attacks took place in 1996 (when 2 of the most powerful Semtex bombs planted in Britain failed to explode) and in 2000, the latter closing the bridge for renovation for a considerable period of time.

Just below the bridge you reach the Thames Path, where you turn right (westwards) into ❷ **Lower Mall**. This stretch of the river bank is well known for its many rowing and sailing clubs. Shortly on the right look out for the ❸ **British Rowing sign** outside number 6 Lower Mall. This is the modest headquarters of the British Rowing organisation, the body in overall charge of the sport in this country and responsible for the GB rowing team that has had such great success at the Olympics and World Championships in recent years.

Rowing clubs along this stretch of the Thames in West London (together with the University clubs of Oxford and Cambridge) helped form the first national rowing organisation – the Metropolitan Rowing Association – in the late 1870s. This was later re-named the Amateur Rowing Association and was the predecessor of British Rowing.

Continue along Lower Mall, passing ❹ **The Blue Anchor**, first licensed in 1722, and its neighbour The Rutland Arms. Both

Hammersmith & Chiswick Walk

are good pubs – the first of many along this route – although given their proximity to Hammersmith they can get very crowded during peak periods. The Blue Anchor is where Gwyneth Paltrow and John Hannah have a drink in the British comedy *Sliding Doors* (1998). It is also where Gustav Holst (1874-1934) spent many hours composing, most notably the *Hammersmith Prelude & Scherzo* (1930) that resulted from a commission from the BBC and was originally meant for their military band. Holst was very familiar with this part of London, teaching at St Paul's School nearby and living for many years in Barnes. Next door is the first of many rowing clubs you will pass, in this case Auriol Kensington Rowing Club which traces its history back to the 1870s. The Rutland Arms, next door, is another fine Victorian riverside pub.

Continue westwards and look out on the right for the ❺ **Furnivall Sculling Club** – and just past the club is ❻ **Furnivall Gardens**. Both are named after the Club's founder Dr Frederick James Furnivall (1825-1910). Furnivall was a remarkable man, a philologist who helped establish the original Oxford English Dictionary. He was also a keen sportsman, and was still rowing from here to Richmond and back until just before his death at the age of 85.

He disliked the discrimination shown by the Amateur Rowing Association against women and working men – the latter not allowed to join the ARA because it was felt they could not abide by the strict amateur ethos. Furnivall set up a new club here in 1896 – principally for women rowers – having already established the National Amateur Rowing Association, designed to encourage working men to take part in the sport. It has been suggested that Kenneth Grahame, author of *The Wind in the Willows*, based the

Hammersmith & Chiswick Walk

character of Ratty on his good friend Furnivall – both certainly liked (in Grahame's words) 'simply messing about in boats'.

The Gardens named after Furnivall were built on the site of buildings destroyed by German bombing during World War II. They also lie on what used to be Hammersmith Creek, an outflow river of the Stamford Brook, one of London's lost rivers. The Brook comprises three streams that converge near Hammersmith. Until the early 19th century Hammersmith Creek was navigable, and known as Little Wapping because of the many barges carrying goods from the Thames. In the mid-19th century there was a wooden bridge in the north-east corner of the park that crossed the Creek. In later years the Creek fell from use and was filled in during the 1930s and suffered further damage during World War II. Furnivall Gardens was laid out in the early 1950s, but over the wall can still be seen an outflow of the long lost Stamford Brook.

Walk around the edge of the gardens away from the river to pass by Grade II listed public house ❼ **The Dove**. This dates back to the early 18th century and was originally a coffee house, popular with the watermen who unloaded their sailing barges near here. The poet James Thomson composed the words to '*Rule Britannia*' in an upstairs room in 1740. Charles II is also said to have entertained Nell Gwyn at the pub.

Other patrons over the years have included Graham Greene, Dylan Thomas, Richard Burton, Elizabeth Taylor and Ernest Hemingway. The pub is also depicted as *The Pigeons* in AP Herbert's novel *The Water Gypsies* (1930). The Dove has the smallest bar in Britain and a plaque showing the height reached by the great flood of 1928.

Hammersmith & Chiswick Walk

Since 1796 it has been owned by Fullers, the famous London brewery whose headquarters will be seen later.

Continue along past The Dove into what is now Upper Mall, again skirting the bank of the Thames. Very shortly on the right at number 26 is ❽ **Kelmscott House**, a substantial Georgian building that was the main London residence of William Morris (1834-1896) for 18 years until his death. Morris was one of the great figures of his age – a poet, craftsman and early socialist. His style contributed to what became known as the Arts & Crafts movement. Morris was involved in artisan manufacture and ran a printing company from a house nearby.

During Morris's era this area was a hotbed for radicals – Morris used to preach political sermons to passers-by from a soapbox near Hammersmith Bridge, and regular attendees at meetings here included Prince Kropotkin, George Bernard Shaw and Keir Hardie. But Morris was not just an intellectual and artist – he was also fairly sporty. In 1880, he once rowed from here all the way to his other house by the Thames, Kelmscott Manor in Gloucestershire. He leased the Manor jointly with the Pre-Raphaelite painter Dante Gabriel Rossetti.

Today the **William Morris Society**, dedicated to perpetuating his memory, occupies the basement and coach house section of Kelmscott House. They are open to the public on Thursday, Saturday and Sunday afternoons (see p.159 for more information).

Kelmscott House dates from the 1780s and other notable people who have lived here include Sir Francis Ronalds (1788-1873) who in 1816 constructed the first electric telegraph in the garden, and the poet and author George MacDonald (1824-1905), best known for the children's books *At the Back of the North Wind* and *The Princess and the Goblin*. A more recent resident of the main house was playwright Christopher Hampton.

Continue westwards and on the right is **9 Laytmer Preparatory School** and beside it the school's boat house. The preparatory school occupies Rivercourt House which dates from 1808. It stands on the site of an earlier residence that was occupied between 1686 and 1692 by Catherine of Braganza (1638-1705), the long-suffering wife of Charles II. She is credited with popularising the drinking of tea and her Catholic faith made her a controversial figure during a period of religious tension. Two servant girls drowned in Rivercourt House in the severe flood of January 1928.

Outside the school's rowing club house is a **10 blue plaque** to **Andy Holmes MBE** (1959-2010). He learnt to row at Laytmer and went on to win gold medals in the sport at the 1984 and 1988 Olympics (alongside Sir Steve Redgrave). He retired from rowing in 1990 and died tragically young from the water-borne disease feared by all regular river users, Leptospirosis – commonly known as 'Weil's disease'.

The school traces its history back to 1624 and a donation by the wealthy merchant Edward Latymer. Other well-known former pupils of this London independent school include Hugh Grant, Alan Rickman, Heston Blumenthal, Lily Cole and Cliff Townshend, father of The Who's Pete and who was expelled and later became a jazz musician.

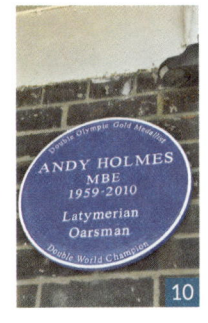

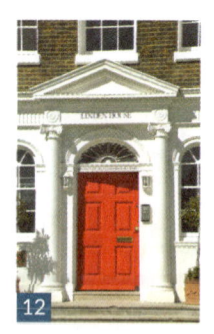

Continue westwards, pausing at the junction with Weltje Road. The house on the corner (there is a blue plaque) was home between 1930 and 1932 to ⑪ **Eric Ravilious** (1903-1942), one of the finest English artists of the 20th century. He served as a war artist during WWII and died when the RAF sea rescue aircraft he was in was lost near Iceland.

Continue on past further fine houses facing the Thames. Ahead is a strange crow's nest style building which serves as the London Corinthian Sailing Club's dinghy racing starting box. The club has been housed since the 1960s at the Grade II listed ⑫ **Linden House** (number 60 Upper Mall), which can be seen just ahead on the right, set back from the river. The house was originally built for a wealthy merchant and dates from 1733. In recent years another rowing club, The Sons of the Thames – formed in 1886 – has also moved into Linden House.

The London Corinthian Sailing Club was formed in 1894, and their original club house stood on the site of Furnivall Gardens, visited earlier. The building was damaged by a V1 rocket during World War II and demolished in the 1960s, causing the club to move to its current home. The Corinthians claim to have been one of the first sailing clubs to admit women boat owners, and notable people associated with the club include the opera impresarios Rupert and Lucas D'Oyly Carte, the renowned oboeist Leon Goosens (1897-1988), athlete and first sub-four minute miler Roger Bannister (b.1929), and MP, humourist and author AP Herbert (1890-1971).

Continue west past the ⑬ **Old Ship public house** with great views of the river. It dates from 1720s, when this was a down-at-heal place of commerce.

Chiswick Riverside

Hammersmith & Chiswick Walk

Shortly you walk slightly away from the Thames and pass ⑭ **The Black Lion public house** which dates from the late 18th century and is said to be haunted by the 'Hammersmith Ghost'. This story goes back to 1803 when a local woman was apparently scared to death by the sight of a ghostly white spectre, thought by locals to be the troubled spirit of a man who had committed suicide nearby shortly before. A few months later, with much of the local population too scared to venture out at night, a local man named Francis Smith loaded up his blunderbuss and went out looking for the ghost.

He came across a bricklayer named Thomas Millwood, who was covered in white dust. Smith mistook Millwood for the Hammersmith Ghost, and shot him. Millwood was carried to The Black Lion where he later died. In a cruel twist of fate, it is said his ghost haunts the pub to this day. Francis was found guilty of murder at the Old Bailey, but given the unusual circumstances of the case, was sentenced to just a year in prison.

The pub has also long been associated with the curious English pub game of skittles which was popularised by AP Herbert (mentioned earlier). Herbert, a regular in the pub who lived on Hammersmith Terrace nearby, is best known for his book *Misleading Cases in the Common Law* (1927). He devoted a whole chapter to skittles in his popular book *The Water Gypsies* (1930), and the pub claims he even brought film star Douglas Fairbanks Jr here to play the game.

Continue west and you will shortly come to ⑮ **Hammersmith Terrace**, which contains 17 tall, elegant Georgian houses that date from the 1750s and which stood alone in open countryside when first constructed. What you see is actually the back of the houses – the gardens and front elevations face the river.

Notable people who have lived in the Terrace include AP Herbert who resided at number 12-13 for 50 years. Apart from popularising skittles, writing books, and serving as an MP, Herbert also found time to make an important contribution to the reform of the divorce laws.

The noted **16** **calligrapher Edward Johnston** (1872-1944) lived at number 3 and there is a blue plaque remembering him. The sharp-eyed will spot that the sans-serif Johnston font he created for London Transport in the 1930s and which was only replaced in the 1980s, has been utilised on the plaque.

Houses here can cost around £4 million and if you are curious to see inside one, and are visiting between April and September, you may be able to visit number 7. This was the home from 1903 to 1933 of **17** **Sir Emery Walker** (1851-1933), a prominent printer and collector. However he is now best remembered for being a close friend of his near neighbour, William Morris. The house boasts a perfectly preserved Arts & Crafts interior that is one of the finest of its kind in the country, many of the furnishings coming from Morris's own manufacturing company. The Emery Walker Trust organises visits, for more information see p.159.

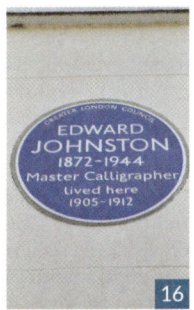

Outside number 12 is a ⑱ **boot scraper** – a relic from when the road outside was just a muddy path. Along the terrace look out for the round metal covers set in the pavement. These are coal hole covers which in former times were opened to allow coal to be delivered down into basements before being used in the homes' many fireplaces.

From the Terrace continue along to reach ⑲ **Chiswick Mall**, the area's most expensive address where properties can sell for over £12 million. You are now also leaving Hammersmith and entering Chiswick – a district whose name is derived from the Old English words for 'cheese farm', probably a trade carried out in the medieval meadows beside the river.

The current district known as Chiswick actually covers what used to be four distinct villages – Little Sutton, Turnham Green, Chiswick itself (which you are now entering) and Strand on the Green (seen later).

For many centuries Chiswick supported a fishing industry and the village grew up around the parish church of St Nicholas Chiswick (seen shortly). In the 18th century the Royal Palace at Kew was popular with the monarchy and Chiswick became a favoured location for second homes among the wealthier classes seeking court patronage. However it remained a largely rural village until the following century, when it was engulfed by London's expanding suburbs. By this time the fishing industry had largely died out, not helped by the pollution afflicting the Thames.

As you walk along Chiswick Mall look out for the small, uninhabited island in the Thames named ⑳ **Chiswick Eyot** (Eyot is pronounced 'eight'). Willows were once harvested on the three-acre island for basket weaving, and the channel between the eyot and the shore was traditionally used for trapping fish. At low tide it is possible to walk to the island, declared a nature reserve in 1993. Anyone attempting the excursion should pay attention to the incoming tide.

Just a little further along is the finest property in the street, ㉑ **Walpole House**. It dates largely from the early 18th century and is named after a former occupant – a nephew of England's first Prime Minister, Sir Robert Walpole. The author William Thackeray (1811-1863) attended an academy for boys within the house in the 1820s, drawing upon this experience when creating the fictional Miss Pinkerton's Seminary for Young Ladies that features in *Vanity Fair* (1848). When leaving the Seminary, Becky Sharpe famously throws her `dixionary' out of the carriage window.

Walpole House was also home to Barbara Villiers (The Duchess of Cleveland) (1640-1709). A mistress of Charles II, she is thought to have borne at least five of his children, and lived here for the last two years of her life. Once renowned as a great beauty, in her last years she was ill and bloated from dropsy, her famous looks having long disappeared. It is said her ghost still haunts the house.

In 1885 Walpole House was purchased by a local shipbuilder named John Thornycroft, more about whom we will learn shortly. Today it is a Grade I listed building, the only others in Chiswick being the better known Chiswick House and Hogarth House. Walpole House was sold in 2008 for over £12 million – almost double its price of two years before.

As you continue along the path you will see on your right-hand side (after Chiswick Lane) the substantial site of ㉒ **Fuller's Griffin Brewery**. Fuller, Smith & Turner Plc and its predecessor companies have been brewing beer on this site for over 350 years. The original brewery was in the gardens of Bedford House and was founded in 1701. It became known as the Griffin Brewery in 1816. During the 19th century the brewery had financial problems and raised money from John Fuller – he later entered into partnership with Henry Smith and John Turner, and their respective families remain involved in the brewery to this day, now controlling around 350 outlets. It is today best known for beers such as London Pride, Chiswick Bitter, ESB and London Porter.

The wisteria on the brewery is said to be around 180 years old, making it the oldest example in England. It originated from one of the two specimens first brought back from China to Kew Gardens in the 19th century. You can visit the brewery on guided tours (telephone 020 8996 2175 for booking).

This is also the oldest part of Chiswick with some of the finest 18th century, Thameside properties. Notable among them is ㉓ **Said House** (easily spotted because of its red urn) and ㉔ **Bedford House** nearby. Said House was rented out to the BBC in 2005 and was home to contestants taking part in the first series of The Apprentice. The landlord at the time complained that £12,000 worth of damage was done by contestants, including a fire resulting from an indoor barbeque.

The actor Michael Redgrave (1908-1985) bought Bedford House in 1945. He lived here for about ten years with his wife, Rachel Kempson, and their three children.

Continue along and shortly on the right pause at the beginning of Church Street with the church of St Nicholas visible further up. Look back to the river and see the ㉕ **Church Street Causeway** leading down into the Thames. This was the site for many centuries of a ferry, and also where the local industries would load and unload their goods, including the hops required by Fuller's Brewery.

It was near to here that the dead body of Montague John Druitt (1857-1888) – one of the main suspects for the Jack the Ripper murders – was found floating in the water on 30 December 1888, just weeks after the last of the infamous Whitechapel Murders.

Hammersmith & Chiswick Walk

This is also near to the site of one of Chiswick's greatest – and most surprising – industries, the shipbuilding business run by the Thornycroft family mentioned earlier.

John Isaac Thornycroft set up the original business in the 1860s at Church Wharf at the west end of Chiswick Mall and – until it closed in the early 20th century – it was one of the leading specialist shipbuilders in the world. By the age of just 17, Thornycroft had built a 36ft long steam launch, which caused a sensation as it was able to keep up with the eights on Boat Race day. Later he built here the first ever torpedo boat ordered by the British Admiralty.

The business designed and built over 200 fast torpedo boats and other ships both for the Royal Navy, and the governments of many other countries including France, Germany and Russia. After being launched the boats would travel under Hammersmith Bridge and then down to the sea. Inevitably as larger ships were developed, the shallow Thames was no longer suitable and the shipbuilding business was transferred to Southampton in 1904.

From here walk up Church Street to ㉖ **St Nicholas Chiswick**, the heart of the original village of Chiswick. St Nicholas is best known as Santa Claus, but he is also the patron saint of sailors and fishermen. The church dominated the medieval village and is thought to have its origins in the 7th century. It was first formally recorded in 1181 and remained the only church in the district until 1843. The tower dates from the 15th century, although most of the current structure dates from a major rebuilding programme in the late 19th century, funded largely by Fuller's Brewery.

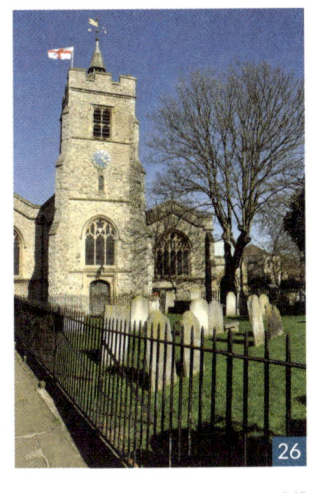

There are a number of tombs in the churchyard that are worth looking out for, most notably that of the artist ㉗ **William Hogarth** (1697-1764). The epitaph on Hogarth's memorial was written by the famous actor William Garrick, and you will see Hogarth's House later in the walk. Other people buried here include the artist James Abbot McNeill Whistler (1834-1903); landscape painter ㉘ **Philip James de Loutherbourg** (1740-1812), whose small mausoleum was designed by Sir John Soane; Sir Charles Tilston Bright (1832-1888), the man responsible for laying the first transatlantic telegraph cable; Private Frederick Hitch VC, hero of Rorke's Drift; and Henry Joy, who may (as staff trumpeter to General the Earl of Lucan) have sounded the charge of the Light Brigade at Balaclava in 1857. Others believe he only sounded the earlier charge of the Heavy Brigade.

Barbara Villiers, Charles II's mistress who was mentioned earlier, was also buried here in 1710. Two dukes and four peers acted as pall-bearers as her body was brought here from Walpole House. Two of Oliver Cromwell's daughters are said to have been buried here, giving rise to a legend that their father was also secretly interred with them. After the Restoration Charles II ordered that Cromwell's body be dug up from Westminster Abbey. It was then symbolically hanged, and his head displayed to the public for twenty years. What happened to Cromwell's body has never been resolved, but perhaps this churchyard is his final resting place. Bernard Montgomery, later Field Marshal Lord Montgomery of Alamein, was married in the church in 1927 by his father Bishop Montgomery.

When finished at the church, continue up Church Street. On the right look out for a timbered old house named ㉙ **Old Burlington**. This dates from the 15th century and was once the Burlington Arms. Aside from the church's tower, it is possibly the oldest structure in Chiswick. The 18th century highwayman

Hammersmith & Chiswick Walk

Dick Turpin is said to have had his marriage breakfast here, and on a separate occasion was almost caught by the authorities but managed to escape through a window. The building is also reputedly haunted by a tall man who wears a large wide-brimmed hat and who rearranges the pictures!

The French philosopher Jean-Jacques Rousseau (1712-1778) is thought to have lived in a house on this street in 1776. He had been exiled from France because of his controversial writings and wrote to a friend: 'I am going to stay at a village near London, called Chiswick'. It is known he lodged with a grocer called James Pullen.

Behind Old Burlington you will see signage that recalls this was once part of the **30 Lamb Brewery**. This was a major rival to Fullers, and originated in or around the site of Bedford House in the 18th century. It was owned for many years by the Sich family who sold out in 1920, and brewing ended here in 1922.

Continue up Church Street to return to the modern world and the horrendous Hogarth roundabout, reputedly the busiest in Europe. Today the centre of Chiswick is no longer around the church, but along Chiswick High Road to the north. Take the underpass and walk along the left-hand side of the A4 – around halfway along the underpass turn left then follow the signs to visit **31 Hogarth House**.

It is named after its most famous resident, the great artist and engraver William Hogarth (1697-1764). He purchased

32 Chiswick House

it as his second home in 1749, and spent most summers in what he called his 'little country box'. While hard to imagine now, the house was then surrounded by open fields. The garden still contains a mulberry tree whose fruit was used by Hogarth's wife to make tarts. Hogarth is best known for his pictorial satires of 18th-century life such as *Gin Lane*, *A Rake's Progress* and *Marriage à-la-mode*, engravings of which you can see inside. He also supported Thomas Coram in setting up the Foundling Hospital in Bloomsbury.

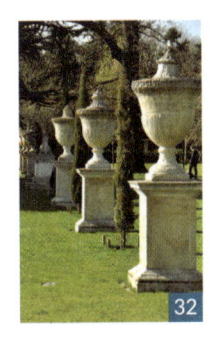

After leaving Hogarth House turn left down Sutherland Road then left again down Paxton Road for a few minutes. At the end you reach Burlington Lane. Turn right along Burlington Lane until you reach on the right the Corney Road Gate entrance to the grounds of ㉜ **Chiswick House**. Head towards the house – or if you want a break – the café just to the north-east of the house. This starkly modern café, designed by Caruso St John was named RIBA London Building of the Year 2011.

Chiswick House was designed by the 3rd Earl of Burlington and built in the 1720s as an extension to a larger Jacobean structure that was later demolished. The 'architect earl', was influenced by the buildings of Classical Rome and the architecture of Andrea Palladio and Inigo Jones. It is one of the finest Palladian buildings in Britain and the gardens, designed by William Kent, are considered the birthplace of the English landscape movement.

After Burlington's death Chiswick House was inherited by the Dukes of Devonshire, and in 1788 the Jacobean house was demolished and an extension to the Palladian villa created. It was later leased out to occupants including the future King Edward VII, and for many years was used as an asylum. It has been open to the public since 1958. Today it is the venue of the annual Chiswick House Festival, described as 'the most middle-class concert in Britain'. Chiswick House has a Beatles connection as on 20 May 1966 the band came here to shoot promotional films for their songs *Paperback Writer* and *Rain*. Another Beatles connection with Chiswick will be seen later on in the walk.

It is worth taking some time to visit the house and the superb surrounding grounds before heading back towards the Thames and the last part of the walk. When finished, follow the map – exiting the gardens through the Burlington Lane Gate. Turn right for a few minutes and you pass near Staveley Road. This is where the first V2 rocket fell in 1944, killing 3 people, injuring 22 and destroying 11 houses. It created a huge crater 40ft across and 20ft deep. The explosion was heard as far away as Westminster and within an hour Winston Churchill had arrived on the scene. The authorities, alarmed by this escalation in the arms race of World War II, initially tried to explain away the disaster as being the result of a gas main exploding. This led to a standing joke amongst Londoners over the next few weeks as more and more 'gas mains exploded'. A memorial was unveiled on the site in 2004.

Follow the map taking the footbridge at Chiswick Station until you reach ㉝ **St Paul's Church**. It was built in 1872 as Chiswick's expansion required more places of worship and its construction was funded by the 7th Duke of Devonshire. Pass the church to continue along Grove Park Road (crossing over a small roundabout) to reach the Thames Path again.

The path takes you along Strand-on-the-Green and a short way along look out for a ㉞ **small fountain** dating from 1880 that was funded by an individual bequest, in conjunction with The Metropolitan Drinking Fountain and Cattle Trough Association. This Association was founded by Victorian philanthropists to provide the public, cattle and horses with free drinking water, and

Hammersmith & Chiswick Walk

other examples can be found throughout London. Such facilities bear witness to the last years of horse drawn transport in the capital, before the rise of the motor car. They were also constructed at a time when the majority of the capital's population did not have clean water supplies at home so were dependent on public fountains like this.

Near the fountain are some pretty cottages that were originally built as ㉟ **almhouses** in the 1720s. A number of plaques on the wall facing the river trace the history of subsequent renovations, and they were renamed the Hopkin Morris homes of rest in the 1930s after receiving funds from the estate of B Hopkin Morris.

Continue along the path beside the river. You are now in ㊱ **Strand-on-the-Green** – one of the most picturesque parts of London (particularly when seen from the river) and containing many buildings that date from the 18th century or earlier. This was first recorded as 'Stronde' in the 14th century, an Old English word for 'shore', and over the centuries what was originally a village has been home to an eclectic mix of fishermen, artisans, aristocrats and artists. It was in fact one of four small villages that merged to form the parish of Chiswick in the 19th century.

Until the middle of the 18th century, the riverside settlement comprised little more than a line of wharves, fishermen's cottages, almshouses, malt houses and pubs stretching several hundred metres south-east from the Kew ferry. A period

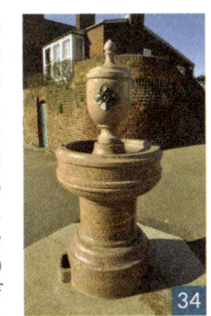

36 *Strand-on-the-Green*

Hammersmith & Chiswick Walk

of rapid gentrification followed as the area became popular with wealthy businessmen and friends of the royal family, fuelled by the completion of the original Kew Bridge in 1759 and the leasing of the Dutch House – subsequently renamed Kew Palace – by Queen Caroline in 1728.

Many of the houses were restored in the 20th century, having fallen into decline in the intervening years, and the riverside terrace today contains some of the finest examples of Georgian residential architecture in west London.

Many houses have ㊲ **miniature doors** raised up to avoid flooding. Despite being many miles from the sea, this part of the Thames is still tidal and the water level can rise and fall by about 7 metres. When the moon is either new or full, the tidal water can cover the path and flood those houses where precautions are not taken. Anti-flood devices include raised-up (in some cases, half-height) doors, glass screens and wooden shutters on rails. These were rendered largely redundant by the opening of the Thames Barrier in 1983, but it seems the residents are happy to keep them just in case.

Continue along, coming upon one of several great pubs along the final stretch of the river bank. If the tide is out you might want to get down from the path onto the shoreline and follow the route this way, although it can be muddy.

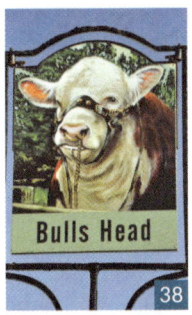

The first pub is ㊳ **The Bull's Head** which was first licensed by at least 1722 and originally belonged to Sich's Lamb Brewery mentioned earlier. By tradition Oliver Cromwell was a frequent visitor here during visits to see his daughter, the Countess of Fauconberg, who lived nearby. There is also supposed to be a secret tunnel out to the little island just along from the pub known today as Oliver's Eyot and where Cromwell is said to have sought refuge on occasion. In reality the Countess did not live here until after her father died and sadly, no tunnel has yet been discovered.

The actor Donald Pleasance (1919-1995), best known for his parts in *The Great Escape*, *Dracula*, *Halloween* and *You Only Live Twice* (as Stavros Blofeld) lived at numbers 10 & 11 during the 1970s and early 80s.

As you continue westwards look out to ❸❾ **Oliver's Island**, known as Strand Ayt until Cromwell's name became attached to it. It has had a variety of uses over time including the building, repair and docking of barges. It is currently leased to the London Natural History Society by the Port of London Authority.

You pass under the ❹⓿ **Kew Railway Bridge** (otherwise known as Strand-on-the-Green Railway Bridge), which carries the District Line and London Overground, and dates back to 1869. The ornate wrought-iron lattice-girders give the bridge some character, though the green paint looks a little faded these days. It featured in the 1964 Doctor Who episode *The Dalek Invasion of Earth*.

Beneath it is the Strand-on-the-Green Sailing Club, which organises races every Sunday between March and November. These can make for a glorious sight on a golden summer evening (see www.strandsailing.org.uk for timings), though as the dinghies thread their way around the course it can be a real challenge for the layman to work out who is actually winning.

Soon you see **41 The City Barge** which has its origins in the late 15th century and was originally called the Navigators Arms. It features in the 1965 Beatles film *Help!* when the band find refuge in the pub after being pursued by Klang. Ringo orders 'Two lagers and lime and two lagers and lime'.

The actual filming took place here on April 24th 1965. In the film Ringo falls through the floor and meets a tiger, although this scene was filmed in a studio. In recent years the pub has been popular with television presenters Ant & Dec whose management company is based nearby. The City Barge, which appeared in the licensing lists by 1787 (as the City Navigation Barge), was partially destroyed in World War II by a parachute mine (which also destroyed or badly damaged over 100 nearby houses). It was subsequently rebuilt, though the original downstairs bar remains intact. It was named after the City of London Navigation Committee's state barge, which regularly moored at Oliver's Island (opposite the pub) in the 18th and 19th centuries.

47 Kew Bridge

Hammersmith & Chiswick Walk

The impressive steel door at the riverside entrance is designed to keep the Thames out during spring tides, when it can flood the path (which is at its lowest point here) to the height of several feet. If you don't like the idea of being trapped in a pub, don't worry, there is an escape route at the end of the upstairs bar.

The poet Dylan Thomas occupied Ship Cottage, behind ㊷ **Ship House** (at number 56), when staying with his friend Professor GM Carstairs. Ship House, which dates from the 1690s, is perhaps the oldest house on the Strand.

Look out for the ornate frontage of what is known, for obviously reasons given its styling, as the ㊸ **Dutch House** at number 60. This was occupied from 1959 to 1964 by director John Guillermin, who best known films include *The Towering Inferno*, *The Blue Max*, *King Kong* and *Death on the Nile*.

German artist Johann Zoffany (1734-1810) occupied number 65 (now named Zoffany House) in the late 18th century. He is best known for his striking painting *The Tribuna of the Uffizi*, and his main patron was George III. The house was also once the home of sitcom writer Carla Lane.

㊹ **Zachary House** (number 70) is a magnificent Grade II listed Georgian house which dates back to 1790. It features the prominent 'Captain's lookout', added by the first owner Captain Zachary. Pop star Midge Ure used to live here, and it was in his studio here in 1984 that he and Bob Geldof co-wrote the Band Aid song *Do They*

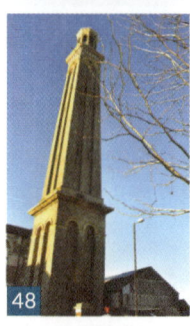

Know It's Christmas. In recent years Zachary House was put on the market for over £6 million by then owner Alan Smith, former editor of the New Musical Express (NME).

Continue along the Strand and you will see ㊹ **The Bell & Crown**, licensed since 1787 and owned by Fuller's since 1814. It is rumoured to have been used by smugglers in the past and to have a resident ghost that turns on the beer pumps during the night. The current building dates from 1907, when the owners – local brewer Fuller, Smith & Turner – decided to demolish the original. The impressive conservatory extension was added in 1984, providing one of the best riverside pub views in London.

The ㊻ **Steam Packet Pub** was originally licensed in 1870 and traded until the 1980s and has now reopened again. It's named after the steam launches that docked at Kew Pier opposite. Pier House beside the pub was a laundry from the 1860s until it was sold in the 1970s.

Ahead is ㊼ **Kew Bridge**, which dates from 1903 – the first bridge here was built in the 18th century. At this stage you can follow the signs around to Kew Bridge Railway Station and the end of this walk.

Alternatively if you still have energy the excellent ㊽ **Kew Bridge Steam Museum** is a five minute walk past the bridge (look out for the 200 foot tall brick tower). Originally built in the 19th century to supply London with water, the museum contains a great collection of steam pumping engines. ●

47 Kew Bridge

VISIT...

Chiswick House & Gardens
Chiswick, W4 2QN (see p.149)
www.chgt.org.uk

Emery Walker House (see p.141)
7 Hammersmith Terr, W6 9TS
www.emerywalker.org.uk

Hogarth House (see p.147)
Hogarth Lane, W4 2QN
Tel: 020 8994 6757

Kelmscott House (see p.136)
26 Upper Mall, W6 9TA
www.williammorrissociety.org

Kew Bridge Steam Museum
(see p.158)
Green Dragon Lane, TW8 0EN
www.waterandsteam.org.uk

EAT, DRINK...

The Bell & Crown (see p.158)
11-13 Thames Road, W4 3PL
www.bell-and-crown.co.uk

The Black Lion (see p.140)
2 South Black Lion Lane, W6 9TJ
www.theblacklion-hammersmith.co.uk

The Blue Anchor (see p.133)
13 Lower Mall, W6 9DJ
www.blueanchorlondon.com

The Bull's Head (see p.153)
373 Lonsdale Road, SW13 9PY
www.thebullshead.com

The Steam Packet (see opposite)
85 Strand-On-The-Green, W4 3NN

The City Barge (see p.155)
27 Strand on the Green, W4 3PH
Tel: 020 8994 2148

The Dove (see p.135)
19 Upper Mall, W6 9TA
www.dovehammersmith.co.uk

Old Ship Public House (see p.138)
25 Upper Mall, W6 9TD
www.oldshipw6.co.uk

Brixton Station Road Market, see p.190

6 Brixton & Brockwell Park Walk

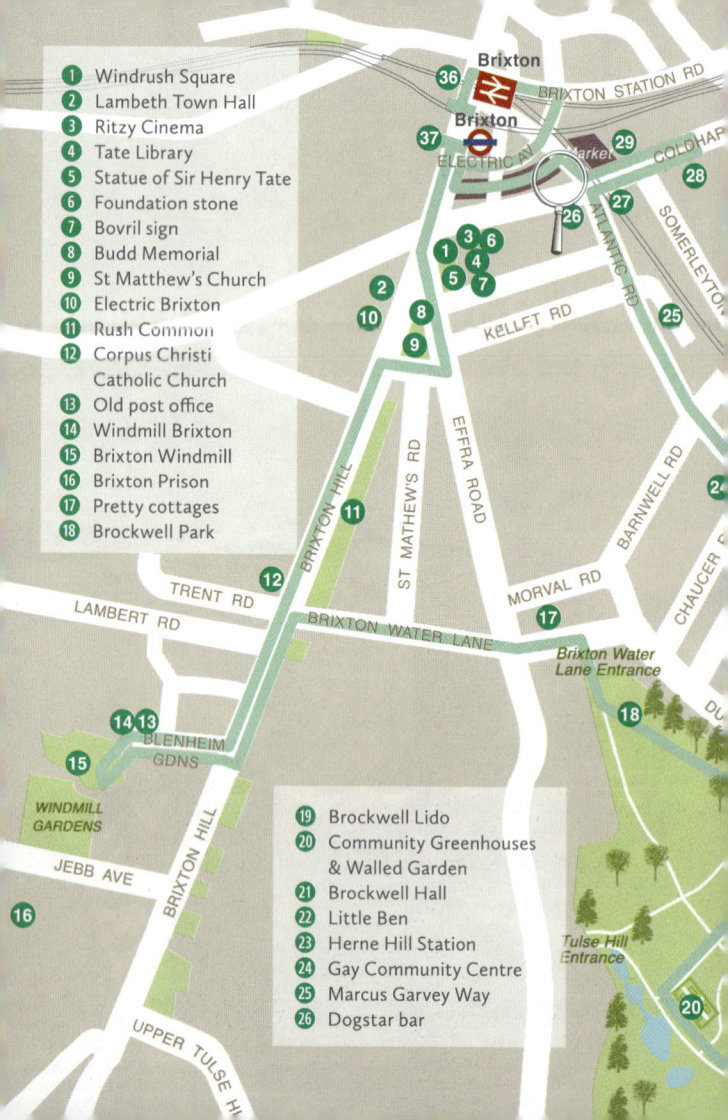

1. Windrush Square
2. Lambeth Town Hall
3. Ritzy Cinema
4. Tate Library
5. Statue of Sir Henry Tate
6. Foundation stone
7. Bovril sign
8. Budd Memorial
9. St Matthew's Church
10. Electric Brixton
11. Rush Common
12. Corpus Christi Catholic Church
13. Old post office
14. Windmill Brixton
15. Brixton Windmill
16. Brixton Prison
17. Pretty cottages
18. Brockwell Park
19. Brockwell Lido
20. Community Greenhouses & Walled Garden
21. Brockwell Hall
22. Little Ben
23. Herne Hill Station
24. Gay Community Centre
25. Marcus Garvey Way
26. Dogstar bar

Brixton & Brockwell Park Walk

- ㉗ Julian Wall (plaque)
- ㉘ Southwyck House
- ㉙ Former Walton Lodge Sanitary Steam Laundry
- ㉚ Brixton Village
- ㉛ Market Row
- ㉜ Reliance Arcade
- ㉝ Morleys of Brixton
- ㉞ Electric Avenue
- ㉟ Brixton Station Road
- ㊱ Bon Marché
- ㊲ David Bowie mural

Brixton & Brockwell Park Walk

Brixton & Brockwell Park Walk
Start/Finish: Brixton underground/rail station
Distance: 4 miles

Turn left down Brixton Road and walk for a few minutes to reach the junction of Coldharbour Lane, Brixton Road, Brixton Hill, Acre Lane and Effra Road. Cross over to enter ❶ **Windrush Square**. It might be worth sitting down in the square to read more about it – and Brixton generally – before continuing on.

Mention Brixton to most Londoners and they tend to have a strong reaction one way or the other. 'Vibrant' is a common description – 'dangerous' is another. Those who actually visit the area usually have a more positive view and hopefully by the end of this walk you will have formed your own impression of what is certainly a unique district of London.

❶ *Windrush Square*

Brixton & Brockwell Park Walk

As you sit in Windrush Square try to imagine the Brixton of 200 years ago. This area was still largely rural then, with a few houses flanking the old country lanes that now form the junction you have just crossed. It was only in the late 18th century that settlements began to grow around these lanes, and even then the area remained just an unimportant backwater in northern Surrey.

The name of Brixton itself has ancient origins, far older than the 'Brixistane' recorded by the Normans in the late 11th century in the famous *Doomsday Book*. The name may refer to the 'stone of Brixi', a Saxon nobleman perhaps. The stone itself could have stood on what is now Brixton Hill, a gathering point for the regular meetings of the 'hundred' – a group of prominent people who lived in this district of Saxon Surrey and who helped run it administratively.

In the early years of the 19th century, Brixton was still just a village. In 1816 there were just a few dozen houses, the new windmill high up on Brixton Hill to the south, and sheep grazing where the square is today. However, things in London were changing rapidly as the population grew out of all proportion to the old housing stock available. An expanding middle class wanted houses away from the over-crowded central areas, but still near enough to get to work easily. A new type of property developer began to build the suburbs to meet this demand.

Estates were bought, fields were ripped up and new houses were built. Brixton became a prime area for development as new bridges over the Thames (particularly Vauxhall Bridge in 1816) opened up south London to the capital's workforce. The age of the London commuter began and Brixton – less than four miles from Charing Cross – was set to benefit.

By the 1820s Lambeth's original parish church, St Mary's (near Lambeth Palace), could no longer properly serve the growing population to the south and so the church authorities founded St Matthew's in Brixton. We will encounter this fine church later in the walk. St Matthew's was consecrated in 1824 and its foundation stone was laid by the Archbishop of Canterbury. From 1190 the Manor of Lambeth belonged to the Archbishops of Canterbury and Acts of Parliament in the early 19th century made it easier for the church authorities to allow developers to build on church-owned land.

Brixton's expansion continued in the 1850s when a large residential estate named Angell Town was built to the north, but the real boost came when the railway station opened in 1862. Within a few decades Brixton became an important town in south London, with a popular commercial centre that drew shoppers from miles around. It became a prosperous, middle class suburb – and remained as such until the period after World War II.

Walk around Windrush Square – the unofficial heart of Brixton. Facing the square you can see the tall tower of ❷ **Lambeth Town Hall**, the municipal centre of the Borough of Lambeth of which Brixton is part. The town hall dates from 1908 and is richly faced in red brick and Portland stone. The modern borough of Lambeth covers a narrow stretch of the capital from the Thames down to Streatham. It is home to a population of around 280,000 and roughly covers the traditional parish of Lambeth that once belonged to the Archbishop of Canterbury.

One of Brixton's most famous former residents – the ex-Prime Minister John Major – served as a councillor here and we will find out more about his life in the area along this walk. Look out for the four stone figures representing Science, Art, Literature and Justice on the tower.

On the north-east corner of Windrush Square you will find the ❸ **Ritzy Cinema**. It opened in 1911 and is the second oldest picture house in London. In the years 1910-1915 nine cinemas were opened in the Brixton area, reflecting a mania for the most revolutionary development in entertainment since the rise of the music hall in the 19th century. After nearly 100 years the Ritzy is the only survivor of that original group.

Brixton & Brockwell Park Walk

It was originally known as the Electric Pavilion Cinema and if you look closely on the wall around the corner you can see figures holding up the letters 'E' and 'P'.

Beside the Ritzy is the ❹ **Tate Library**, an elegant classical style building that was erected in 1892. It was named after the sugar merchant and philanthropist Sir Henry Tate (1819-1899). He sponsored three libraries in this part of London in between inventing the sugar cube and building up a hugely successful business that – after his death – would merge with a rival to become today's world-famous Tate & Lyle. Tate also donated his art collection to the nation and this formed the basis of London's Tate Britain gallery (see page 281 for more about Henry Tate and his sugar empire).

You can see a ❺ **statue of Tate** in the square, although old pictures show the bust once stood on a much more substantial plinth. Shortly after the library was built this area was still surrounded by fields upon which sheep grazed but Tate's widow bought the land in 1905 and donated it for public use. It was then known as Brixton Oval, later becoming Tate Gardens and more recently it was re-named Windrush Square. Tate knew this area well, having lived on Streatham Common and is buried in West Norwood Cemetery nearby.

Between the Ritzy and the Tate Library used to stand Brixton Theatre which opened in 1894 and staged serious theatrical productions for consumption by the middle class of Brixton. However, it was destroyed during the Blitz and today all that remains is the ❻ **foundation stone** (near the library) which was laid by the great Victorian actor-manager Henry Irving.

You may be curious as to why Tate Gardens became Windrush Square. The answer is closely linked to an event that had a fundamental impact on the next phase in Brixton's history. After World War II Britain was facing a labour shortage, and encouraged workers from its Empire to come here. In 1948 a group of Jamaican immigrants arrived at Tilbury Docks on the SS Empire Windrush – 493 people who would change the course of English history.

Initially many of the immigrants were housed in the nearby Clapham South deep shelter, the nearest job centre (then known as a Labour Exchange) being on Coldharbour Lane in Brixton. Unsurprisingly many decided to settle nearby, seeking safety in numbers during an era when it was totally normal to see signs in London boarding house windows stating 'No dogs, no blacks, no Irish'. The area soon became south London's centre for the British Afro-Caribbean community and so began another chapter in Brixton's history. Blitz damage to residential streets, the introduction of housing estates and the changing demographic resulted in many white middle-class families moving away from the area during the 1950s and 60s. Today, nearly one-quarter of Brixton's population is of Afro-Caribbean descent, nearly double the average in London, and the district has become known as the heart of the Afro-Caribbean community in London.

Unsurprisingly, the issue of race is never too far from the surface in Brixton, with many physical reminders of the community's sense of solidarity with oppressed minority groups or heroes of the civil rights movement. Besides Windrush Square's name – introduced to coincide with the 50th anniversary of the ship's arrival at Tilbury

Brixton & Brockwell Park Walk

– there is also (opposite the library) a monument to the victims of the Sharpeville Massacre of 1960 when 69 black protestors were shot dead by policemen serving the Apartheid regime of South Africa.

It was only by chance that this area was not named Monte Rosa Square – that was the Empire Windrush's original name when she began her life as a German cruise ship. During World War II she carried German troops and even some Jews who were being deported to concentration camps. The ship was later captured by the British who renamed her.

Windrush Square has been criticised for being rather soulless, attracting alcoholics and drug users and a far cry from the days when Tate's money made this an attractive location. But Brixton is on the way up, and the square can only get better.

Just beside the library look out for one of London's 'ghost' advertisements – an old ❼ **Bovril sign** high up on the wall. Underneath the sign is a war memorial commemorating the men and women from Africa and the Caribbean who served in World War I and II. While here, look out for the mile stone that tells travellers they are 4 miles from the Royal Exchange.

Head out of the square aiming for St Matthew's church visible on the south side (in the triangle between Effra Road and Brixton Hill). At the junction between those two roads (opposite Lambeth Town Hall) is the ❽ **Budd Memorial** that was erected in 1825 by the theologian Henry Budd in memory of his father Richard, an eminent doctor, who was born in Brixton in 1748.

Continue on to reach the church. As mentioned above, ❾ **St Matthew's** was consecrated in 1824. It was one of a number of so-called 'Waterloo' churches – built using money provided by Parliament in 1818 and 1824 to bolster the presence of the Church of England in the newly created urban areas. The latter, in the decades following the French Revolution and Napoleon's regime, were seen as potential breeding grounds for atheism and revolution and so the Church of England and politicians were keen to maintain the status quo by drawing the new urban dwellers into the arms of the establishment.

This substantial building was no doubt meant to impress upon the residents of Brixton that the Church of England was still a force to be reckoned with. It was designed by the architect CF Porden in a Greek revival style and was one of four new Lambeth parish churches built during the same period. In 1970 John Major married Norma here.

In recent years the church's dwindling congregation has resulted in parts of the building being used for distinctly secular purposes, and for a time this was the venue for the Mass nightclub. These days there are more wholesome activities like children's play groups.

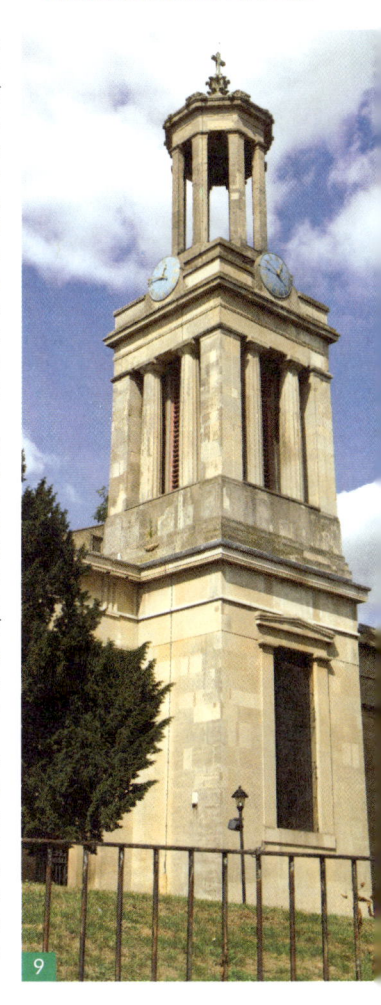

Brixton & Brockwell Park Walk

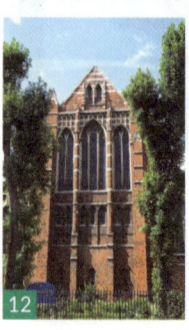

Leave the church and walk for a few minutes south up Brixton Hill as we aim for the Brixton Windmill and Brixton Prison. Just after the church you will see (on the same side as Lambeth Town Hall) the ❿ **Electric Brixton**, until recently better known as The Fridge. Founded in 1981, and based here from 1985 to 2010, The Fridge was one of London's most famous nightclubs. In the early 1980s it was at the centre of the New Romantic movement, featuring many then obscure artists such as the Pet Shop Boys, Boy George, Frankie Goes to Hollywood and the Eurythmics. Bands such as The Clash and The Smiths also played here. The core of the building dates from 1913 when it was known as the Palladium Cinema which, along with the Ritzy, was one of the early cinemas opened in Brixton.

Continue south up Brixton Hill and walk through ⓫ **Rush Common** on the left-hand side. This was originally land that was part of the Manor of Lambeth and the common land here was enclosed by Parliament in the early 19th century.

After a few minutes cross over to see ⓬ **Corpus Christi Catholic Church** on the right-hand side. It dates from 1887 and was designed by John Francis Bentley (1839-1902). This was his first important church commission and he was later responsible for arguably London's finest modern church, Westminster Cathedral. For many years Corpus Christi was run by the Jesuits who had established a mission here a few years before.

Brixton & Brockwell Park Walk

After a further short walk up Brixton Hill head right up Blenheim Gardens and continue along. On the right-hand side is an ⑬ **old post office** dating from the 1891 and still being used as a delivery office. At the end is the ⑭ **Windmill Brixton**, well-known for its excellent gigs.

Just past here is the Blenheim Gardens Estate. Unfortunately problems on Brixton's many housing estates have helped create a negative impression of the area over the years. The newspaper headlines about drugs gangs, violence and disorder overlook the conscientious local residents working to make Brixton a pleasant place to live. This particular estate is a prime example, as in recent years it has become recognised as one of the best-run estates in Lambeth after its residents took more control over its organisation.

Many old streets were bulldozed in the late 1960s to make way for the Blenheim Gardens Estate but if you want to see how they looked, watch the Alfred Hitchcock film *The Man Who Knew Too Much* (1956) – several scenes featuring Doris Day and James Stewart were filmed on Cornwall and Vicary Streets that once stood here.

15 Brixton Windmill

At the end of Blenheim Gardens bear left into Windmill Gardens. You will soon see ⑮ **Brixton Windmill**, an extraordinary survivor of old Brixton. It dates from 1816 and was originally known as Ashby's Mill – after the Ashby family who ran it for many decades. It continued to function as the fields around it were slowly built on by developers, however these new properties literally took the wind out of Ashby's sails. In the 1860s the Ashbys moved their main production of flour to windmills in Mitcham, Surrey. However in 1902 the Ashbys once again began to use their mill here, replacing wind power with steam and then gas power.

The mill finally ceased production in 1934, a year before the death of the last Ashby miller – Joshua. Despite suffering over the years through vandalism and general neglect, the windmill is now in the capable hands of the Friends of Windmill Gardens who help maintain this Grade II listed building and offer guided tours to the public (see www.brixtonwindmill.org for more details).

In the 1860s the area south of the windmill was the site of a reservoir owned by the Lambeth Water Works Company. This enterprise began in 1785, supplying South London with water taken from the Thames, and establishing a reservoir in this part of Brixton in the 1830s. However growing Victorian concerns about water-borne diseases and the polluted Thames led to legislation restricting the use of the river for domestic consumption and so the Company moved its reservoir elsewhere.

Directly south of the windmill is ⑯ **Brixton Prison** – you can just see the roof from Windmill Gardens. It was opened in 1820 as the Surrey House of Correction, with Brixton Hill chosen because it was so out of the way. From the start the prison had a brutal reputation, and was one of the first to introduce the treadmill which sacrificed the health of many prisoners in return for cheaply milled wheat that could be sold.

In the 1850s it became a female-only institution, with new inmates forced to spend their first four months in the prison in solitary confinement. It was later used as a military prison before reverting back to its current use for male prisoners, principally those awaiting trial or serving short sentences.

The 3rd Earl Russell, better known as Bertrand Russell (1872-1970), the famous philosopher, mathematician and social critic, was jailed here twice. The first time was in 1918 for six months after he publicly expressed anti-war sentiments. He used his time to write one of his best-known works, *Introduction to Mathematical Philosophy*. Incredibly, 43 years later, he was locked up here again in 1961 after being convicted of a breach of the peace for failing to obtain a permit to organise public protest meetings. He was then aged 89 and in one of his letters sent shortly after he was released he wrote of how 'when I got to Brixton all the officials remarked gleefully "you've been here before", and I wanted to reply "yes you're welcoming an old lag". They were all friendly'.

Mick Jagger also stayed here for just one night in 1967 after his drugs conviction following the infamous police raid by the police on Keith Richards' house Redlands. The conviction sparked off a huge national debate about what was the suitable punishment for the drug offence, with even *The Times* regarding the conviction as being too harsh. In 1991 two IRA prisoners escaped from the prison after scaling the walls and hijacking a prison officer's car.

In recent years the prison's reputation has declined even further, with widespread public criticism of the harsh conditions that have resulted in an unusually high level of suicides among its prisoners. At one stage it was due to be privatised – normally a sign that the authorities have lost faith in their attempts at reform from within.

Return down Blenheim Gardens and re-trace your steps back down Brixton Hill. Opposite Corpus Christi church turn right into Brixton Water Lane, passing a sign for St Matthew's Estate. This estate is one of those with a notorious reputation for violence, prostitution and drug dealing. In 2004 the St Matthew's Project was founded by local resident Lee Dema to help tackle such problems and make the estate safer for the local children.

Brixton & Brockwell Park Walk

Continue along Brixton Water Lane aiming for Brockwell Park (it is about a ten minute walk and you will need to cross over Tulse Hill Road). Brixton Water Lane follows the course of the River Effra, one of London's lost rivers, which has long been covered over. The Effra has its source in Crystal Palace and passes under Brixton and eventually reaches the Thames near Vauxhall Bridge.

As you cross over Tulse Hill Road look out on the left-hand side for some ⓱ **pretty cottages** (numbers 56 to 66) – rare survivors of old Brixton which date from around 1820. Their original purpose was to house workers at nearby Brockwell Hall – which we will find out more about shortly.

In May 1900 a notorious murder took place just near here at number 44 when Mrs Kate Wakenell's body was discovered with 27 stab wounds from a pair of scissors. The case was reported around the world and shocked London, perhaps for some stirring up memories of Jack the Ripper who had disappeared just 12 years before. Like the Whitechapel murders, the brutal killing of Mrs Wakenell remains unsolved.

Very shortly are gates to enter ⓲ **Brockwell Park** with more of the cottages just to the left. Inside the park, bear left along the footpath. This is a very pleasant public space of 125 acres that is popular with Londoners either running, practising yoga, growing vegetables, swimming in the Lido, playing tennis or just taking stroll and enjoying the view across London.

This lovely park is fortunate to exist at all as in the 1880s the owners – the Blades Blackburn Estate – wanted to sell it. It would almost certainly have been transformed by ambitious developers into yet another urban residential area were it not for local MP Thomas Lynn Bristowe (1833-1892). He led a hard-fought campaign to save the land for the public, even providing a guarantee for the purchase price. Bristowe won the battle but tragically died from a heart attack on the steps of Brockwell Hall during the park's opening ceremony in 1892.

After a few minutes' walk you pass ⓵⓽ **Brockwell Lido** on the left – a superb Grade II listed art deco outdoor swimming pool that dates from 1937. The 1930s was the decade when swimming became very popular in England, and many lidos were constructed around the country. It is known locally as 'Brixton Beach' and is seemingly always busy, regardless of the weather. It had an identical counterpart in Victoria Park in Hackney, both designed by the now defunct London County Council, but this was sadly demolished in 1990. Brockwell Lido however has

Brixton & Brockwell Park Walk

recently been renovated and has an excellent café with an outdoor terrace next to the pool if you're in need of refreshment (see Lido Café p.191 for more information).

From the Lido walk up the hill aiming for the tennis courts at the top. Remember to look back to get a superb view of London – from Battersea Power Station in the west to Canary Wharf in the east. In 2011 the singer Adele was asked why she was not performing at music festivals that year and replied that she preferred 'sitting in Brockwell Park with my friends, drinking cider'. Her years here inspired the song *A Million Years Ago*.

At the top of the hill bear left (around the edge of the tennis courts) to reach the ⓴ **Community Greenhouses** and the **Walled Garden**, the old kitchen garden for Brockwell Hall. They are lovingly maintained by local residents, and a testament to the community spirit of this area that does not always come across in the media's portrayal of south London. Beyond the walled garden are the tranquil ponds and a children's play area complete with paddling pool.

Head across the park to the Grade II* listed ㉑ **Brockwell Hall** which sits at the brow of the hill and offers fantastic views of London's most prominent landmarks. It dates from 1813 and was built by John Blades (c. 1751-1829), a wealthy glass manufacturer who first bought 60 acres of land here in 1809 and then demolished the original mansion. There is a fantastic café on the ground floor if you are in need of a refuel.

179

Brixton & Brockwell Park Walk

As you near the Hall look out for ㉒ **Little Ben** – a clock resembling Big Ben that was donated by MP Charles Tritton in 1905. The Hall contains a bust of Bristowe, who was one of the key figures behind the foundation of this tranquil green space.

When finished at Brockwell Hall follow the path down the hill towards the Herne Hill park entrance. Follow the map onto Railton Road. This pedestrianised zone makes up the centre of Herne Hill and is a pleasant place to stop, shop and refuel before we head back to the centre of Brixton. ㉓ **Herne Hill Station** on your right was opened to traffic in 1862, and the entrance listed Grade II in 1999. Just by the station is the excellent Herne Hill Bookshop.

Continue to walk up Railton Road. The first section feels very gentrified, containing many refurbished Victorian houses. However, during the dark days of the early 1980s, Railton Road became known as the 'front line' as locals took on the police in a series of major riots that lasted two days and destroyed around 30 buildings. The riots were reported around the world and the subsequent public enquiry, headed by Lord Scarman, lead to significant changes in police arrest procedure.

As you continue up Railton Road the apparent gentrification masks this particular area's radical and bohemian past. In particular in the 1970s, not that long after homosexuality was de-criminalised in the UK, a radical gay squatting movement was based along here. It was focused around the

Brockwell Park ponds

㉔ **South London Gay Community Centre**, an empty shop at 78 Railton Road that was squatted by gay activists from 1974 until evicted two years later. During this time they shared similar concerns about police harassment as their West Indian neighbours. There were also other activist groups based nearby, including feminist groups, anarchists and militant squatters. Many of those affiliated to these various movements squatted at several houses on Railton Road and Mayall Road (just to the east) and developed a shared communal garden in the space in between.

As you continue northwards look out on the right for ㉕ **Marcus Garvey Way**, named after the Jamaican black rights activist. Marcus Garvey (1887-1940) presented his often radical ideas about race to the American public in the oppressive political climate that prevailed after World War I. He most controversially advocated the return of millions of black people to a new nation in Africa. Many of Garvey's plans remained unfulfilled and he died a disappointed man in Hammersmith in 1940 and was buried in Kensal Green Cemetery. However he remains an important figure in the early black rights movement hence the local authorities remembering him in this street name.

As you continue northward Railton Road becomes Atlantic Road and you will start to notice more shops serving Afro-Caribbean inspired food and probably see some of the many Rastafarians who have made Brixton their home.

On your left at the corner of the junction with Coldharbour Lane is the ㉖ **Dogstar bar**. Today this bar is one of Brixton's favourite venues, but during the riots of 1995 it was gutted by a mob, angry that it had replaced the original popular Afro-Caribbean pub, the Atlantic. Many felt then, and still feel today, that the gentrification of the area often marginalises local people. The local press regularly reports stories about yet another old Brixton pub being closed or redeveloped.

John Major, partly responsible for the creation of some of Brixton's less attractive estates, himself lived on Coldharbour Lane when he was a child. His father, Tom Major-Ball, was then a struggling music hall performer plagued by ill health and they lived in a damp two-bedroom flat on the corner of Coldharbour Lane and Eastlake Road. The Conservative Party later played heavily on Major's humble Brixton origins during his election campaigns.

Before television helped kill off variety theatre, many stage performers such as Tom Major-Ball, Max Wall and Dan Leno lived in Brixton. It offered cheap digs and proximity to the West End and local theatres such as the Brixton Empress and Camberwell Palace.

Turn right to walk along Coldharbour Lane and under the railway bridge. Immediately on your right is a fine Victorian buildng with a ㉗ **plaque to Julian Wall** who 'lived here 1979-1989; Totter, squatter, a true individual. Much Loved.' Wall was a founding member of a local housing cooperative who was renowned for the help and advice he gave to Brixtonians struggling to find a roof over their heads. Perhaps only in Brixton would you find such a memorial.

Look at the external wall on this building to see a huge mural by Brian Barnes and Dale McCrea that dates from 1981 and depicts a Nuclear Dawn – a protest against the siting of Cruise missiles in Britain at the height of the Cold War. The mural was one of many commissioned by the local council in the wake of the 1981 riots.

Continue down Coldharbour Lane, crossing over Somerleyton Road which was once the route of the tram service. Stop outside the brutal-looking housing block on the right named (28) **Southwyck House**, which stands on the edge of the Somerleyton Estate. The estate dates from the 1970s and during that decade there was a radical plan to build a six-lane inner city motorway through this part of London. Southwyck House was intended to stand on the edge of the new road system and became known as Barrier Block – its zig-zag design was supposed to act as a sound break between the traffic and residents on the rest of the estate. Thankfully the motorway did not go ahead but Barrier Block – already squatted – unfortunately did. Since then it has endured a terrible reputation and continues to be one of the most troubled estates in Brixton.

In 2003 the prominent black rights activist Darcus Howe wrote of the Barrier Block in the New Statesman that he 'would like to see it blown up so that the whole of London could see the mushroom of smoke and the flames, so they'd know that its like would never be seen again.'

The contrast between such a blighted part of Brixton and the gentrification of the area is well illustrated by the new 'Brixton Square' development directly opposite on Coldharbour Lane. Built by Barratt Homes, this recent plush construction sits uneasily between Southwyck House and the equally infamous Loughborough Estate which lies just to the north of here.

Brixton & Brockwell Park Walk

Return down Coldharbour Lane, stopping on the right-hand side outside the richly coloured ㉙ **former Walton Lodge Sanitary Steam Laundry**. It dates back to 1880 and has been based here since 1895. The laudry traded for over 120 years until its recent conversion into a pleasant café bar called (unsurprisingly) The Laundry.

Beside the laundry is the entrance to ㉚ **Brixton Village,** one of three indoor arcade-style markets created in the 1920s and 30s when street stalls were moved to make more space for traffic. **Brixton Village** (formally the Granville Arcade) was built in 1937. The markets today are a buzzing culinary and cultural hub but their story could have been very different.

The markets narrowly avoided being demolished in 2007 when Market Row and Brixton Village were sold to developers. The new owner's plans included the development of a 10 storey privately-owned residential tower block, above a new market building. Local residents and traders ran a campaign against the proposals and in April 2010 the government overturned its previous decision and awarded heritage protection to these three arcades.

Brixton & Brockwell Park Walk

Brixton & Brockwell Park Walk

The markets were rundown after years of neglect with many empty units but the last few years have seen them burst back into life with the help of urban visionaries – the nonprofit organization Space Makers Agency in cooperation with Friends of Brixton Market and the local authority. A revitalization project has transformed the empty shops into a rolling programme of temporary pop-ups, weekly events and community driven businesses.

Brixton Village is now thriving but its charm lies in its warm community atmosphere, the small restaurants that feel like you're stepping into someone's living room for dinner, the hand-painted signs, vintage shops and colourful meat, fish and vegetable stalls.

Another innovation is the use of the Brixton Pound – a local currency that is available as an alternative to the pound sterling. It works by encouraging shops and shoppers to source goods and services locally meaning money spent in Brixton stays there, helping local businesses thrive and fostering a community spirit.

When finished in Brixton Village follow the map and take the exit onto Atlantic Road. Atlantic Road is where Brixton Market first began in the 1870s before moving to Station Road in the 1920s to ease traffic congestion. The David Greig grocery shop opened at 54-58 Atlantic Road in 1870, its popularity such that it became a major influence on Brixton's shopping centre, and it went on to become a rival to the early Sainsbury's chain with over 200 shops by the late 1960s. The family sold the company in the early 1970s, but if things had turned out slightly differently the Greig empire – started in Brixton – could still rival Tesco's or Sainsbury's today.

Opposite and slightly to your left you will see another of Brixton's indoor markets – Market Row. Cross Atlantic Road and pause outside Market Row and look to your right towards the railway bridge. The view has not changed significantly since Michael Caine walked along Coldharbour Lane while playing the title character in the controversial film *Alfie* (1966).

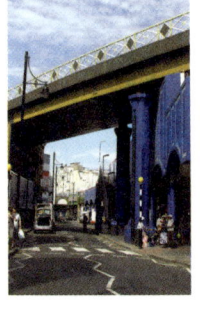

31 **Market Row** is worth visiting both to see the glass roofed arcade designed by Andrews and Peascod in 1928 and also to perhaps have a rest at one of the many fantastic eateries and delis to be found here, including Franco Manca – one of the best pizzerias in London.

Exit at the other side of Market Row, crossing Electric Lane to reach the third covered market in Brixton – the **32** **Reliance Arcade**. More traditionally focused than the increasingly gentrified Market Row, it provides a narrow pedestrian route from Brixton Road to Electric Lane. Built in 1925-6, it was Brixton's first indoor market. The distinctive façade was inspired by the fashion for all things Egyptian following the discovery of Tutankhamen's tomb in 1922.

Exit the Reliance Arcade onto Brixton Road. Turn right and walk until you reach Electric Avenue. This road dates from the 1880s and its name reflects that fact it was one of the very first London streets to be lit by electricity. Such innovations led to Brixton becoming the key shopping district in this part of London, which by the 1920s boasted three large department stores. One still survives today – **33** **Morleys of Brixton** at 472-488 Brixton Road.

In April 1999 a neo-Nazi named David Copeland, who sought to spark off a race war in London, planted a nail bomb in Brixton Road. The bomb was moved by a suspicious market trader into Electric Avenue and later exploded injuring around 50 people. Copeland's wave of terror also targeted Asians in Brick Lane, as well as the gay community in Soho. He was caught and given a long sentence the following year.

Walk down ❹ **Electric Avenue** with its many fruit and veg stalls and local traders including butchers and fishmongers selling all kinds of exotic and unusual produce. It's a great place to see a vibrant week day market, when so many have declined in recent years.

Reggae star Eddy Grant made this street world famous with his massive 1982 hit 'Electric Avenue'. Another rock song associated with this area is The Clash's *The Guns of Brixton* (1979) which reflects some of the tensions between the police and locals that would erupt during the riots of 1981.

Cross into Pope's Road opposite – lined with market stalls – and follow this around to turn left into ❺ **Brixton Station Road**. This is the final part of Brixton market visited on this walk so if you have resisted the temptation to buy some food along the way, this may be the time to give in. On weekdays it is a food market but on Saturdays it hosts a variety of rotating monthly markets including a vintage and retro market, craft, flea and bread market and weekly Sunday farmers' market (*www.brixtonmarket.net*).

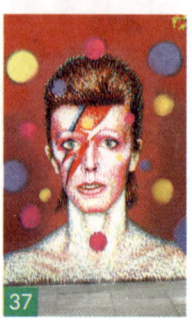

At the end you join Brixton Road. On the other side of Brixton Road you see an elegant building named ㊱ **Bon Marché**. Originally a department store, it was founded by Mr James Smith from Tooting who in 1876 won a fortune after his horse won two races at Newmarket. He decided to invest his winnings in a commercial venture, and Bon Marché – the first purpose built department store in the country – opened in 1877. Unfortunately Smith later became bankrupt and later owners of the store included Selfridges and John Lewis. Bon Marché finally ceased trading in 1975 and the building is now largely occupied by TKMaxx.

Before taking the tube or bus home it's worth taking a moment to note the musical heritage of Brixton with the famous Brixton Academy nearby on Stockwell Road. The Academy began life in 1929 as a cinema and theatre named the Astoria, and opened with an Al Jolsen film. The Astoria declined over the years and was nearly demolished in the 1970s. However it survived to be re-invented as a concert venue and became the Brixton Academy in 1983. Over the years the Academy has hosted concerts by some of the biggest names in the music industry including Madonna, Bob Dylan, Franz Ferdinand and Two Door Cinema Club and dozens of bands have released live albums from gigs at the venue.

Brixton & Brockwell Park Walk

Probably Brixton's most famous son is the pop star David Bowie, who was born David Robert Jones just a few streets from the Brixton Academy in 1947. The young David Jones moved from Brixton to Bromley at the age of six, but the London borough is still very proud of the connection. In 2013, to coincide with the *David Bowie is* exhibition at the V&A, an impressive ㊲ mural by artist Jimmy C depicting the cover of Bowie's *Aladdin Sane* album was installed at the side of Morley's Department Store, just opposite Brixton tube station. Since Bowie's death in January 2016, the mural has become a shrine for fans and has recently been accorded listed status. The walk concludes here, you can now return to the underground or railway stations and the end of this walk. ●

SHOP...

Brixton Markets, SW9
www.brixtonmarket.net
See list below:

• **Electric Avenue
& Pope's Road Market,** SW9 8JX

• **Brixton Station Road Market,**
Street Food all week

• **Covered Markets including
Brixton Village, Market Row
& Reliance Arcade,** SW9 8PR

EAT, DRINK...

**Brixton Village
& Market Row** (see p.185)
www.brixtonmarket.net

Brockwell Hall Café (see p.179)
Brockwell Park, SE24 9AF

Dogstar
389 Coldharbour Ln, SW9 8LQ
www.dogstarbrixton.com

Lido Café (see p.178)
Dulwich Rd, SE24 0PA
www.thelidocafe.co.uk

Roupell Street, see p.199

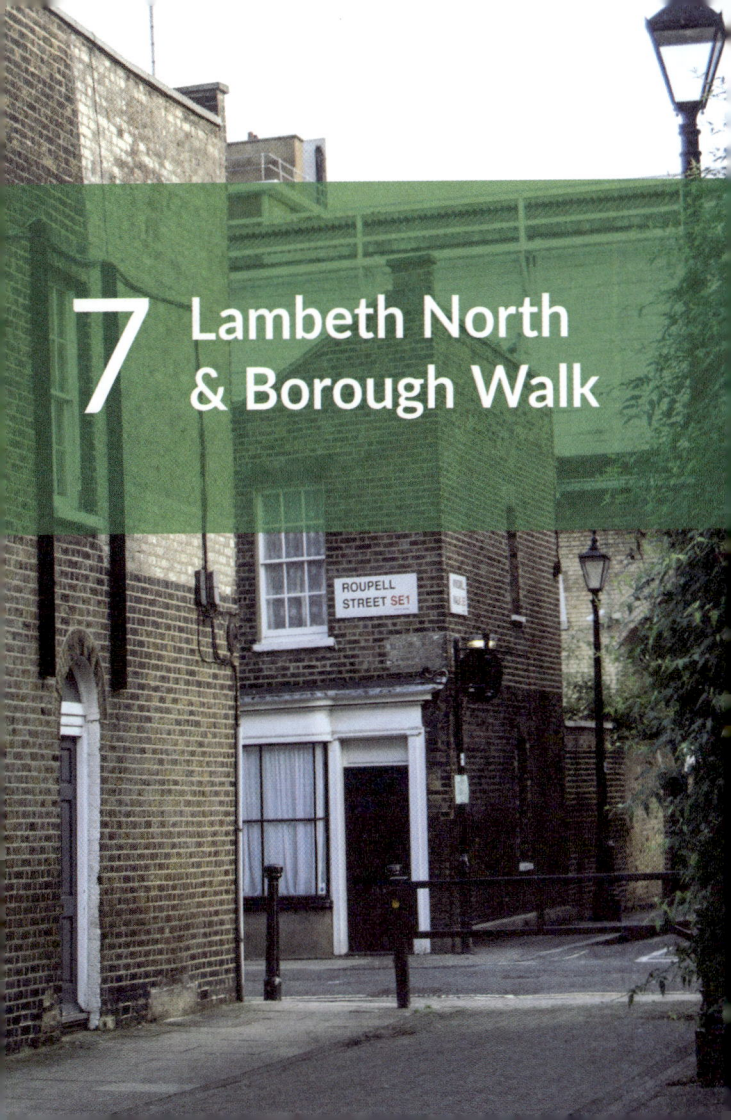

7 Lambeth North & Borough Walk

1. Waterloo Station
2. Royal Waterloo Hospital for Children & Women
3. St John The Evangelist Church
4. Roupell Street
5. King's Arms public house
6. Cons Street
7. Young Vic Theatre
8. Ufford Street
9. The Stage Door public house
10. Morley College
11. Archbishops House and Cathedral House
12. St George's Catholic Cathedral
13. Imperial War Museum
14. Geraldine Mary Harmsworth Park
15. Charlotte Sharman Primary School
16. West Square
17. J.A.R. Newlands (blue plaque)
18. Charlie Chaplin
19. No 36 West Square
20. Horse scratching post
21. Churchyard of St Mary's Newington
22. Red brick circular tower
23. Jam Yang Buddhist Centre

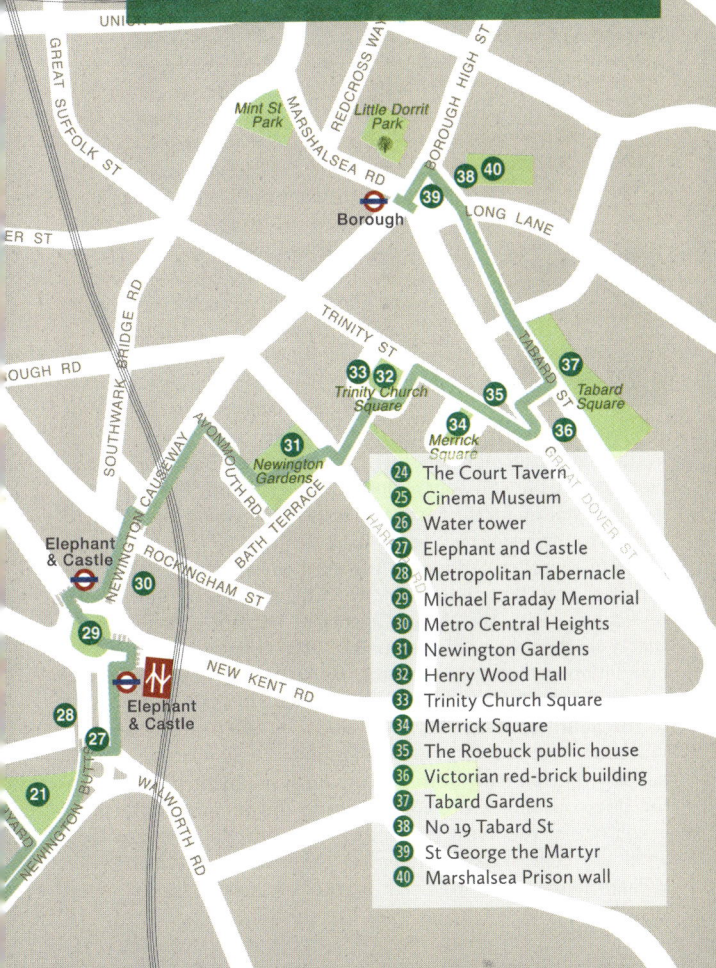

Lambeth North & Borough Walk

- 24 The Court Tavern
- 25 Cinema Museum
- 26 Water tower
- 27 Elephant and Castle
- 28 Metropolitan Tabernacle
- 29 Michael Faraday Memorial
- 30 Metro Central Heights
- 31 Newington Gardens
- 32 Henry Wood Hall
- 33 Trinity Church Square
- 34 Merrick Square
- 35 The Roebuck public house
- 36 Victorian red-brick building
- 37 Tabard Gardens
- 38 No 19 Tabard St
- 39 St George the Martyr
- 40 Marshalsea Prison wall

Lambeth North & Borough Walk
Start: Waterloo rail/underground station
Finish: Borough underground station
Distance: 3.6 miles

This walk begins from the cavernous and impressive ❶ **Waterloo Station**. The station may appear a dauntingly complex place now, but the current station is a product of the early 20th century, designed to simplify the 18 platforms that were previously scattered over 4 stations on this site. The new building, consisting of red brick and Portland stone, took over 20 years to plan and complete and was finally opened in 1922. The station kept its original name, but the impressive main entrance with its 'Victory Arch' is to commemorate the First World War and not the defeat of Bonaparte. As a main terminus, Waterloo was an important target during the Blitz and suffered 50 bomb blasts, but still went about its business. After the war it was the main station for the Festival of Britain, disgorging thousands of visitors to the newly built South Bank Centre.

Exit Waterloo Station via the main entrance and walk down the steps and through the pedestrian subway leading to the busy roundabout with the IMAX Cinema at its centre. It was here that a cardboard city of the homeless stood for 20 years until its demolition in 1998. On the other side is the ❷ **Royal Waterloo Hospital For Children & Women**. Founded in the City, it moved to the South Bank in 1823 and was one of the first buildings on Waterloo Road. Like Waterloo Station, this is not the original building, but an early 20th century redevelopment. The ornate red brick building with ceramic façade and terracotta dressings is still one of the finest in the area. The hospital closed in 1976 amid the controversy surrounding the work of psychiatrist Dr William Sargant, who used high doses of tranquillisers and electroconvulsive therapy (ECT) to 'repattern' the brains of mostly young women suffering from illnesses including anorexia and depression. In some cases patients were put to sleep for several weeks in what was called the Narcosis Room. Dr Sargant's work has long been discredited and it is now thought that he may have been supported by the Ministry of Defence. His books are still referenced by terrorists and intelligence services wanting to engage in the sinister practice of 'brain washing'. The name of the hospital still remains in large metal letters on the top storey, but the building is now part of a university campus with many students blissfully unaware of the building's troubling past.

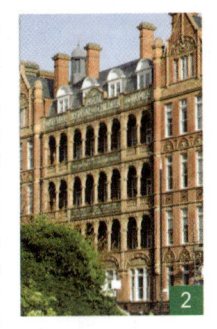

Follow the map to the junction with Waterloo Road where you will find ❸ **St John The Evangelist Church**. St John's is a fine example of Greek Revival church architecture complete with Doric columns, portico and elegant steeple. St John's was one of four churches designed by Francis Octavius Bedford following victory in the Napoleonic wars and was completed in 1824. The church's roof and interior were almost entirely destroyed by a German bomb in 1940, but the outer walls and Italian white marble font survived, as did the people sheltering in the crypt below. In 1950, the building was restored by Thomas Ford, who made significant changes and adaptations to the interior including the commissioning of a mural by German-Jewish emigre, Hans Feibusch. The church was rededicated as the Festival of Britain Church the following year.

In more recent years St John's underwent a further renovation that cost £5.5 million and was undertaken by the award winning architect Eric Parry. The sensitive work has adapted the nave into a

3 *Parterre Garden, St John The Evangelist Church*

Lambeth North & Borough Walk

flexible space and transformed the crypt. You may wish to explore the new interior of the church but one of the best things about St John's is its fabulous gardens which form an oasis of calm in busy Waterloo.

Follow the path behind the church and exit onto Exton Street. Follow the map and continue along ❹ **Roupell Street** with its well preserved early 19th century, Grade II listed buildings which were once workers' houses. These two-storey terraces with 'double-pitched' (two slopes rising to a point) roofs were built by and named after John Roupell and his son Richard who made their fortune trading in scrap metal and property development. It was John Roupell's illegitimate grandson, William, who was later investigated as a corrupt Member of Parliament and convicted of embezzling the family fortune. The houses on Roupell Street were originally rented to local artisans, but the street is now very desirable with properties here sell for over a million pounds. Those with a sweet tooth should take the opportunity to visit the original Konditor & Cook bakery (at 22 Cornwall Street).

Look out on the right for the atmospheric ❺ **King's Arms pub**, a traditional real-ale pub with open fires. In the mid-19th century the pub was used for official business including inquests. Turn right immediately after the pub and walk down Windmill Walk. This area was for many years a place of industry and trade and Windmill Walk is named after the windmills that once stood here and were an important part of the local

Lambeth North & Borough Walk

economy. The local Horn Brewery also used a windmill for power. The brewery has long since disappeared but its tap house has now become a great pub called 'The Windmill', which you will encounter shortly on the junction with The Cut.

Continue down Windmill Walk, looking out on your left for ❻ **Cons Street** which used to be called Little Windmill Street, but was re-named after Emma Cons, a 19th-century social reformer and Suffragette who is best remembered for her attempts to reform the 'Old Vic' Music Hall which she bought in 1880. Like the puritans of the 17th century, Cons disapproved of alcohol and a good deal of the theatrical repertoire (including Shakespeare) and transformed the Old Vic into a place serving nothing stronger than coffee and hosting lectures praising sobriety. The venture was not popular, but she did enjoy some success founding Morley College which you will see shortly.

On reaching The Cut turn left to encounter a more successful theatrical venture – ❼ **The Young Vic Theatre**. This was set up by Laurence Olivier and Frank Dunlop for emerging actors and directors to present theatre to a younger audience. The theatre was housed in an old butcher's shop which had survived a direct hit during the Blitz and was initially considered a temporary venture. More than 50 years later the Young Vic is still going strong. Its updated exterior – clad in steel mesh, customised concrete blocks and glass – won the RIBA London Building of the Year in 2007.

Lambeth North & Borough Walk

Cross The Cut (directly opposite the theatre) to walk down Short Street turning right at the end into Ufford Street. A stark contrast to the steel and concrete of the refurbished Young Vic, the cottages on ❽ **Ufford Street** were built at the turn of the 20th century by the Church commissioners and named after a medievel cleric. This well preserved street has been granted Grade II listing from English Heritage.

Continue to the end of Ufford Street turning left to walk along Webber Street. Ahead on your right at the junction with Gray Street is ❾ **The Stage Door pub**. Until 1985 this pub was called The Halfway House and was very probably the 'Half-the-Way' inn referred to in Samuel Pepys' diary of 1665. The name is inspired by the proximity of the Old Vic Theatre, a short walk away down Webber Street.

Follow the map along Gray Street, crossing Waterloo Road and walk down Pearman Street (to the right of the London Ambulance Service building) and you will eventually reach ❿ **Morley College**. This is the lasting legacy of Emma Cons (whose story was covered earlier in the walk). The more genteel activities of the unsuccessful Old Vic Music Hall included 'penny lectures', opera recitals and generous servings of tea and cake. It is these events that drew in the crowds and received such funding that it opened as a college for working men and women in 1889. The original building was destroyed during the Blitz, but Sir Edward Maufe's 1937 extension still survives. Inside are murals painted by Edward Bawden in the early 1960's, depicting scenes from the Canterbury Tales. Gustav Holst and Michael Tippett were both music directors here and the Lilian Baylis Theatre has its origins at the college.

Just opposite Morley College is an unusual corner building with a crenellated roof. This is the ⑪ **Archbishops House and Cathedral House**. Designed by F A Walters in a Gothic style, it was completed in 1887 but incorporates parts of an earlier clergy house and school that is the work of A W Pugin. The building is now recognised as a fine example of Victorian ecclesiastical architecture and has a Grade II listing.

Lambeth North & Borough Walk

Follow the map down St Georges Road until you see on your left ⑫ **St George's Catholic Cathedral** which dates from 1848 and is also the work of Augustus Pugin (1812-1852), best known for his neo-Gothic designs within the Palace of Westminster. Until the opening of Westminster Cathedral, St George's was the most important Catholic church in London and the first to be granted cathedral status since the English Reformation. Pugin became the first person to be married in the cathedral on 10 August 1848 when he married his third wife. On 10 May 1768 there was a famous riot near here protesting against the imprisonment of the radical John Wilkes for criticising King George III. The Riot Act was read out and a half dozen people were shot dead by troops, the incident becoming known as the Massacre of St George's Fields.

Cross over St George's Road and bear right to follow the map along Lambeth Road to enter Geraldine Harmsworth Park. The land was gifted to the 'splendid struggling mothers of Southwark' by Harold Harmsworth, the 1st Viscount Rothermere. Harmsworth was the proprietor of the Daily Mail and a supporter of Hitler in the 1930s.

Ahead is the dome of the ⑬ **Imperial War Museum**. This was originally home to the Bethlehem Hospital that began as the Priory of the New Order of St Mary of Bethlem in the mid-13th century. The oldest existing psychiatric institution in the world, it was originally based in the City – moving to Moorfields, before opening on this site in 1815. It became notorious for the conditions the patients were held in and was popularly known as Bedlam – a term that has become part of the English language as meaning a place of uproar. Referred to in countless literary works, including the plays of Shakespeare, the famous hospital eventually moved out to the suburbs in the 1930s. In that same decade the building you see (despite being partially demolished) was re-opened as home to the Imperial War Museum.

13 *Imperial War Museum*

Lambeth North & Borough Walk

After the Second World War two guns from former Royal Navy warships were mounted outside the museum's entrance. Both the 15" naval guns had been fired in action during the Second World War.

You may wish to visit the Museum at this point, but you may want to stay outdoors and explore the surrounding ⓴ **Geraldine Mary Harmsworth Park.** The park was opened in 1934 on land gifted by Viscount Rothermere, named after his philanthropist mother and dedicated to the 'splendid struggling mothers of Southwark'. The park contains The Soviet War Memorial commemorating the 27 million Russian citizens who lost their lives in World War II. There's also the very lovely Songbird Café from where you can admire the famous 15" guns. The park is also near the start of the subterranean River Neckinger that flows about 1.5 miles from here to join the Thames at St Saviours Dock.

Exit passing alongside the park's tranquil peace garden onto St George's Road and walk east turning right along Geraldine Street – again named after Mrs Harmsworth – to reach West Square.

As you walk towards West Square you skirt the ⓯ **Charlotte Sharman Primary School** which still occupies its original Victorian school building with the old 'Boys' and 'Girls' signs above the entrances. You will also see (on the north side of West Square) the monogram 'LSB' which stands for the London School Board. This body ran the school system in London when education for children was made compulsory after 1870, and continued this role until being replaced in 1904. Charlotte Sharman (1832-1929) was a well known local social reformer who founded several homes for destitute children including several on this square.

Lambeth North & Borough Walk

Continue walking down the path parallel to the school until you reach ⓰ **West Square**, named after the Temple West family who owned land here in the late 18th century. This elegant square was built around 1800 and as you walk around look out for a blue plaque outside number 19 which recalls ⓱ **J A R Newlands** (1837-1898), who discovered the Periodic Law for the chemical elements.

The old mulberry trees propped up in the centre are as old as the square itself and would have been seen by the square's most famous resident ⓲ **Charlie Chaplin** (1889-1977), who is believed to have lived at number 39. Chaplin's dramatic early life was played out on the streets you will walk through today. His story illustrates the incredible hardship faced by the poor of the late Victorian period. Born on East Street to the south, his mother and father were music hall performers. They moved to West Square shortly after Charlie's birth when the family were still reasonably prosperous. However his alcoholic father soon abandoned the family. Charlie's mother, Hannah, struggled to look after her two boys but experienced further setbacks when she lost her singing voice, Charlie witnessing the night when she was booed offstage on her last performance.

Unable to work, the family ended up in the workhouse, the boys separated from their mother and sent to harsh schools. Hannah, buckling under the pressure, was eventually confined to an asylum and for a time the young Charlie stayed on the streets to avoid getting sent to the workhouse school. He survived long enough until his brother – now with some money – returned to help him. Charlie Chaplin's meteoric rise from the slums of Kennington to becoming the world's first great film star remains one of London's greatest rags-to-riches stories.

16 Old mulberry trees, West Square

Look out for ⑲ **number 36** (the centre house on the east side). In 1795 the Admiralty installed shutter telegraph apparatus to relay messages between the Navy in Kent and Whitehall. In 1812 the erection of a dome on the roof of the new Bethlem Hospital obstructed the view from Whitehall and a tower had to be added. It is still distinctive with its bow window and raised top storey. The house has another naval connection as the niece of Captain Bligh also lived here.

Follow the map down Orient Street, in the south-east corner of West Square. Number 1 predates most of the buildings on the square and boasts an elaborate portico. The adjoining houses are the survivors of a once extensive range of cottages most likely intended for grooms and coachmen. You can see in the distance a ⑳ **horse scratching post** at the end of the street, an unusual relic from a forgotten age.

Take the first turning on the left. Don't be put off by the fact it looks like a dead-end! Follow the footpath which goes left between high garden walls at the end of the alley. Follow the path turning right on Hayles Street and left into Lamlash Street, with allotments on either side. At the end, turn right and walk down Elliott's Row, turning left at Brook Drive and then right to walk down Churchyard Row.

On your left is the ㉑ **old churchyard of St Mary's Newington** that stood nearby from the 13th century until it was eventually demolished in the 19th century. At the end

Lambeth North & Borough Walk

of the lane you reach the busy A3 and an area known as Newington Butts. The churchyard is one of the very few reminders of the old rural village of Newington Butts that was part of Surrey until the expansion of London in the early 19th century. Newington is the correct name for this southern part of Southwark, most generally known as Elephant and Castle. The name Newington means 'new farmstead' and 'Butts' may refer to archery butts – or practice field. One of its most famous offspring was Michael Faraday (1791-1867), son of a blacksmith, who overcame his modest beginnings to undertake pioneering work in the fields of chemistry and electro-physics that made him one of the most famous figures in scientific history.

One of the earliest theatres in England was founded around here in the 1580s. In 1572 plays were banned in the City itself, thus leading to the creation of new theatres outside the City walls in Shoreditch, Bankside and Lambeth. The theatre here probably predated the more famous theatres to the north and it is likely Shakespeare would have performed in the Newington Butts theatre as well having his plays performed there.

Turn right on Kensington Lane, staying right at the fork and then right again along Renfrew Road. Walk up the road, looking out for a ㉒ **red brick circular tower** on the right. This building adjoining the road was originally a fire station dating from 1868.

As you continue along, you pass a former court house (which contains prison cells) dating from 1869. The is now occupied by the ㉓ **Jam Yang Buddhist Centre**. Don't miss their wonderful Courthouse Garden Café – a great place to stop for lunch. The café is situated in the old courtyard, once

23 Jam Yang Buddhist Centre

the exercise yard for prisoners, however the only guards you might see on patrol today are the two resident cats (see p.221 for more information).

Take the next right down Dugard Way, looking out on the corner for the former pub ㉔ **The Court Tavern** (the signage remains up high). This building dates from the 1860s when a terrace was built here, but it is the only survivor after the Blitz flattened the rest of the buildings. The Blitz did huge damage to Newington and the Elephant and Castle, destroying many of the buildings that would have been familiar to Charlie Chaplin just 40 years before. Walk through the gates at the end of Dugard Way and turn left to find a solid Victorian brick building on the left. Today this is home to the ㉕ **Cinema Museum** which is open for pre-arranged tours, mainly on weekdays (call 020 7840 2200 for further details).

However, as good as the Museum is, the main purpose of visiting it on this walk is that its premises are all that remain of the Lambeth Workhouse. It was built in the early 1870s and looked after the poor and destitute until the workhouse system was shut down nationally in the 1920s. The building was then home to Lambeth Hospital for many decades. The workhouse was built under the governance of the local Board of Guardians, and received men and women although they were separated from each other. As you approach the entrance to the Cinema Museum look out for the original foundation stone. The inscription states it was laid by John Doulton, chairman of the Board of Guardians, and a member of the famous Royal Doulton pottery firm that was originally based in Lambeth.

Life at the workhouse was meant to discourage inmates, who were forced to carry out tedious tasks and live in degrading circumstances. In those days many expectant mothers, too poor to survive without assistance, would come to the workhouse in order to give birth. Their babies were officially listed as having been born in 'Renfrew Road' – respecting the fact that no one wanted to be stigmatised in the future by having Lambeth Workhouse on their birth certificate. In 1898 Charlie Chaplin, aged just eight, arrived here with his family and was duly separated from his mother. He also spent time at another workhouse in the area.

One of Jack the Ripper's victims, Mary Ann Nichols, is also known to have stayed at the workhouse. A prostitute, she died in 1888 on the streets of Whitechapel. Oddly Chaplin also had a Ripper connection – he recalled how as a child he had been offered, but declined, a glass of water by George Chapman. Weeks later Chapman was arrested for the murder of a number of women, and was hanged in 1903. However, many experts think Chapman may have been behind the Whitechapel Murders of 1888 as well.

Before you leave, look around the left corner of the cinema at the 99 foot ㉖ **water tower** belonging to the old workhouse. This was recently converted into a private residence, giving the occupants an unparalleled view of London and one of the most spectacular homes in the capital.

Retrace your steps along Renfrew Road and Kennington Lane, heading north along Newington Butts, past St Mary's Churchyard. You will shortly see the imposing classical façade of the Metropolitan Tabernacle ahead on your left – but before you reach the Tabernacle take the pedestrian crossing to reach where once stood the Elephant and Castle Shopping Centre.

Lambeth North & Borough Walk

27 Elephant and Castle consists of two major traffic junctions connected by a short road called Elephant and Castle, where you are now standing. It is named after a blacksmith's shop that stood at the junction, and which later became a tavern that displayed the sign of an elephant and castle. The exact reason for such a sign is unclear, but it matches the coat of arms used by the Cutlers' Company – an ancient livery company that once monopolised the trade of making knives and weapons. Shakespeare also mentioned the Elephant tavern in *Twelfth Night*, 'In the south suburbs, at the Elephant, is best to lodge.' The Shopping Centre that stood here for over 50 years with its famous fibreglass Elephant & Castle monument has now been demolished as part of this area's regeneration.

As the skyscrapers and house prices begin to rise, it is worth remembering that in the early and mid-20th century this part of London was famous for its violent gangs. The Elephant & Castle Mob were dominant in the interwar years and fought many bloody battles with London rivals. One of the leaders of the Mob, Wag McDonald, eventually left for the US and became a minder for Hollywood celebrities, among them a fellow son of the Elephant & Castle – Charlie Chaplin.

This area is also the birthplace of the Teddy Boys – a youth movement that shocked conservative post-war Britain in the 1950s. In about 1951 working class boys in gangs around the Elephant and Castle started wearing clothes that aped the Edwardian style of their parent's generation. The injection of rock and roll from the mid-1950s added to a heady mix that created Britain's first teenage sub-culture.

Lambeth North & Borough Walk

You can get a good view here of the ㉘ **Metropolitan Tabernacle**, run by an independent reformed Baptist church group. It has its origins in the 1650s when the tabernacle non-conformist fellowship began to meet, despite religious persecution from the authorities. They congregated in a number of sites in London before opening a new tabernacle here in 1861. It was later burnt down, except for the frontage, and rebuilt a number of times – including after damage caused during the Blitz. Following the map, use the pedestrian crossings to reach the centre of the northern junction island.

Here can be found the ㉙ **Michael Faraday Memorial**, a large stainless steel box built in honour of the scientist and inventor, who was born nearby. It is fitting that such an unusual monument to the father of electromagnetism serves a dual purpose, containing an electrical substation for the Northern Line of the London Underground. The structure is the work of Brutalist architect Rodney Gordon, himself inspired by the work of Mies Van Der Rohe. The building was completed in 1961 and has been Grade II listed by English Heritage. This is a good place to stop and look around to see the numerous hi-rise residential buildings that have sprung up here in recent years.

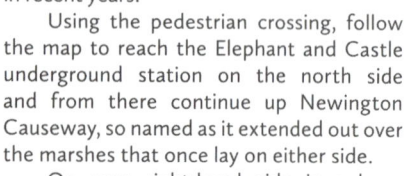

Using the pedestrian crossing, follow the map to reach the Elephant and Castle underground station on the north side and from there continue up Newington Causeway, so named as it extended out over the marshes that once lay on either side.

On your right-hand side is a large structure called ㉚ **Metro Central Heights** that was designed in the 1960s by one of the greatest modernist architects to operate in London during the mid-20th

29. Michael Faraday Memorial

century, the Hungarian-born Erno Goldfinger (1902-1987). He was also responsible for 2 Willow Road in Hampstead and – perhaps most famously – the Trellick Tower in Ladbroke Grove. Legend has it that Ian Fleming named his famous villain Auric Goldfinger after the architect in revenge for the architect building 2 Willow Road despite objections from Fleming and other local residents.

Stop opposite the entrance to Rockingham Street. In the 1750s a windmill stood on the other side of Newington Causeway surrounded by open fields. Continue north – passing Gaunt Street (on the west side) – where you will find the Ministry of Sound, which was founded in 1991 and is one of London's best-known nightclubs.

On this walk we turn right and walk down Avonmouth Road; directly ahead is the entrance to ㉛ **Newington Gardens**. Walk through the park, bearing right to walk past the tennis courts. This was once the site of Horsemonger Lane Jail, which operated between 1791 and 1879. It was the largest jail in Surrey, and around 135 executions of men and women

Lambeth North & Borough Walk

took place here in the 19th century. Charles Dickens attended the public hanging here in November 1849 of Frederick Manning and his wife Maria, a local couple who had poisoned their lodger and buried him under the floor. Dickens complained about the hanging in the *Times*, helping change public opinion which in turn led to executions taking place privately. Dickens is said to have based the character Hortense in *Bleak House* on Maria Manning.

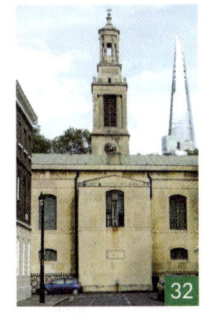

Exit on the north-east side and walk down Brockham Street, the view dominated by **32 Henry Wood Hall** straight ahead. As you reach the hall you enter **33 Trinity Church Square**, perhaps the finest square on the walk. This and neighbouring Merrick Square, are owned by the Corporation of Trinity House – a historic body that was granted a Royal Charter by Henry VIII to organise pilot ships and lighthouses throughout the country. It continues to oversee lighthouses to this day.

Trinity House bought the land here in 1660 from London merchant Christopher Merrick for £1,694 with the requirement to hold it on charitable trust 'for Relieving comforting Easing & Maintaining of the poor Aged Sick Maimed Weak and decayed Seamen and Mariners of this Kingdom, their Wives children and Widowes where most need was'. Today larger houses on the square sell for nearly 900 times that original purchase price.

Henry Wood Hall was originally the Holy Trinity Church. The foundation stone of the church was laid by the then Archbishop of Canterbury and consecrated in 1824. The church is by Francis Octavius Bedford, who also designed St John's Waterloo, visited earlier in the walk (see p.197). It continued to be used as a church until the late 1960s. Today, named after the famous conductor

Lambeth North & Borough Walk

who is most associated with the London Proms, it is the capital's premier classical rehearsal and recording venue. The principal orchestra to use the hall is the London Philharmonic.

With the hall behind you, head right along Trinity Street, looking out for the smaller, but still majestic, ㉞ **Merrick Square** (named after the merchant who sold the estate to Trinity House in 1660). After a short walk you reach a junction with Great Dover Street. ㉟ **The Roebuck**, an excellent and ornate Victorian pub, stands on the corner and is worth a stop if you are weary. The pub claims Charlie Chaplin used to perform here.

On the other side of Great Dover Street (the A2) stands another ㊱ **Victorian red-brick building** (no 165). Just beside here is the site of a Romano-British cemetery that was discovered in recent years. In 1996 the remains of what was thought to be a 'female gladiator' were found. On the front of this building (dating from 1897) are ornate carvings. If you look closely you can also see a carved head of Queen Victoria in profile in between the dates 1837 and 1897.

Lambeth North & Borough Walk

1897 was the year of Victoria's Diamond Jubilee and many new buildings of that era incorporated decorative features like this to remember the historic occasion.

From here walk up Becket Street to reach Tabard Street. Turn left and walk along Tabard Street with ㊲ **Tabard Gardens** on your right. The gardens stand on what were once Victorian tenement streets that became slums and were cleared away in 1929. These are all associated with Geoffrey Chaucer, the 14th century poet and writer. His greatest work *The Canterbury Tales* followed a group of pilgrims who leave the Tabard Inn in Southwark on their way to visit the shrine of Saint Thomas à Becket in Canterbury.

Leave the gardens and continue for some distance up Tabard Street. Look out for ㊳ **number 19** on the right-hand side. You can see the signage for 'Japanners' and 'Harding & Sons Hardware Merchants'. This Grade II listed building dates from 1891, though the original business was founded by George Harding nearby in 1835. The signage is the only reminder of the long-forgotten art of Japanning – a varnishing treatment once in widespread use that protected household and artistic products. As a trade it went into decline in the late 19th century due to the introduction of electroplating and changing fashions. Today this is one of the few visible reminders left in the capital of a once important profession.

At the top of Tabard Street is the church of ㊴ **St George the Martyr**. First recorded in the 12th century, the current classical-

40 *Marshalsea Prison wall*

Lambeth North & Borough Walk

style building dates from the 1730s. Henry V was welcomed by the aldermen of London on the steps of the church after he returned from his victory over the French at Agincourt in 1415. Charles Dickens knew the church well, living in misery nearby as a 12-year-old when his father and the rest of his family were imprisoned inside Marshalsea Prison (which once stood beside the church) because of his father's debts. Dickens never forgot the experience and used it when writing *Little Dorrit*, with William Dorrit imprisoned in Marshalsea for debts and his children growing up in and around the prison. There are several references to the church in the book and the church itself contains a Dorrit window.

If you exit the church on the north side you can cross over Tabbard Street into a small park to see the remains of the ㊵ **Marshalsea Prison wall**. The prison, that had such a traumatic influence on the young Charles Dickens, opened in the 14th century and closed in 1842.

From here you can follow the map for a short walk to Borough underground station and the end of this walk. ●

SHOP...

Konditor & Cook (see p.199)
22 Cornwall Rd, SE1 8TW
www.konditorandcook.com

VISIT...

Cinema Museum (see p.211)
2 Dugard Way, SE11 4TH
www.cinemamuseum.org.uk

Imperial War Museum (see p.203)
Lambeth Rd, SE1 6HZ
www.iwm.org.uk

Young Vic Theatre (see p.200)
66 The Cut, SE1 8LZ
www.youngvic.org

EAT, DRINK...

Jam Yang Buddhist Centre (see p.209)
43 Renfrew Rd, SE11 4NA
www.jamyang.co.uk

The King's Arms (see p.199)
25 Roupell Street, SE1 8TB
www.windmilltaverns.com

The Roebuck (see p.218)
50 Great Dover St, SE1 4YG
www.theroebuck.net

The Stage Door (see p.201)
28-30 Webber St, SE1 8QA
www.thestagedoor.co.uk

Grand Square, Old Royal Naval College, see p.250

8 Greenwich Walk

Greenwich Walk

1. Almshouses
2. Greenwich Station
3. West Greenwich Library
4. Former Town Hall
5. Burney Street Park
6. Dougie Mullins (plaque)
7. Royal Hill
8. No 80 Royal Hill
9. Old ghost advertisement
10. Whitbread & Co
11. The Point
12. Ranger's House
13. Princess Caroline's sunken bath
14. Macartney House
15. Greenwich Park
16. Flamsteed House
17. Royal Observatory
18. Prime meridian
19. General Wolfe statue
20. Queen Elizabeth's Oak
21. Roman temple or villa
22. Vanbrugh Castle
23. One Tree Hill
24. Park Vista
25. Greenwich Power Station
26. Cutty Sark public house
27. Ballast Quay
28. Harbour Master's Office
29. Trinity Hospital
30. Plaques
31. The Yacht public house
32. Trafalgar Tavern public house
33. Steps
34. Water Gate entrance
35. Grand Square
36. Queen's House
37. The Chapel
38. Painted Hall
39. National Maritime Museum
40. Greenwich Visitor Centre
41. Cutty Sark
42. Greenwich Foot Tunnel
43. Greenwich Market
44. Church of St Alfege
45. Sir Daniel Day-Lewis
46. The Fan Museum
47. No 24
48. No 26
49. Gloucester Circus
50. Dr Alfred Salter (plaque)

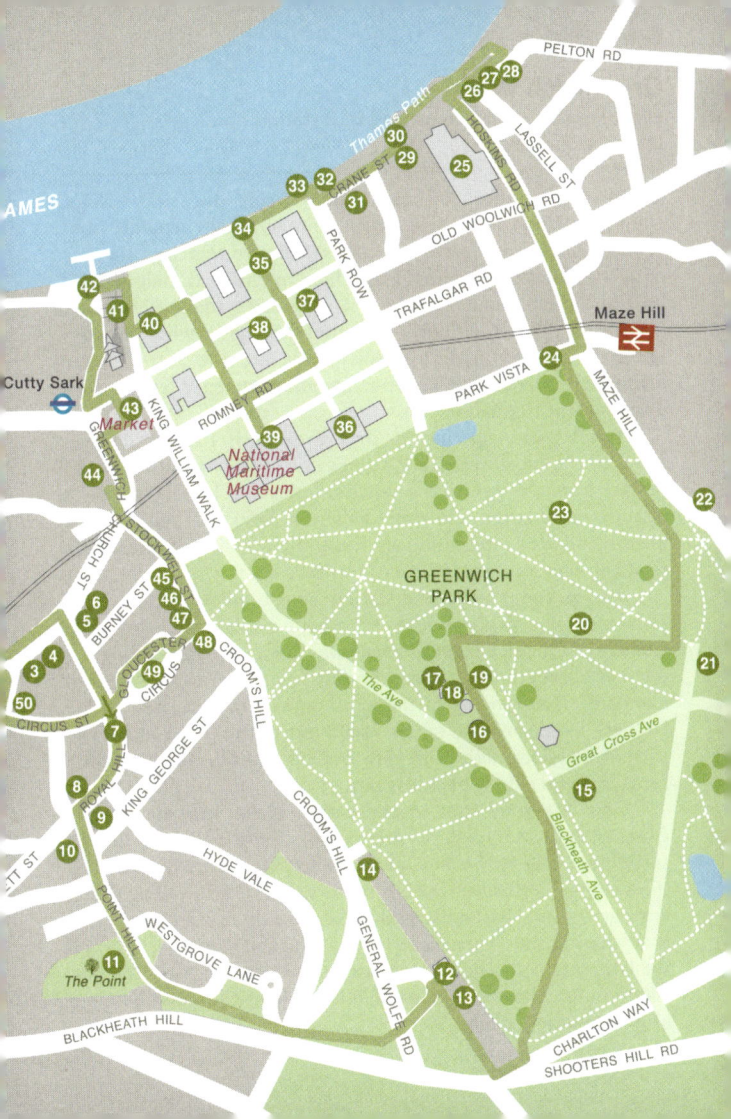

PELTON RD
27 28
26
LASSELL ST
Thames Path
30
33 32 29
CRANE ST
31
25
HOSKINS RD
34
OLD WOOLWICH RD
PARK ROW
35
THAMES
37
TRAFALGAR RD
38
42
41
40
Maze Hill
PARK VISTA
24
Cutty Sark
43
ROMNEY RD
MAZE HILL
KING WILLIAM WALK
Market
39 36
Greenwich
44
National Maritime Museum
CHURCH ST
22
GREENWICH PARK
23
STOCKWELL ST
45
6
BURNEY ST
46
5
20
47
3 4
GLOUCESTER
48
17 19
21
50
CIRCUS
49
18
CIRCUS ST
CROOM'S HILL
16
7
The Ave
Great Cross Ave
ROYAL HILL
KING GEORGE ST
8
15
9
Blackheath Ave
TT ST
10
HYDE VALE
CROOM'S HILL
POINT HILL
14
GENERAL WOLFE RD
WESTGROVE LANE
11
12
The Point
13
CHARLTON WAY
BLACKHEATH HILL
SHOOTERS HILL RD

Greenwich Walk
Start/Finish: Greenwich rail and DLR station
Distance: 4 miles

Greenwich lies south of the Thames, facing the Isle of Dogs. Until the railway age, it was always quite physically separate from central London, an impression that remains to this day. Its ease of access for ships, high hills and hunting grounds, help explain its Old English name 'Grenewic' – or 'green trading settlement' or 'harbor'. These attributes attracted the Tudors who, from the late 15th century, turned a sleepy hamlet into one of the Royals' favourite residences and thus fundamentally changed Greenwich's development thereafter.

Royal patronage meant that Greenwich has featured in some of the most important scenes in British history. While its heyday from the 15th to the 19th centuries may be long gone, its historic importance and outstanding architectural legacy have been recognized internationally and Greenwich is one of Britain's relatively small number of World Heritage sites.

As you come out of the station almost directly opposite are some charming ❶ **almshouses** set around a courtyard. This is the **College of Queen Elizabeth** which was founded in 1576 during the reign of Elizabeth I by a philanthropist and lawyer named William Lambard. The running of the almshouses was entrusted to the Drapers' Company, one of the wealthiest of the City guilds. The current buildings date from 1819 and this almshouse charity still cares for local elderly people today.

This is a good spot to pause and read a little about early Greenwich's history before carrying on. There was some Roman settlement here, however Greenwich was first properly settled by the Saxons – probably in the 6th century. In 1012 an invading Viking army arrived and based themselves here for three years, anchoring their ships in the Thames and camping on the high hills. You will see later a famous church dedicated to Alfege, the Archbishop of Canterbury, who the Vikings held hostage in Greenwich, before brutally murdering him.

However, Greenwich was still just a small fishing village when the Duke of Gloucester first built a palace, named Bella Court, by the river on a 200 acre site in 1447. He was known as the 'son, brother and uncle of kings' on account of being the son of King Henry IV, the brother of Henry V and the uncle of Henry VI. Henry VI's wife, Margaret of Anjou, took a fancy to this palace and later made it her home, renaming it the Palace of Placentia or the 'pleasant place'. However it was still a fairly insignificant palace until the late 1400s when Henry VII (using around 600,000 bricks) built a spectacular new building.

The Palace of Placentia, otherwise known as Greenwich Palace, remained one of the Royal family's favourite residences until the Civil War. You will find out more about the site of the palace, and what happened to it next, later on in the walk.

Greenwich Walk

As you leave the almshouses, look back to the ❷ **railway station**. The world's very first commuter railway line ran between London Bridge and Greenwich. Construction of the line began in 1836 and was operated by the London & Greenwich Railway. The line was constructed over a huge viaduct comprising around 900 arches (some of which can still be seen). In a panorama painting of London dating from 1845, Greenwich appears as a very small town, still surrounded by woods and fields with nothing in between it and Borough except for the huge elevated railway viaduct rising from the landscape. It must have been an astonishing sight for those living through the earliest years of the railway age. Greenwich station is also historic – designed in a classical style by George Smith, it dates from 1840 and is one of the oldest train stations in the world.

Follow the map along Greenwich High Road. On the right is ❸ **West Greenwich Library**. This dates from 1907 and was one of 2,811 such establishments in the English speaking world that were funded by Andrew Carnegie (1835-1918). Carnegie was the son of a weaver who left Scotland for America when he was 12. He spent many hours reading in a library which was open to working boys each Saturday evening. Carnegie later become a steel-magnate and one of the richest men in the world, but he never forgot his homeland and his debt to libraries, and Greenwich was one of the recipients of his philanthropy.

Greenwich Walk

Just beside the library, and on your right as you walk up Royal Hill, is the ❹ **former Town Hall** (dominated by a clock tower). It was built in 1939 in what was then seen as an innovative style by architect Clifford Culpin. It was described by architectural historian Pevsner as 'the only town hall of any London Borough to represent the style of our time adequately'. The Culpin architectural practice was established by Ewart Culpin in 1918 and continues to this day.

Turn right up Royal Hill. Opposite the police station on the left, look out for the tiny ❺ **Burney Street Park** with a memorial declaring it was built by Greenwich people in 1981-82. The park is home to one of London's most obscure but charming recent memorials, dedicated to ❻ **Dougie Mullins** (1932-1991), a master dairyman, who was born in a shop on the site. Mullins was by no means famous, but he was by all accounts a well-loved local character whose father, Bill, had founded a dairy on this spot. Dougie was a familiar sight pushing an old fashioned red and white handcart carrying milk around the town.

Continue up ❼ **Royal Hill**, lined with pleasant houses of which a fair number date from the 18th and 19th centuries. Many visitors to Greenwich do not get a chance to see anything other than the main tourist attractions, but along Royal Hill you will encounter some impressive houses that are highly individual in character. Number 70, now a dilapidated shop front, was originally a Masonic building in the mid-19th century, and was later a munitions factory during World War I. Look out particularly for ❽ **number 80** with its unusual ogee arched windows; it is part of a terrace that dates from the 1830s.

Continue up Royal Hill and at the junction with Point Hill on the left pause to see an ❾ **old ghost advertisement** on the side of one building (just up Point Hill) and also the vintage ❿ **Whitbread & Co** sign visible above the entrance to a restaurant on the corner.

Walk up Point Hill which leads you up to Greenwich Park and Blackheath. As you climb Point Hill you can take a detour to ⓫ **The Point** – a pleasant green area that has fantastic views over London and is a great spot for a picnic if you need to gather your strength before facing the busier parts of Greenwich.

Not far from here is the site of the legendary Jack Cade's Cavern (between Maidenstone Hill and Hollymount Close). Used in medieval times as a chalk pit, it was re-discovered by accident in 1780 and re-opened as a popular drinking club and brothel, infamous for its naked masked balls. During World War II it was used as an air raid shelter, but was then sealed up. In the 1960s it was secretly opened again for a while as a concert venue and it is said Jimi Hendrix played a gig here. All that can be seen today is a ventilation pipe buried in undergrowth behind a fence at the end of an alley.

When finished at The Point, or if you just want to continue on, at the top of Point Hill, you will see the A2 road along Blackheath Hill ahead. Bear left, following the map along the grass, keeping the road well to your right. You are walking through Blackheath, named after the colour of its earth. For many centuries this was an important gathering place for people in this district and a site where rebel armies would muster before descending upon London, such as during the Peasant's Revolt of 1381 and the Kentish Rebellion of 1450.

In the 18th and 19th centuries the area was famous for its raucous biannual fairs that were ostensibly for local farmers to sell cattle and sheep, but were in reality dominated by drinking, wild sports and particularly notorious for their freak shows. One advert from 1741 advertised 'a woman, 38 years of age alive, with 2 heads, one above the other, having no hands, fingers nor toes, yet she can dress, undress, knit, sow, read and sing'. As with many traditional London fairs, the increasingly prudish Victorian authorities closed down Blackheath Fair in the late 19th century.

The roads around here – particularly the old Watling Street built originally by the Romans – were plagued for centuries by highwaymen before the area was developed into a suburb. Many

Greenwich Walk

travellers would have once followed this route anxiously on a dark night, counting down the minutes to reach the safety of central London. Their anxiety may not have been helped by the then common sight of the corpses of hanged highwaymen rotting away in gibbets as a deterrent. The London diarist Samuel Pepys wrote in the late 17th century of seeing one disintegrating corpse as he travelled along – 'a filthy sight'.

Soon you reach General Wolfe Road. This is named after Major General James Wolfe (1727-1759), who famously died aged just 32 whilst leading British forces to victory over the French at The Battle of Quebec and so securing Canada for the British Empire.

Already a major in the army at the age of just 18, this remarkable man moved to Greenwich with his family in 1738, living in Macartney House on Chesterfield Walk – near to the Ranger's House seen shortly. Like many of the greatest war heroes, Wolfe was a restless, intriguing figure, regarded with suspicion by many of his contemporaries. Some less gifted, and no doubt jealous military men, questioned his sanity which caused a scornful George II to remark 'Mad, is he? Then I hope he will bite some of my other generals'.

Follow the map along General Wolfe Road, bearing to the right to reach ⑫ **Ranger's House**. This imposing Georgian villa dates from 1723 and today houses the Wernher Collection – works of art assembled by the diamond magnate Sir Julius Wernher (1850-1912). Among the 700 items in the collection are Old Masters, Renaissance bronzes and portraits by Sir Joshua Reynolds and George Romney (see page 261 for information regarding visiting). Early residents of the house included senior Navy figures, but its current name relates to the office of the Ranger of Greenwich Park – a largely honorary title bestowed under Royal patronage. In 1815 the house was used as a grace and favour residence for the then Ranger, Princess Sophia Mathilda; the last Ranger left the house in 1896.

⑫ *Ranger's House*

Greenwich Walk

Just beside the House are some remains (at ground level) of ⓭ **Princess Caroline's sunken bath**. Caroline came from Brunswick and married George, the Prince of Wales, in 1795. Despite her status as the Princess of Wales, she was very publicly spurned by her husband although popular with the masses. When he became King George IV in 1820, they had lived apart for over 20 years and he refused her desperate attempts to attend the coronation ceremony. The bitter marriage both appalled and fascinated the chattering classes of the country. George's camp blamed Caroline for the split, due in part they claimed because of her awful hygiene problems and love of raw onions and garlic.

Caroline lived in a grand building on this site known as Montague House between 1798 and 1814. She hosted many decadent parties here, allegations of the orgies leading to various enquiries into her behaviour by politicians. Her estranged husband later vindictively demolished the house after she moved abroad and the remnants of the bath (discovered in 1909) are all that survive of her era.

When Caroline died thousands accompanied her coffin and the authorities shot dead two men in the crowd as the mob tried to travel through Kensington. Unsurprisingly some have drawn parallels with what took place 200 years later between another Prince and Princess of Wales – Charles and Diana.

⓮ **Macartney House** on Chesterfield Walk, where Wolfe lived as a child, is just

Greenwich Walk

a five minute walk if you continue north along General Wolfe Road. It dates from 1676 and was recently on the market for £10 million. However on this walk we retrace our steps and again walk parallel to the A2 – known as Shooter's Hill Road. Shooter's Hill is the highest point in south London and was first recorded in 1223, its name being Old English for 'hill of the shooter' or 'archer'. Whether this refers to its medieval use as an archery site, the fact that robbers frequently lurked in the vicinity, or the hunting that used to take place in what was once a heavily wooded district, is unclear. Shooter's Hill is also mentioned in Charles Dickens' *A Tale of Two Cities* and Byron's poem *Don Juan*.

Follow the map to continue down Charlton Way and almost immediately left through a gate into ⑮ **Greenwich Park**. Covering 74 hectares, this is the oldest enclosed Royal park, having its origins in the 1400s. Henry VIII spent much of his youth hunting here, and he introduced the deer whose descendants can still be seen today (principally in the eastern corner of the park known as 'The Wilderness'). James I later enclosed the park with a 12 foot high wall that ran for two miles. The formal gardens were laid out in the 1660s, although the public were only allowed access in the 18th century. Early Stone Age tools have been found in the park, as well as evidence of Roman and Viking settlements.

Follow the map in a general north-easterly direction across the park, with the Ranger's House on your left. Shortly you reach Blackheath Avenue (where thousands of runners queue up before the start of the London Marathon) and walk towards the Royal Observatory (there are signs). You should also see the Wolfe Statue ahead. There is a pleasant, although often busy, café (Pavilion Tea House, see p.235) just on the right of the Avenue if you would like to have a break (there are also toilets here).

Greenwich Walk

As you approach the Royal Observatory you begin to see one of the finest views in London (see below), with the sites of central Greenwich below, the Isle of Dogs and Canary Wharf development to the north of the river, and the O2 Arena (previously known as the Millennium Dome) to the north east.

The first Astronomer Royal was John Flamsteed, appointed in 1675, aged only 28, and the Observatory's original building is now known as ⓰ **Flamsteed House**. His successor as Astronomer Royal was Edmund Halley, best known for his prediction of the return of Halley's Comet. Look out for the red ball at the top of the Observatory building – this drops at 1pm each day and was once crucial for shipmasters on their vessels moored on the Thames to the north. They set their ship's chronometers to it– essential to accurate navigation.

This is also a reminder that the principal aim behind the foundation of the Observatory was to assist in the spread of the fledgling British Empire. When the Observatory was built Britain was not yet a world power, and was dependent on its navy and merchant ships to take British colonists and traders to new lands.

View from Royal Observatory

However navigation at sea was still a rather hit and miss affair and sailors often struggled to find out accurately where they were along the lines of latitude (north/south) and longitude (east/west).

Finding out a ship's place on the line of longitude was the real problem. The early astronomers at the Observatory were able to work out the angle of stars to the moon at certain times in Greenwich. This angle – known as the lunar distance – could, when observed by navigators on ships using a sextant, be compared to tables in the Navy Almanac that showed what the corresponding time was in Greenwich – known as Greenwich Time. The navigator could then calculate his position east or west by using a marine chronometer to work out the difference between his local time and Greenwich time – each hour of difference representing about 15 degrees east or west.

The problem was then finding an accurate enough marine chronometer to tell local time on board a ship. Navigational errors caused the 'Scilly Disaster' of 1707 when four Royal Navy ships were lost at sea along with around 1,400 sailors. The resulting national outcry spurned Parliament into action and they set up the

Board of Longitude, which offered a prize of £20,000 to the first person to construct an accurate ship's chronometer. This was eventually won in 1773 by John Harrison (1693-1776). A Yorkshire watchmaker of humble origins, Harrison's heart-wrenching efforts over 31 years to win the prize were brought to life in Dava Sobel's bestselling book *Longitude* (1998).

The ⑰ **Royal Observatory** was founded in 1675 during the reign of Charles II and was the first purpose-built scientific research facility in the country. It is a lasting reminder of a great age of scientific and architectural innovation in Britain that the King was keen to promote – the Observatory was of course effectively in the King's back garden as the Royals still occupied the Tudor palace below. The Age of Enlightenment produced men such as Sir Isaac Newton, Robert Hooke and Sir Christopher Wren, and the latter (possibly with Hooke's help) was responsible for designing the Observatory.

The work of the Observatory, and Harrison's invention, helped expand the British Empire and thus change the history of the world. This was clearly shown even before Harrison died, when Captain James Cook took an early version of Harrison's new chronometer with him during some of his voyages of exploration. Greenwich has no direct link with Harrison himself, but the Observatory contains his early chronometers in its museum – numbered H1 to H4 in order of their construction. H4, which is completely different to the others in that it is more of a large pocket watch than a clock, was the device that won him the prize and is arguably the most precious timekeeper on display anywhere in the world. The Observatory also has an excellent planetarium.

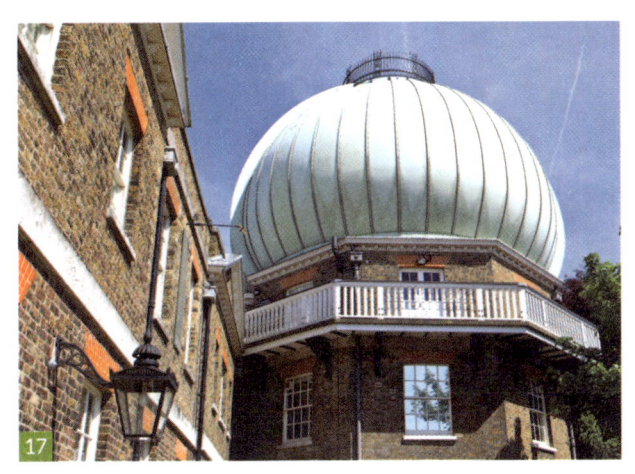

During the 19th century it became clear that world trade required a standardised system of deciding what local time was in any one place, although many nations used Greenwich Time. In 1884 Greenwich Mean Time (GMT) was voted upon by a number of countries as being the preferred method at the International Meridian Conference in Washington D.C. It was also decided here to establish one ⓲ **prime meridian**, meaning a line of longitude, at Greenwich. This is still today the line by which every place on Earth is measured in terms of its distance east or west. For example, Greenwich is the common zero of longitude, while Washington is 77 degrees to the west of this, and Jerusalem 35 degrees to the east.

You will no doubt see many people being photographed with their legs either side of the line marked on the ground by the Observatory, enjoying the feeling of standing in both the eastern and western hemispheres at the same time. The Russian President Vladimir Putin was photographed doing exactly the same thing during his trip to the Observatory in 2003, part of the first visit by a Russian leader to Britain since Tsar Alexander II in 1874. The Equator of course divides the northern and southern hemispheres.

Greenwich Walk

The Royal Observatory organisation moved out of Greenwich shortly after World War II and now use powerful telescopes all around the world. The original Observatory building can be visited today (see p.261 for further details).

Beside the Observatory is a ⑲ **bronze statue of General Wolfe** which was erected in 1930 and is the work of Canadian sculptor Robert Tait McKenzie. The statue bears the inscription 'This monument, a gift of the Canadian people, was unveiled by the Marquis de Montcalm'. The statue was hit by a V1 bomb during World War II and the base still bears the scars.

In 1894 the first international terrorist incident in Britain took place near here when a young 26 year old French Anarchist named Martial Bourdin accidently killed himself by detonating a bomb. His motives are unclear, however it seems more than likely he had been hoping to blow up the Observatory. The event inspired Joseph Conrad, whose book *The Secret Agent* (1907) features an anarchist who plots a bomb attack on the Observatory.

From the statue head eastwards across the park, following signs for ⑳ **Queen Elizabeth's Oak**. You will reach this after a few minutes. The tree dates back to the 12th century, and according to legend Henry VIII danced around it with Anne Boleyn, and Elizabeth I took refreshments in its shade. Although the tree died sometime in the 19th century, the patchwork of ivy that had grown around it held it upright until

Greenwich Walk

1991 when a heavy storm brought it down. Nearby is a young oak tree planted by The Duke of Edinburgh in 1992.

Bear right following signs for the Roman Remains. At this point you are walking over a network of hidden tunnels – or conduits – whose existence has never been fully explained, although it is thought they carried natural groundwater to the buildings of the Royal palace and later Greenwich Hospital. Urban myths abound about their actual purpose, usually concerning kings having a secret route from the Royal Palace. There are at least three such conduits under the Park (some entrances are still visible), built of brick and almost large enough to walk upright in.

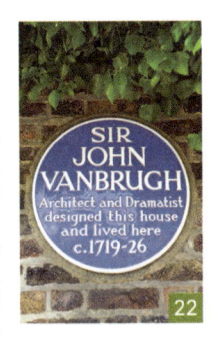

You soon should reach the site of a **㉑ Roman temple or villa**. Excavations in 1902 uncovered hundreds of 4th century AD coins and the site was also the subject of a dig by Channel 4's *Time Team* that was broadcast in 2000. One theory is that the building was an isolated temple, used by travellers who passed nearby along Watling Street, which linked London to the Roman ports in Kent.

Follow the map and look out on the east side – outside the park itself – to see **㉒ Vanbrugh Castle**. It is named after John Vanbrugh (1664-1726), the architect and dramatist. He is most famous for his Baroque masterpieces such as Castle Howard and Blenheim Palace. Vanbrugh succeeded Wren as the Surveyor to Greenwich Hospital in 1716 and lived here. It has been suggested he based the Gothic design of his house on the notorious Bastille in Paris where, earlier in his life, Vanbrugh had been imprisoned. The house appeared in a few scenes in the film *Mona Lisa* (1986).

Do not walk towards Vanbrugh Castle but continue downhill, heading directly north towards central Greenwich.

Greenwich Walk

Several films have used Greenwich Park as a location including *Layer Cake* (2004) starring Daniel Craig, and *Longitude* (2000), a TV film about John Harrison. It is also where in 1970 the future multiple Oscar winning actor Daniel Day-Lewis (b.1957) received his first experience of acting when he was one of a number of local children used as extras in John Schlesinger's film *Sunday, Bloody Sunday*. Daniel Day-Lewis, the only actor to win three Oscars, grew up at number 6 Crooms Hill (seen later).

You should pass ❷❸ **One Tree Hill**, a famous viewing spot, and walk towards the north-east corner of the park (by a children's playground). The actual 'one tree' that gives the hill its name was blown down in 1848.

The Greenwich Fair once took place in this part of the park, its origins as a 'hiring fair' beginning in medieval times when servants congregated twice a year to find employers. By the 19th century it had become a raucous affair and was eventually banned in 1857 after local residents became concerned about the disruption caused by the 200,000 visitors who thronged the dancing booths, puppet shows, plays and travelling menageries.

Charles Dickens loved this fair, describing at length in *Sketches by Boz* (1836) how visitors would arrive from all over London in 'Cabs, hackney-coaches, shay carts, coal-waggons, stages, omnibuses, sociables, gigs, donkey-chaises'. He also described the dangerous game of 'tumbling' undertaken by young men, 'The principal amusement is to drag young ladies up the steep hill which leads to the Observatory, and then drag them down again, at the very top of their speed, greatly to the derangement of their curls and bonnet-caps, and much to the edification of lookers-on from below'.

Exit the park onto ㉔ **Park Vista** with its lovely 18th and 19th-century houses and turn right, then left along Maze Hill. This is probably named after Sir Algernon May ('May's Hill') who lived near here in the late 17th century. The tunnels that run under Greenwich have sometimes been exploited by criminals and in 1847 the Kentish Gazette reported how three 'blackguard fellows' – two of whom were sailors – were caught by police attempting to use tunnels to rob houses in Maze Hill. They were discovered after one alarmed house owner and his servants heard strange noises and smoke coming out of the ground – initially thought to be the result of ghostly activities.

At the bottom of Maze Hill cross over the busy Trafalgar Road and continue north along Hoskins Street, crossing Old Woolwich Road, which – as its name suggests – was the original connecting road between Greenwich and Woolwich to the east until the wider Trafalgar Road was laid out in the 1820s. The new road allowed the rapid urbanization of this part of Greenwich to take place during the subsequent years of the 19th century.

Greenwich Walk

As you near the river bank you skirt along the north-east side of the hulking ㉕ **Greenwich Power Station** which is an imposing sight when viewed from the river or the Isle of Dogs. It was designed and built by London County Council between 1902-10 in order to power the Council's electric tramways. The chimneys were originally meant to have been much taller but were reduced in size after objections from the astronomers at the Royal Observatory. The coal-fired, steam-powered plant was replaced by gas turbine generators in the 1960s and it now acts as a standby station to provide back-up power to London Underground. The huge, sinister-looking jetty once used by colliers to deliver coal and take away the residual ashes, now sits unused and unloved.

Shortly you reach the path by the Thames and bear right. Just here you will see the large bow window of the ㉖ **Cutty Sark pub** which claims to date from around 1695 and is a good place for a stop. This area is Ballast Quay, so named because it was here that ship crews, after unloading their cargoes, would then have to take on tons of ballast in the form of stones and gravel (dug from Maze Hill). This ballast was essential to ensure empty ships were stable in the water on the return leg of their journey.

Walk past the pub along ㉗ **Ballast Quay**, one of the prettiest streets in Greenwich, with many of the houses dating from the 17th century. Look out for the signage over

Greenwich Walk

the building at the end that marks it out as the **㉘ Harbour Master's Office**. There are also old insurance company signs outside some of the houses, one (outside number 10) dating to 1695. In the days before a publicly funded fire brigade, fire insurance companies operated their own crews – often refusing to help a house owner if they turned up to find a rival insurer's sign on the outside of the burning dwelling.

Retrace your steps past the pub and then keep along Thames path (the Thames to your right), passing the power station. Immediately after on the left is **㉙ Trinity Hospital**. This traces its history back to 1613 and is the oldest building in central Greenwich. It was founded by the Earl of Northampton to help poor people in the area (although its rules excluded 'common beggars, drunkards, whore hunters, haunters of taverns'). It was rebuilt in 1812 in the present Gothic style and remains a charity run by the Mercers' Company. Today it offers 41 apartments to those in reduced circumstance who have lived in Greenwich for at least 4 years.

Greenwich Walk

Opposite the entrance look out for **30 plaques** by the wall facing the Thames that recall historic high tide marks reached in past years. The increasing flooding of the banks of the Thames led to the construction of the Thames Barrier (operational since 1984) just to the east of here.

From here you also get a good view of the Isle of Dogs to the north. Continue to follow the map along Crane Street, passing Curlew Rowing Club (established 1866) and Globe Rowing Club (established 1923) – two of the many rowing clubs based beside the Thames. You also pass another cosy pub, **31 The Yacht**. This may be a better bet on a busy day compared to the Cutty Sark and Trafalgar Tavern if you want a good atmosphere with river views.

At the end of Crane Street you reach Park Row and ahead you see the first part of the Old Royal Naval College which occupies the site of the Tudor Greenwich Palace. Turn right here and pause outside the **32 Trafalgar Tavern** on the corner facing the Thames. It is worth reading a little of the history about the Old Naval College before continuing on, and you might want to do this over some lunch in the Trafalgar.

Greenwich's most famous pub the Trafalgar Tavern, dates from the 1830s, and became legendary in the 19th century for its whitebait suppers that attracted notable diners such as Charles Dickens, Lord Palmerston and William Gladstone. The wedding breakfast scene in Dickens' *Our Mutual Friend* takes place in the tavern.

31 *The Yacht*

Greenwich Walk

As mentioned earlier, the Tudors, from Henry VII, chose Greenwich Palace as one of their principal residences. Henry VIII was born here in 1491 and spent much of his youth hunting in the forests, jousting at tournaments and engaging in the complex politics and dramas that led to the English Reformation. Henry's daughters Mary (1516) and Elizabeth (1533) were also born here, and his sickly son Edward VI died at the palace in 1547. It was at a jousting festival held here in 1536 that Anne Boleyn allegedly gave her lover a secret signal. This was the last straw for Henry VIII and Anne's arrest papers were signed in Greenwich Palace, her execution for adultery and treason following soon after. Elizabeth I spent most of her time at Greenwich, and no doubt Shakespeare and his company of players performed for their Queen within the palace building. It was also here that Walter Raleigh is said to have famously placed his cloak over a puddle so the Queen would not wet her feet.

James I also lived at Greenwich Palace and his Queen, Anne of Denmark, sponsored the finest remaining feature of that era – the Queen's House – seen shortly. However with the Civil War, the palace was turned into a biscuit factory supplying the Parliamentarian navy, and became dilapidated. With the Restoration, Charles II commissioned Wren to rebuild the palace on an epic scale. However after Charles II died, his successors James II and then William and Mary, began to lose interest in trying to resurrect Greenwich as a Royal residence. In the early 1690s William and Mary gave up the palace, and instead sponsored the building of a new Royal Hospital for Seamen on the site. This Hospital (known as Greenwich Hospital) looked after navy veterans from around 1685 until its closure in 1869. The site was then used between 1873 and 1998 to train officers in the Navy as part of the Royal Naval College. After the Navy left the buildings were taken over by Greenwich University and the Trinity Laban College. Slightly confusingly the complex is often described as the Old Royal Naval College, even though it was originally Greenwich Hospital.

Work on Greenwich Hospital, located on the site of the demolished Tudor palace, began in 1694 under Wren's supervision. Its purpose was to look after veteran sailors just as the Royal Hospital

Greenwich Walk

at Chelsea looked after army veterans. Building work took many decades, and employed some of the greatest architects of the age including Hawksmoor and Vanbrugh. At its peak in 1814 around 2,700 navy veterans lived at Greenwich Hospital, enjoying a daily allowance of four pints of beer a day but subject to strict rules of behaviour.

The Hospital's veterans seem to have retained a robust sense of humour despite many suffering from war wounds. For example in 1867 there was much public excitement about a cricket match at the Oval between two teams drawn from the Hospital's ranks – one side comprising men with just one arm, the other side made up of men with one leg.

The need for the Hospital faded over time, probably because naval engagements became less common. While the Hospital was closed in 1869, the original charity, established under a Royal Charter granted by William and Mary in 1694, continues to this day. It supports various causes, most notably the Royal Hospital School. This school (founded in 1712) moved to Suffolk in 1933 and the old school buildings are now occupied by the National Maritime Museum.

When ready to continue, walk along the path by the Thames. There are some ❸❸ **steps** (near the Trafalgar) that lead down to the shoreline. Only go down if the tide is out (and be careful, it can be slippery); however, if the shoreline is visible you can continue along for a few hundred yards to get an unusual view of the College and what is happening out on the river that most tourists do not normally see.

Continue along (either on the path or if walking along the shoreline until you reach another set of steps and ascend) to reach the ❸❹ **Water Gate entrance** into the College.

249

Greenwich Walk

Walk through the Gate into the majestic ㉟ **Grand Square**, dominated by a statue of George II at the centre. Wren designed the Naval Hospital so it was built in four separate wings, with Queen Anne and Queen Mary Courts on your left (as you look south towards Greenwich Park) and King Charles and King William Courts on your right.

If you look south towards Greenwich Park from the Grand Square you will see the ㊱ **Queen's House**. This was commissioned by Anne of Denmark (1574-1619), queen to James I, and was built between 1616-1619. The architect was Inigo Jones (1573-1652), and as the first true classical style building to be constructed in this country it represents one of the most important milestones in British architectural history.

Later, when Wren and his fellow architects were constructing Greenwich Hospital, they were required by Queen Mary II to split the design to ensure the view from the Queen's House down to

㉟ Grand Square with Queen's House far right

the Thames was uninterrupted. Today the finest view of this site is from the Isle of Dogs side, with the wings of Wren's design framing Inigo Jones's masterpiece.

James I and Anne famously did not get on, and it is said he gave her the land in Greenwich as an apology after swearing at her in public – although she had apparently just shot one of his favourite hunting dogs by accident.

The Queen's House is also where one of the most famous 'ghost photographs' was taken by a tourist named Mr Hardy from Canada in 1966. He took a picture of the elegant Tulip Staircase and when he returned to Canada found the developed photograph contained the image of a shrouded spectre ascending the stairs.

At this point in the walk there are a large number of attractions in the vicinity that you could spend several hours visiting and describing them all in detail is beyond the scope of this book (see p.261 for more information on local attractions).

㊲ The Chapel (just to the south by Queen Mary Court) is certainly worth taking time to appreciate. Noted for its stunning, neo-classical, design, the Chapel was the last major part of Greenwich Hospital to be completed in 1751. It was also where the second wedding took place in *Four Weddings and a Funeral* (1994), with Rowan Atkinson playing the bumbling vicar.

The **㊳ Painted Hall** (by King William Court) is just as impressive. Often described as the finest dining hall in Europe, it was designed by Wren and Hawksmoor. Sir James Thornhill spent 19 years from 1708 painting its ceilings and walls with scenes celebrating the British monarchy and maritime power. He was paid £3 per square yard for the ceiling, and £1 per square yard for the walls. The body of Lord Nelson lay in state in the Hall following his death at the Battle of Trafalgar in 1805 – a plaque marks the spot where his coffin rested before it was taken for burial at St Paul's Cathedral.

You may find the Painted Hall, and other buildings and exteriors of the Naval College strangely familiar. This is because their epic scale has made them very popular with film makers, most notably in productions such as *The Bounty* (1984), *Octopussy* (1983), *Patriot Games* (1992), *The Madness of King George* (1994), *The Golden Compass* (2007), *The King's Speech* (2010), *Pirates of the Caribbean: On Stranger Tides* (2011), *Sherlock Holmes: A Game of Shadows* (2011), *Les Miserables* and *Skyfall* (2012); as well as episodes of *The Crown* and *Bridgerton*.

The Pirates of the Caribbean film's connection with the site is oddly appropriate. The infamous pirate Captain Kidd (1645-1701), hanged just over the river at Execution Dock in Wapping, left over £6,000 in treasure on his death. This was a huge sum in those times and Queen Anne donated it to the Greenwich Hospital meaning that some of the buildings used in the film were in fact paid for out of a real pirate's ill-gotten gains.

In 2010, Johnny Depp was on location at the Old Royal Naval College filming his part as Captain Jack Sparrow. He turned up in full costume to surprise pupils at a local primary school after one of the children had written to the star asking that he help them stage a mutiny against the teachers.

Daniel Defoe (c1660-1731), author of *Robinson Crusoe*, also benefitted from Kidd's treasure – Defoe was a manufacturer of bricks which were used in the construction of Greenwich Hospital.

When you have finished at the Old Royal Naval College site, I would suggest you exit through the North Gate and

Greenwich Walk

turn right, until you soon reach the entrance to the ❸❾ **National Maritime Museum**. What began life in 1807 as a school for the children of seafarers is now one of London's finest museums and tells the story of Britain's maritime history. The museum is probably too large to be incorporated within this walk, but opening details can be found on page 261.

Follow the map to reach the ❹⓿ **Greenwich Visitor Centre** housed in the recently refurnished Grade II listed Pepys building. Its exhibitions explain the royal and maritime history of Greenwich and the local area. The adjoining Old Brewery is a good spot to stop for a refreshing beer or bite to eat (see page 261 for more information).

Next to the visitor centre sits the ❹❶ **Cutty Sark**. She was launched in 1869 in Dumbarton on the Clyde with the aim of being the fastest ship or 'clipper,' in the annual race to bring home the first of the new season's tea from China. The ship was named after a garment known in Scotland as a cutty sark and worn by a witch named Nannie in Robert Burns' 1791 poem *Tam o' Shanter*. The ship's figurehead which adorns her bow represents Nannie.

Sadly the Cutty Sark, for a while the fastest ship in the world, only had a short period of glory. The opening of the Suez Canal meant steam ships could challenge the clippers, and avoid having to go around Cape Horn or the Cape of Good Hope. The Cutty Sark was almost instantly obsolete

41 Cutty Sark

given her original purpose. After many different uses, often undistinguished, the ship was restored and brought to Greenwich for permanent display in 1954. However she was badly damaged by a fire in 2007, possibly arson, and the current visitor centre opened in 2012 after a painstaking restoration that cost over £50 million.

Continue down to the Thames and see the entrance to ㊷ **Greenwich Foot Tunnel**. The tunnel opened in 1902 to allow men living south of the river to easily reach their jobs on the docks on the Isle of Dogs. If you have time it is worth going into the tunnel, even just to be able to tell people you have walked 33 feet under the Thames (at low tide) and 55 feet (at high tide). The tunnel is slightly narrower on the far north side – the result of a German bomb that caused damage and required rebuilding work.

From the Foot Tunnel follow the map to reach College Approach. Cross over to enter ㊸ **Greenwich Market**. There has been a market at Greenwich since the 14th century, although this site has been in use since around 1700. The current market buildings are Grade II listed and date from the early 1830s. Look out for the sign near the entrance that reads 'A False Balance is Abomination to the Lord but a just weight is his delight' – taken from Proverbs 11.1. The market contains a nice selection of food and craft stalls and is open all days except Monday and Tuesday with a busy craft and food market at the weekend.

Greenwich Walk

When you have finished exploring the market walk down Durnford Street to join Greenwich Church Street and head left. Stop on the left at Turnpin Lane to see one of the oldest and narrowest streets in Greenwich. Continue along Greenwich Church Street, one of the busiest shopping streets in the area with lots of cafés to stop at if you need a rest. After a short while you will see on the right-hand side the **44 church of St Alfege**.

Alfege was the Archbishop of Canterbury from 954-1012, a period when the Vikings still dominated much of the eastern part of the country. In 1011 they besieged Canterbury and captured Alfege, returning with him to their base at Greenwich and demanding a ransom of £3,000. Alfege refused to help his captors in their demands, famously saying 'the gold I give you is the Word of God'. This did not go down well with the pagan Vikings who, after heavy drinking at a feast, decided to bludgeon their prisoner to death using meat bones and the shafts of their axes. Alfege was canonized in 1078 and a church was first constructed on this site around that time.

The church was rebuilt between 1712-1714 by Nicholas Hawksmoor, Wren's pupil, and master of the Baroque style. Hawksmoor was one of the great architects of the age in his own right, and his Masonic interests have given rise to many theories that his designs contained hidden Masonic meanings. The church was gutted by enemy bombing during World War II but has since been extensively restored. It is seen to its best advantage from Roan Street. Henry VIII was baptized in the old church, and General Wolfe buried here. Thomas Tallis (1505-85) – the 'father of English church music' – was an organist at the church and was also buried here.

From the church follow the map up Stockwell Road and then into Crooms Hill. Crooms Hill is one of the nicest streets in Greenwich, with many notable people having lived here over the years in its elegant Georgian houses that now sell for over £3 million.

At number 6 is the former home of the great film actor and winner of three Oscars ㊺ **Sir Daniel Day-Lewis**. His family lived here from 1957 to 1972, and he later recalled standing by the front door in 1968 while press reporters assembled outside, because his father Cecil Day-Lewis (1904-1972) had just been chosen as Poet Laureate. There is a blue plaque to commemorate Cecil Day-Lewis.

㊻ **The Fan Museum** at number 12 is unique, the only one of its kind in the country dedicated to the art and history of

Greenwich Walk

fan-making. It contains over 4,000 items, and is housed in a beautiful Grade II listed building dating from 1721 that is worth a visit even if you have no particular interest in the subject matter (for more information see page 261).

Continue up Crooms Hill to number 24, looking out for any dangerous holes. In recent years a number of holes have appeared in the road along Crooms Hill and Blackheath Hill roads, thought to be connected to the mysterious tunnels and caverns underneath the park. ❹ **Number 24 Crooms Hill** was home in the 1930s to Laurence O'Shaughnessy, a distinguished thoracic surgeon, and the brother of Eileen O'Shaughnessy. Eileen married Eric Arthur Blair (1903-1950) – better known as George Orwell – and the writer spent a great deal of time at the house. It has been suggested Eileen's own poem entitled *End of the Century, 1984* helped inspire Orwell's famous book *Nineteen Eighty-Four*. Laurence died during the Dunkirk Evacuation in 1940 and Eileen – who was extremely close to her brother – never really recovered from the shock. Combined with upset caused by Orwell's numerous affairs, her health took a turn for the worse and she died during surgery in 1945. Orwell died just five years later of tuberculosis, a disease on which Laurence was a world authority.

❹ **Number 26 Crooms Hill** was the home of Benjamin Waugh – founder of The National Society for the Prevention of Cruelty to Children (NSPCC). Working as a minister in Greenwich, Waugh was appalled at the deprivation inflicted on children by the workhouse system and prison. The charity he helped found is still in existence today, helping alleviate the suffering of children in desperate situations.

Greenwich Walk

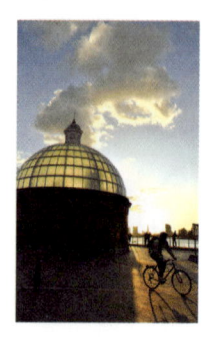

Follow the map through ㊾ **Gloucester Circus**. The Circus has a slightly split personality – one half has elegant townhouses dating from the 18th century, while the other contains less attractive looking 1950s flats. You may suspect this was due to bomb damage during World War II, however the reality is that when the circus was first constructed by architect Michael Searles between 1791 and 1809, there were not enough people to buy the expensive new properties so only one side was built, leaving a highly unusual 'D' shape. The older houses today sell for several million pounds and make this one of the best addresses in the area. It is also popular with film crews who are attracted – at least from one angle – to the period feel. The film *Sense & Sensibility* (1995) starring Emma Thompson, Kate Winslet and Hugh Grant had some scenes set here.

Walk along Circus Street. Turn right into Greenwich Street and immediately on your right above a shop (nos. 23-25) you will find a plaque commemorating the former residence of ㊿ **Dr Alfred Salter** (1873-1945) who was a pioneering doctor and philanthropist who became Bermondsey's first Labour MP.

Just a few doors further down is a wonderful junk shop, aptly named, The Junk Shop which is well worth visiting. Don't be deceived by the modest façade as it's much bigger than it appears.

When finished proceed across Greenwich High Street to return to the station and the end of this walk. ●

SHOP...

Greenwich Market (see p.256)
Greenwich Church St, SE10 9HZ
www.greenwichmarketlondon.com

The Junk Shop (see p.260)
9 Greenwich South St, SE10 8NW
www.thejunkshopandspreadeagle.co.uk

EAT, DRINK...

Cutty Sark (see p.244)
4-6 Ballast Quay, SE10 9PD
www.cuttysarkse10.co.uk

The Old Brewery (see p.254)
The Pepys Building,
Old Royal Naval College,
SE10 0AR
www.oldbrewerygreenwich.com

Astronomy Café (see p.239)
Royal Observatory, Blackheath Avenue, Greenwich Park, SE10 8XJ

Pavilion Tea House (see p.235)
Charlton Way,
Greenwich Park, SE10 8QY

The Trafalgar Tavern (see p.246)
Park Row, SE10 9NW
www.trafalgartavern.co.uk

The Yacht (see p.246)
5-7 Crane Street, SE10 9NP
020 8858 0175

VISIT...

The Cutty Sark (see p.254)
Cutty Sark Gardens, SE10 9HT
www.cuttysark.org.uk
www.rmg.co.uk

Discover Greenwich Visitor Centre (see p.254)
The Pepys Building,
Old Royal Naval College,
SE10 9LW
www.ornc.org

Fan Museum (see p.258)
12 Croom Hill, SE10 8ER
www.thefanmuseum.org.uk

National Maritime Museum (see p.254)
Romney Road, SE10 9NF
www.rmg.co.uk

Painted Hall & Chapel (see p.252)
Old Royal Naval College, SE10 9JF
www.ornc.org

Queen's House (see p.250)
Greenwich, SE10 9NF
www.rmg.co.uk

Ranger's House (see p.232)
Chesterfield Walk, SE10 8QX
www.english-heritage.org.uk

Royal Observatory & Planetarium (see p.238)
Greenwich Park, SE10 8XJ
www.rmg.co.uk

IFS Cloud Cable Car

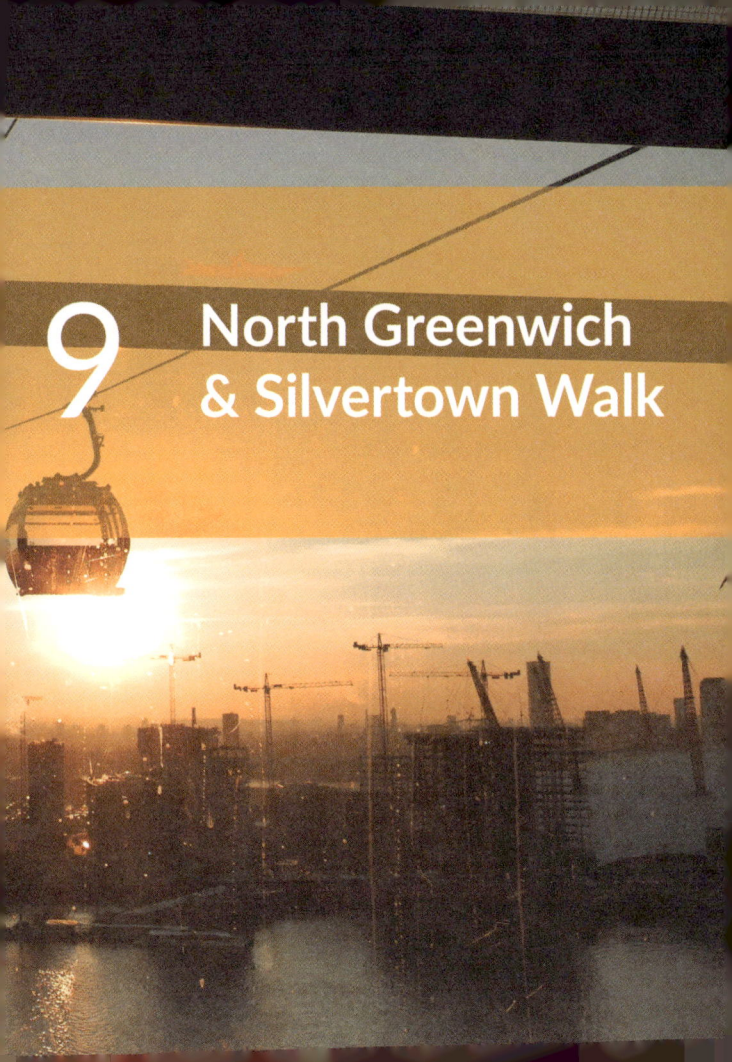

9 North Greenwich & Silvertown Walk

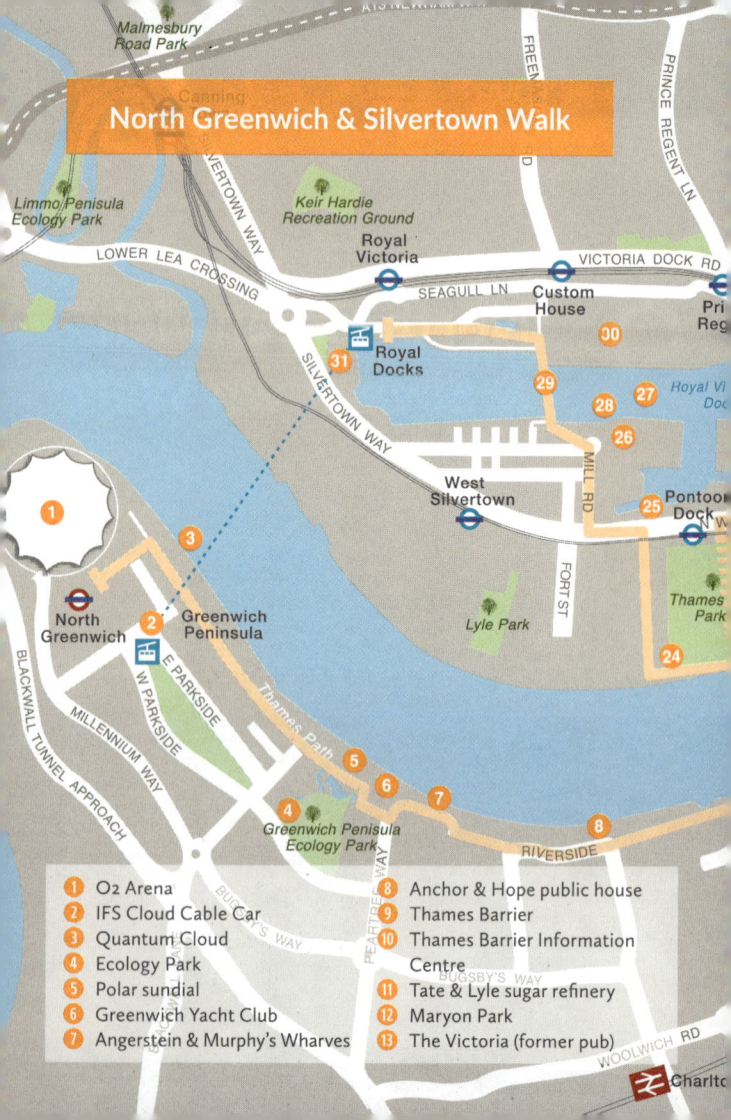

North Greenwich & Silvertown Walk

1. O2 Arena
2. IFS Cloud Cable Car
3. Quantum Cloud
4. Ecology Park
5. Polar sundial
6. Greenwich Yacht Club
7. Angerstein & Murphy's Wharves
8. Anchor & Hope public house
9. Thames Barrier
10. Thames Barrier Information Centre
11. Tate & Lyle sugar refinery
12. Maryon Park
13. The Victoria (former pub)

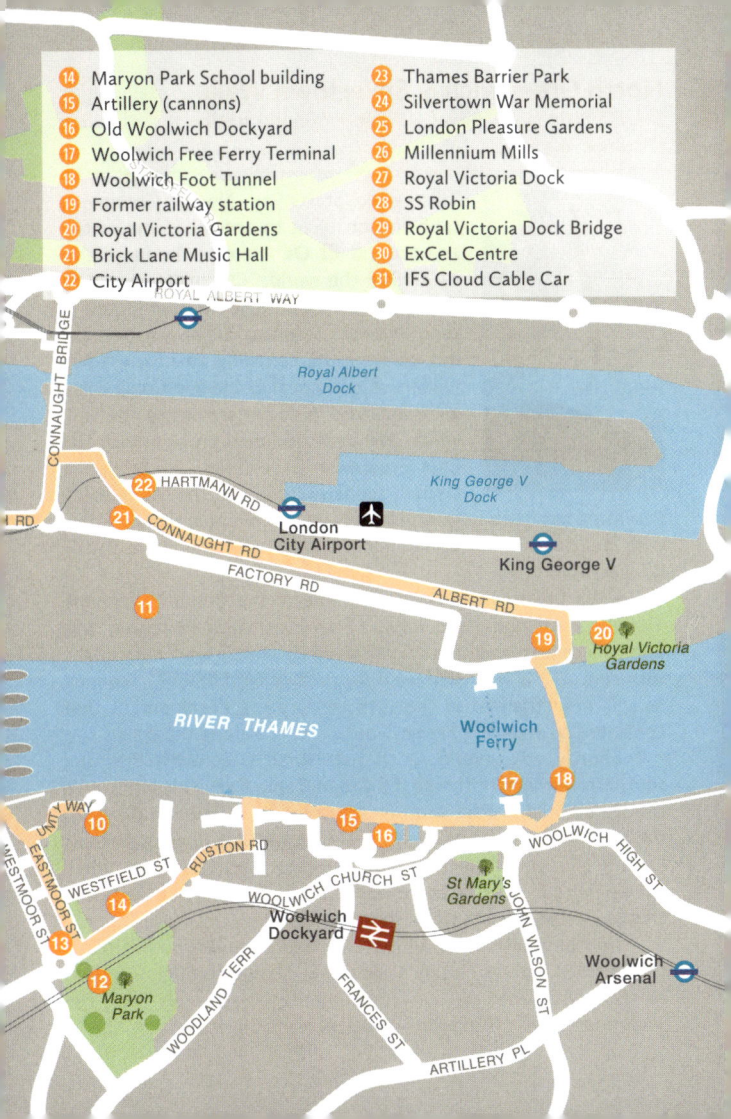

- ⑭ Maryon Park School building
- ⑮ Artillery (cannons)
- ⑯ Old Woolwich Dockyard
- ⑰ Woolwich Free Ferry Terminal
- ⑱ Woolwich Foot Tunnel
- ⑲ Former railway station
- ⑳ Royal Victoria Gardens
- ㉑ Brick Lane Music Hall
- ㉒ City Airport
- ㉓ Thames Barrier Park
- ㉔ Silvertown War Memorial
- ㉕ London Pleasure Gardens
- ㉖ Millennium Mills
- ㉗ Royal Victoria Dock
- ㉘ SS Robin
- ㉙ Royal Victoria Dock Bridge
- ㉚ ExCeL Centre
- ㉛ IFS Cloud Cable Car

North Greenwich & Silvertown Walk

Start/Finish: North Greenwich underground station
Distance: 6.3 miles

This walk starts at North Greenwich tube station. Exit to see the dome of the 20,000 seat ❶ **O2 Arena** – the largest of its kind in the world. Originally known as the Millennium Dome, it was completed in 1999 and was a controversial construction due to its costs spiralling to nearly £800 million. A great deal of the additional costs were incurred in decontaminating the site, which had been occupied previously by the East Greenwich Gas Works. However the Dome's construction on the Greenwich Peninsula has had a huge and largely beneficial impact on the area, with thousands of visitors coming to a part of London previously off any tourist map.

Walk towards the right-hand side of the dome to find the Thames Path and head east. The Greenwich Peninsula was originally marshland, and was drained by Dutch engineers in the 16th century. It was then used for pasture land before becoming heavily industrialised in the 19th century – a development that continues to mark this area as you will notice along the walk.

Shortly you should reach the North Greenwich Pier and southern terminal of the ❷ **IFS Cloud Cable Car**. This innovative service opened in 2012 and takes passengers to the Royal Docks, the final destination on this walk. (Make sure it is open on the day you travel as you should be taking the cable car to return to North Greenwich tube station at the end of this walk – the website www.tfl.gov.uk contains the latest information).

Continue eastwards, and for the next few miles you will follow the Thames Path as closely as possible, passing through Charlton to reach Woolwich before crossing under (or possibly over) the Thames itself to reach North Woolwich and Silvertown.

2 IFS Cloud Cable Car

North Greenwich & Silvertown Walk

You will soon pass a sculpture by artist Antony Gormley (b.1950) titled ❸ **Quantum Cloud**. This stands 30 metres high, and is taller than his better known creation, *The Angel of the North*. It was completed in 1999 to accompany the opening of the Millennium Dome, and was inspired by Gormley's interest in mathematics and space-time.

Continue on. While Greenwich to the west is a World Heritage Site (see Greenwich Walk pages 222-261), this stretch of London heading eastwards was once a bleak industrial area with an old gas works and power station. This all changed in the 1990s with continued development transforming this area into a smart, if rather characterless, residential area.

Following the map and after about ten minutes you will see the ❹ **Greenwich Peninsula Ecology Park** on the right. It is made up of two lakes surrounded by marshes and wet woodlands, and was originally known as Greenwich Marsh. The area became industrialised from the late 1880s, dominated by a shipbuilding yard and gas and chemical works but, beginning in the 1970s, the works were gradually closed down. A regeneration project began in 1997 covering 121 hectors including this park. As you can see, the area has been transformed and has perhaps gone through more change than any other part of London.

Opposite is a ❺ **polar sundial**, one of three designed by Piers Nicholson which were built by the Royal Engineers in late 1999 to commemorate the new millennium. The other two are in the City and outside the Royal Engineers' Museum at Chatham.

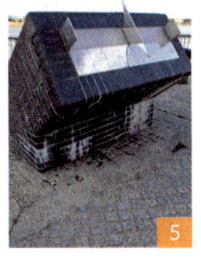

Continue eastwards passing through the rear of ❻ **Greenwich Yacht Club**. This was founded in 1908 by Thames watermen and river workers who lived nearby. The club moved into its current home in 2000 when the Millennium Dome was built on the site of the old clubhouse. Designed by Frankl and Luty the new clubhouse is a contemporary timber and aluminium building which stands high out of the water on a concrete platform supported on stilts. It is open to the public on Tuesday evenings and at weekends. You can also visit through the London Open House scheme (*www.londonopenhouse.org*).

You now pass through a bleak, yet strangely fascinating industrial landscape. Some 33 acres around here are dominated by aggregate companies. Aggregate (largely comprising sand and gravel) is brought in by boat and then processed for use in building materials.

The ❼ **Angerstein and Murphy's Wharves** (just after the yacht club) receive boats daily bringing in aggregate dredged from the coastline around Britain. Over 2.5 million tonnes of material arrive here annually by boat, making this Europe's largest sea-dredged aggregate terminal. Aggregate may not seem the most glamorous industry in London but it is a vital one – materials from here were used in the new buildings designed for the 2012 London Olympics, the Emirates Stadium (home to Arsenal), the Canary Wharf development and the Channel Tunnel.

North Greenwich & Silvertown Walk

Angerstein Wharf is now controlled by a huge cement company, Cemex. It was named after John Julius Angerstein (1732-1823), a local entrepreneur and art collector who lived nearby in Westcombe Park. Angerstein, who became known as the 'Father of Lloyd's' (the famous insurance market in the City), and whose legacy of paintings formed the basis of the National Gallery's collection, built his own branch line in order to connect his wharf to the main railway line a mile to the south.

After a few minutes you pass the ❽ **Anchor and Hope**, a real old-fashioned local with a pleasant terrace providing views over the river. The building dates from 1899 but the pub was founded in the 16th century. The name is said to originate from the sailors drinking here and hoping the wind would pick up. This area is Charlton and it lies between Greenwich and Woolwich. In the 1830 a large three-armed gibbet stood near here. The bodies of executed pirates were suspended from the gibbet, as a deterrent for anyone passing by.

Continue along the Thames Path and you will see the ❾ **Thames Barrier** ahead. The world's second largest moveable flood barrier, it officially opened in 1984, 10 years after construction began. Its origins go back to the 1950s, and in particular the North Sea Flood of 1953. This occurred after a huge storm surge caused flooding in England, Scotland, Belgium and the Netherlands and killed 2100 people, including 53 in Canvey Island. The disaster led to an official report in the UK that recommended the construction of what you see today. The Barrier spans 520 metres across the Thames and its 10 steel gates protect 125 square kilometres of central London from flooding by tidal surges.

Your path winds past the Barrier along a covered path. Look out for the etching on the wall that plots the 215 mile course of the Thames – try to find out where you are now.

Following the map down Unity Way to reach the ⑩ **Thames Barrier Information Centre** which contains useful information about the Barrier and its history, but is unfortunately now only open on Saturdays (10.30-15.30, April-October). Look over to the north shore and you will see the vast ⑪ **Tate & Lyle sugar refinery** in Silvertown. There will be more about the factory later but this spot provides an excellent vantage point.

From here you need to go inland as the Thames Path does not go right along the river edge. Follow the map down Eastmoor Street. Alternatively, if you fancy a greener experience – you can walk through the parks that run parallel (to your left) of this street, continuing directly south until you reach the busy Woolwich Road.

On the other side of the road is ⑫ **Maryon Park**. It was once a wild wooded area and together with Maryon Wilson Park was known as Hanging Wood – a retreat for highwaymen who plied their trade on nearby Shooters Hill and Blackheath. Those caught were hanged here – hence the name. Today's park was created by the London County Council in 1891 from disused sand and gravel pits donated by the Maryon-Wilson family. It is perhaps best known in popular culture as a key location in the cult film *Blowup* (1966), directed by Michelangelo Antonioni.

9 Thames Barrier

North Greenwich & Silvertown Walk

Just west along the Woolwich Road is the shell of another 19th-century pub – ⑬ **the Victoria**, which displays a black eagle emblem. This was the logo of the now-defunct Truman's Brewery, which was founded around Brick Lane in the Spitalfields area, and which for many years was one of the biggest brewers in the country.

From here walk along the side of Woolwich Road for a short while to get back to the Thames Path. Look out on the left for the 'SBL' monogram on the frontage of the ⑭ **Maryon Park School building**, which opened as a school in 1896 and is now part of Greenwich Community College. The sign stands for 'School Board for London', and is a reminder of the beginning of universal education in this country. The board was set up directly after the Elementary Education Act of 1870, which required all children aged between five and 12 years to receive an education, and it continued to supervise many schools in the capital until 1904 when its role was taken over by the London County Council (LCC).

After a few minutes you reach a roundabout, where you take the second turning up Ruston Road and follow the map left to reach Harlinger Street.

Walk straight across through a large opening in a block of flats to reach the Thames Path once again, then head right (eastwards). The Tate & Lyle factory is opposite on the north side of the Thames.

Shortly you will see ⑮ **two pieces of artillery** on moveable foundations pointing out over the Thames. This is the first sign you are in Woolwich, a district whose military connections were critical to its development.

The name Woolwich is probably derived from an Anglo-Saxon word meaning 'trading place for wool'. It was just a small Kentish fishing village when Henry VIII decided to build a Royal Naval Dockyard here. This was founded in 1512, and Henry – living just up the river at his palace in Greenwich (see page 248) – also built another great dockyard at Deptford. The Woolwich Dockyard operated until 1869, by which time the ships the Navy needed were too large to make it this far down the Thames. The Woolwich dockyard was responsible for some of the Navy's most famous ships, including Henry's flagship *Henri Grâce à Dieu* (*Henry Grace of God*, more commonly known as *Great Harry*) and *HMS Beagle*, which carried Charles Darwin on his great voyage of discovery.

Continue eastwards looking out for a sign to the grim looking Woolwich Dockyard Estate. This dates from the 1970s and occupies part of the site of the ⓰ **Old Woolwich Dockyard**. As you continue eastwards you will see the last real remnants of Henry's institution – two water-filled docks – originally dry docks – that lie beside the estate. Situated next to the first dock, you will encounter what looks like an abandoned lido. This was the Southeast London Aquacentre which was a popular facility for canoeists and anglers. Although swimming was prohibited, the kids from the local estates would climb the walls and swim here in the evenings. The centre closed in the 1990s and now looks rather forlorn as it gradually falls into dereliction.

If you had stood here in the late 18th century you would have seen great prison hulks moored out on the Thames. The loss of the North American colonies after the 1770s meant many convicts who would once have been transported there had to stay in this country and were kept on the hulks of old warships at night, and forced to work in the Woolwich docks during the day.

As you continue eastwards you will see the ⓱ **Woolwich Free Ferry terminal**. A ferry across the Thames has operated here since at least the 14th century, and the free ferry began in 1889. It was supplemented by a foot tunnel that opened in 1912 and which, if open on the day you visit, you will walk through later in the walk.

Woolwich has a centuries' old association with Britain's army and navy with the Royal Arsenal, the Royal Military Academy and the Royal Artillery all having long histories in the area. The Royal Arsenal was principally concerned with the production of armaments and research into explosives and was resident from the Napoleonic Wars until its closure in 1967. The Royal Military Academy was founded here in 1741 and Woolwich trained all army officers until

North Greenwich & Silvertown Walk

1939 when Sandhurst became the military's training headquarters. For a brief period Woolwich lost its link with the active military when the last artillery regiment left in July 2007, but The Princess of Wales's Royal Regiment was stationed in Woolwich after their return from Cyprus in 2010. In 2012 the King's Troop, Royal Horse Artillery moved barracks from St John's Wood to new quarters and stables in Woolwich.

The link between Woolwich and the army was further strengthened in the public mind when Private Lee Rigby of the Royal Regiment of Fusiliers was murdered near his barracks on Wellington Street by two Muslim converts in May 2013.

If you want to reach the site of the Arsenal retrace your steps to Woolwich High Street and continue along a little while, crossing over towards the Thames and bearing right. Until the end of 2016, Firepower (a museum dedicated to the link between Woolwich and the British military) stood just to the east of the Woolwich Foot Tunnel. The museum has been relocated to Wiltshire and the land is now the site of luxury flats which bare the name of the Royal Arsenal.

Woolwich has been a place for the storage of ordinance since the reign of Henry VIII. The first building on the Royal Arsenal site dated from 1545 in an area known as the Warren. Gun manufacturing had originally taken place mainly within the City, but concerns about public safety resulted in the industry moving out to Woolwich, then still an isolated site. It became known as the Royal Arsenal in 1805 after a suggestion made by George III and continued to produce armaments until 1967 before finally closing in 1994. During World War I, the Royal Arsenal extended over some 1300 acres and employed around 80,000 people.

Its most famous offshoot is Arsenal football club, whose own origins began in 1886 when workers at the site started a team that entered the professional league in 1893. The team later moved to North London, but is still known as the 'Gunners' and has a cannon on its crest.

Look out for signs behind the leisure centre for the ⓲ **Woolwich Foot Tunnel**, and descend. Before you enter the tunnel, look out to the Thames and over to the east. It was around a mile away from where you are standing that the *SS Princess Alice* sank on 3 September 1878 at around 7.40pm after colliding with a steam collier ship, the *Bywell Castle*. The *Princess Alice* was returning to her dock near London Bridge after taking day-trippers out to Gravesend and Sheerness, and sank in about five minutes. It is thought that at least 600 people drowned, many almost certainly overcome by the toxic outflow from the sewage works at Beckton, and various chemical factories by the river edge. Around 500 bodies were recovered from the Thames in the week following the disaster, with dozens more found by the exit doors of the ship when it was eventually pulled from the riverbed weeks later.

You should now descend to the foot tunnel. In recent years the tunnel has been shut for restoration. If it is open on the day you visit you are in for a treat. If no one

North Greenwich & Silvertown Walk

else is in the tunnel, which is quite common (unlike the Greenwich foot tunnel to the west), it is quite an eerie experience. If the tunnel is shut, then you can continue a little further on to take the Woolwich Free Ferry to the north bank of the Thames.

The building of this 504m tunnel was designed to assist workers in south London to reach the factories and Royal Docks to the north, and, like the Greenwich foot tunnel, was largely constructed due to the efforts of the remarkable working-class politician Will Crooks (1852-1921). As a child Crooks had spent time in the workhouse, and later worked on the docks. He overcame his tough upbringing to enter politics and chaired the LCC's Bridges Committee – the body responsible for the tunnel. Crooks, also helped found Island Gardens (on the Isle of Dogs) and the Blackwall Tunnel, and would later become the MP for Woolwich, the fourth-ever Labour MP.

When you reach the other side you are in North Woolwich – a rare example of a single district separated by the Thames. Follow the map along Pier Road to reach Albert Road. Look out on your left for the ⑲ **former railway station building** that dates from the 1840s. After the railway line was closed the building housed a museum that closed a few years ago.

As you approach Albert Road, look out on your right for the ⑳ **Royal Victoria Gardens.** These were opened by the LCC in 1890 on land acquired with funds raised through public subscription, including a

279

donation of £50 from Queen Victoria. Until the 19th century, this part of North Woolwich was malarial marshland, formerly part of the ancient manor of Hammarsh and owned by Westminster Abbey for some 800 years. It was only really developed from the 1840s after the introduction of the steam ferry and a rail link between here and Canning Town.

In 1850 a man named William Holland, who owned the Pavilion Hotel at North Woolwich, laid out a pleasure garden here. Holland was apparently a bit of a character, once (like the fictional Wizard of Oz) escaping his creditors by leaving the park in a balloon. He put on entertainments such as trapeze artists, fireworks, and 'monster baby shows'. However, pleasure gardens – once the most popular entertainment in London – fell out of favour in London as the 19th century progressed, prey to competition from the music hall and public house. The gardens closed in the 1880s, and the land was converted into the public park you see today.

Head left (westwards) along Albert Road. You are walking through Silvertown, named after a rubber factory that opened here in 1852. SW Silver & Co. (owned by Samuel Winkworth Silver) began in Cornhill in the City in the 18th century, and was originally an outfitter for people working in the colonies and Army. It later developed into a business producing waterproof fabric from a factory in Greenwich and diversified into rubber cable covering. The factory moved north of the Thames in 1852 to where you are now, before the Royal Docks were opened and when road connections were very poor. The company grew rapidly, dominating the neighbourhood so that by 1859 the area became known as Silvertown. By 1887 the factory occupied 15 acres and employed 2,800 people, and from its own wharf on the Thames ran four cable-laying ships one of which was called *The Silvertown*.

The Silvertown was then the second largest ship in the world, the largest being Brunel's *Great Eastern*. The factory's owners were commissioned to produce and lay telegraphic cables under most of the world's oceans; however, after reaching a peak in the early 20th century, the company was badly impacted by the recession of the 1920s and 1930s and went into steady decline.

The rubber factory that gave the area its name has long gone, but Silvertown is still dominated by a small number of companies and institutions such as the Tate & Lyle sugar refinery, the Royal Docks, City Airport, the Excel Centre and the University of East London to the north.

This is a unique community, physically still quite remote from the rest of London, and for many decades split into tribes determined by each tribe's respective workplace. You are unlikely to meet many people (even those living in London) who have actually been to Silvertown.

The area reached national prominence in 1917 with the 'Silvertown Explosion' – the greatest explosion in London's history, when 50 tons of TNT caught fire in a munitions factory. Upwards of 70,000 buildings were damaged, 73 people were killed and around 400 were injured. You will encounter the Silvertown War Memorial later in the walk (see p.285).

Continue along the road. After a few minutes you reach the ⑪ **Tate & Lyle sugar refinery**, which was seen across the Thames earlier in the walk and is a place where many generations of Silvertown residents have worked. Henry Tate (whose art collection helped establish Tate Britain) first set up a manufacturing site here in 1878, famously producing the original white sugar cube. This business was merged in 1921 with rival Abraham Lyle's own enterprise. The original Lyle factory, home of Golden Syrup, is just further along to the west at Plaistow Wharf and opened in the 1880s. In recent decades the number of workers, at the refinery has declined and so its influence on the area has waned.

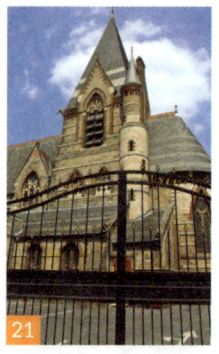

If you are interested in finding out more about life at Tate & Lyle, I would recommend *The Sugar Girls: Tales of Hardship, Love and Happiness in Tate & Lyle's East End* (2012). Written by Duncan Barrett and Nuala Calvi, it explores the lives of the girls and women who worked at Tate & Lyle from the mid-1940s onwards. Many girls first came here to the 'Sugar Mile' aged 14 and lived within an enclosed community, socialising with each other, speaking of themselves as coming from 'Tate's' or 'Lyle's' (depending on which site they worked at).

After a few minutes look out on the left-hand side for a church building which is currently obscured by the high walls of another building development. This is the home of the ㉑ **Brick Lane Music Hall**, the only music hall still operating regularly in London. While the music hall tradition is a long one, this theatrical experience only dates back to the early 1990's at the Truman Brewery in the East End. It has now found a permanent home in Silvertown, but has kept its original name (see p.289 for more information).

The former church of St Mark's was built in a Gothic style in the 1870s and is Grade II listed. It was deconsecrated in the 1980s and not long after was nearly destroyed in a fire, but it was saved after accumulated pigeon droppings on the roof fell down and extinguished the flames.

21 Brick Lane Music Hall

North Greenwich & Silvertown Walk

23

24

25

284

North Greenwich & Silvertown Walk

Continue on. To your right you will see the entrance road to ㉒ **City Airport**. This began to operate in 1987 and is built on the site of the Royal Docks (of which more later). It says something about the scale of the docks that an international airport could fit within the perimeter of the site.

At a roundabout (with a huge sculpture of a woman) head left down Connaught Bridge, and then right into North Woolwich Road. Walk along until you reach Pontoon Dock DLR station to visit the wonderful ㉓ **Thames Barrier Park** – the first riverside park to be opened in London in 50 years. Access to the park is via the station's car park.

The work of French landscape architect Alain Provost, the park was carved out of a 22 acre, de-contaminated brownfield site on the north bank of the Thames. It was opened in 2000 and affords incredible views of the flood defences of the same name. The park's most photographed feature is the Green Dock, a 16 foot deep sunken garden that runs diagonally across the rectangular site. Referencing the area's industrial maritime past, the canal-like Green Dock ripples with undulating topiary. With a ringside view of the Thames Barrier, a children's play area, and coffee shop, it's a great place to stop for a coffee or spot of lunch (see page 289 for more information).

After enjoying the views of the Thames and its barrier walk along the riverside until you see the ㉔ **Silvertown War Memorial** which has been relocated to this smart residential estate. The memorial commemorates the 72 workers killed on the 19th January 1917 when the Brunner-Mond & Co factory exploded. The factory had recently been converted to purify TNT for the war effort. The fatal explosion could be heard one hundred miles away and is still the largest in London's history.

Continue to walk through this recently completed development until you reach North Greenwich Road again and opposite look out for the ill-fated ㉕ **London Pleasure Gardens** that opened and closed in 2012 after failing to persuade Londoners that pleasure gardens – which had fallen out of favour during the 19th century – deserved a second chance.

27 *Royal Victoria Dock &* 29 *bridge*

Follow the map and take the first right along Mill Road, heading directly north – towards the soaring 19th-century chimney stack in the middle of a roundabout. On the right you will see the vast ㉖ **Millennium Mills**. A former flour mill, it was built in the early 1930s on the site of an earlier mill. It has become a distinctive landmark and symbol of post-industrial Britain, and has been used as a backdrop for a number of films, television programmes and music videos. These include the BBC's *Ashes to Ashes*, Derek Jarman's *The Last of England*, and videos for bands like The Smiths, Coldplay and Arctic Monkeys.

In the early 20th century the flour millers, W. Vernon & Sons, in Birkenhead, became famous for their 'Millennium' flour. They later joined forces with Spillers, and built here a vast complex of reinforced concrete granaries. The location was perfect as grain ships would arrive in the Thames and berth at the Royal Docks. The wheat was then removed from the ship by suction at the rate of two hundred tons an hour. With the closure of the Royal Docks in the 1980s the mill, as with many other industrial sites, closed or moved away.

Continue on to the reach the edge of ㉗ **Royal Victoria Dock**, the western dock of the Royal Docks complex. This was originally marshland, but the construction of great docks further west of here in the early 19th century led to vicious competition between the dock owners. They sought to outdo each other in building ever larger docks that could keep up with the increasing size of shipping, and also leapfrog their rivals. This was the first dock (opened in 1855) to accommodate large steam ships and was followed by the Royal Albert Dock to the east (1880), and the King George V Dock (1921) (south of Royal Albert Dock).

The three together formed the largest enclosed dock complex in the world with a water area of nearly 250 acres and an overall estate of 1100 acres. This is equivalent to the whole of central London from Hyde Park to Tower Bridge. The docks specialised in the import and unloading of foodstuffs, with rows of giant granaries and refrigerated warehouses being sited alongside the quays.

The opening of the Royal Victoria Dock in 1855 attracted many industries to this part of London. With easy access to raw materials, Silvertown and nearby Canning Town and West Ham together formed the largest manufacturing centre in the South of England, best known for engineering, chemical and food production.

Competition between the private dock owners in London resulted in ever-decreasing profits, with the economic future of the docks generally looking doubtful. A Royal Commission was appointed in 1900 to look into this problem, and the result was the creation of the Port of London Authority (PLA) in 1909 which took over the main docks in London, including the Royal Docks. The PLA continues to function to this day.

The Royal Docks were finally closed to shipping in 1981 after the introduction of containerisation by global shipping lines which required larger docks nearer the sea, such as at Tilbury. This closure – along with the decline of manufacturing in the area – has had a long-term impact on employment that is still being felt today.

By the water's edge you will see the 300 tonne steam coaster ㉘ **SS Robin**. Built in 1890 in the Thames Ironworks on the River Lea, it is the oldest example of its kind in the world. This is also the site of the launch of the battleship *HMS Albion* in 1898 which was one of the first such events to be filmed. The footage seems peaceful but the ship's launch created a large wave which destroyed a jetty and drowned 39 spectators.

From here walk over ㉙ **The Royal Victoria Dock Bridge** to the north side of

North Greenwich & Silvertown Walk

the dock. This spectacular high level footbridge was opened in 1998 and was designed to resemble the great ships that once filled the now-empty acres of water all around.

From here you can see the huge cranes that stand redundant along the dock edges, and planes taking off at City Airport to the east. You can also see the ③⓪ **ExCeL Centre** on the right as you cross the bridge. This exhibition space occupies 100 acres and opened in 2000. During the 2012 London Olympics a number of events were hosted here.

When you get down from the bridge on the other side, head left (westwards) along the edge of the dock until you reach the north side of ③① **IFS Cloud cable car**. From here you can return to North Greenwich Station and the end of the walk. ●

VISIT...

O2 Arena (see p.266)
Peninsula Square, SE10 0DX
www.theo2.co.uk

Brick Lane Music Hall (see p.282)
443 North Woolwich Rd, E16 2DA
www.bricklanemusichall.co.uk

**Greenwich Peninsula
Ecology Park** (see p.269)
SE10 0QZ
www.greenwichmarketlondon.com

**Thames Barrier
Information Centre** (see p.272)
1 Unity Way, Woolwich, SE18 5NJ
Open: Sat 10.30-15.30 (April-Oct)

Thames Barrier Park (see p.285)
North Woolwich Rd, E16 2HP

IFS Cloud Cable Car
Edmund Halley Way, SE10 0FR
www.tfl.gov.uk/modes/london-cable-car/

EAT, DRINK...

Anchor & Hope (see p.271)
2 Riverside Walk,
Charlton, SE7 7SS

Greenwich Yacht Club (see p.269)
Pear Tree Wharf, SE10 0BW
www.greenwichyachtclub.co.uk

View Café (see p.272)
North Greenwich Pier,
The Royal Arsenal Woolwich Pier,
SE7 8LX

Tower Hamlets Cemetery, see p.325

10 Whitechapel & Bow Walk

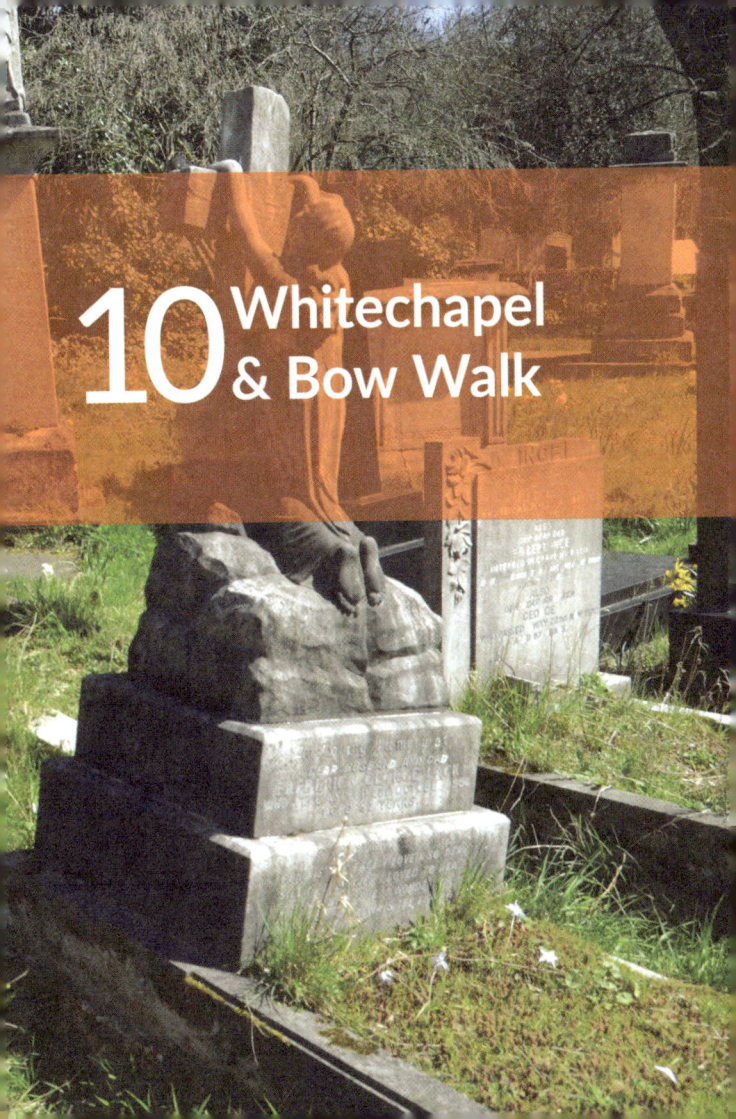

Whitechapel & Bow Walk

1. Working Lads' Institute
2. Former Royal London Hospital
3. Drinking fountain
4. Albion Brewery
5. Whitechapel post office
6. Blind Beggar public house
7. Mile End Waste
8. William Booth

9. Trinity Almshouses
10. Tower Hamlets Mission
11. Edward VII bust
12. Captain James Cook Memorial
13. Former Ocean Somali Community Centre
14. Wickham's department store
15. Genesis
16. Stepney Green
17. Daren Bread
18. Stepney Green Gardens
19. No 37 Stepney Green
20. Stepney Jewish School
21. Stepney Green Court
22. Dunstan Houses
23. Anchor Retail Park
24. former Adams House office block
25. Charrington House
26. Malplaquet House
27. Stepney Green underground
28. Mile End Place

- ㉙ Betahayim Velho cemetery
- ㉚ Albert Stern House
- ㉛ Mile End Hospital
- ㉜ Workhouse
- ㉝ Ashkenazi Jewish cemetery
- ㉞ Tower Hamlets local history library
- ㉟ Great Hall
- ㊱ Clock tower & drinking fountain
- ㊲ Betahayim Nuevo cemetery
- ㊳ Clement Attlee (monument)
- ㊴ Daniel Mendoza (blue plaque)
- ㊵ Ocean Estate
- ㊶ Regent's Canal
- ㊷ Mile End Park
- ㊸ Church of the Guardian Angels
- ㊹ Green Bridge
- ㊺ Onyx House
- ㊻ Tredegar Square
- ㊼ No 40 Tredegar Square
- ㊽ Morgan Arms
- ㊾ Boundary stone
- ㊿ Dr Barnardo's first lodgings
- 51 Charles Coborn (plaque)
- 52 St Clements's Hospital
- 53 Tower Hamlets Cemetery
- 54 Central Foundation School
- 55 George Lansbury (monument)
- 56 Sikh Gurdwara
- 57 Byas House
- 58 Green and gold clock
- 59 London mile post
- 60 Bow Road underground station
- 61 Police station
- 62 Bow Bells pub
- 63 Poplar Town Hall
- 64 Stratford Co-Operative & Industrial Society
- 65 Bryant & May match factory
- 66 Grove Hall Park
- 67 The Nunnery
- 68 St Mary's Church of Bow
- 69 William Gladstone (monument)

Whitechapel & Bow Walk

Start: Whitechapel underground station
Finish: Bow Road underground station
Distance: 5.25 miles

Leave the station to enter Whitechapel Road, normally crowded due to the street market. This was started by Irish immigrants in the 1850s, and later dominated by the Jewish community who arrived in London in large numbers from the 1880s. Today this is primarily a Bangladeshi market, their community making up more than 40% of the local population. Evidence of the constant waves of immigration that have passed through the East End will be a constant theme throughout this walk.

Right beside the underground station is a tall red-brick building – step back to look up at it. You can just make out the lettering at the top that indicates this was once the ❶ **Working Lads' Institute**. There are also old signs above the entrances that once led to a gymnasium and lecture hall. The Institute was founded in the 1870s by a merchant named Henry Hill, and moved to this building in the following decade. Its purpose was to provide distractions for boys over 13 years old after they had finished work, and keep them away from the temptations of the hundreds of local pubs that formed the social hub for many Eastenders.

In the 1890s the Institute was facing financial problems and was sold to a Methodist minister and social reformer named Revd Thomas Jackson. He developed it into the Whitechapel Mission, which today continues to look after hundreds of homeless people and is based at number 212 Whitechapel Road. The Lads' Institute building was the location for some of the inquests that took place into victims of Jack the Ripper in the late 1880s.

On the other side of the road is the facade of the ❷ **former Royal London Hospital** which opened on its present site in

1757, but has recently been converted into the Whitechapel Civic Centre which also serves as the headquarters for Tower Hamlets Council. Its most famous patient was Joseph Merrick (1862-1890), better known as the 'Elephant Man'. Merrick was terribly deformed through an illness that most medical experts think was neurofibromatosis. He was discovered appearing in a freak show on Whitechapel Road (very near the tube station) by a surgeon named Frederick Treves.

Treves managed to have Merrick admitted as a long-term patient at the hospital and he lived there until his death. He became something of an attraction for London's great and good, and his story was told in the film *The Elephant Man* (1980) starring John Hurt (as Merrick) and Antony Hopkins (as Treves). The inquest into his death was held by Wynne Edwin Baxter, who two years earlier in 1888 had conducted inquests on some of Jack the Ripper's victims.

On the side of the underground station, and opposite the former hospital building, is a ❸ **drinking fountain** erected in 1911 to commemorate the life of King Edward VII (1841-1910) – 'in grateful and loyal memory by the Jewish inhabitants of East London'. Edward was seen as being sympathetic to the Jewish community in an era when anti-Semitism was rife, and attracted criticism from some quarters for socialising with prominent Jews such as the financier and philanthropist Baron Nathaniel Rothschild, who he first met when they were students together at Cambridge.

Between 1880 and 1914, 150,000 Eastern European Jews arrived in the East End, fleeing the anti-Semitism that was triggered in Russia after the assassination of Tsar Alexander II in 1881. Among the immigrants were a small number of radicals and anarchists, who came to national prominence in late 1910 when a gang of Latvian Jewish anarchists killed three policemen and wounded two others during a robbery in nearby Houndsditch – the incident becoming known as the 'Houndsditch Murders'.

The gang escaped, but in January 1911 were tracked down to a house in nearby Sidney Street (seen later). They were attacked by the police and army under the command of the then Home Secretary, Winston Churchill. The gang members in the house, except for the enigmatic Peter the Painter, all died after the house caught fire, in what became known as the siege of Sidney Street. These brutal events shocked Edwardian London and this memorial was partly an attempt by the Jewish community to demonstrate their loyalty to the monarchy and state.

Retrace your steps east back towards the underground station (north side) and continue until on your left you pass the yellow brick structure and gates that are the remains of ❹ **Mann Crossman & Paulin's Albion Brewery**. You can still see the brewery name above the entrance gate. The brewery was founded in 1808 and later taken over by James Mann, who was joined by Robert Crossman and Thomas Paulin in the 1840s. It became one of London's great breweries, and employed hundreds of people. The brewery was the first place in Britain to produce bottled brown ale. It was later taken over by Watney's in 1959 and finally closed in 1979 – the building has now been converted into flats.

If you look over to the south side of Whitechapel Road (just past the hospital) you can see the ❺ **Whitechapel post and sorting office**. In 1927 a tiny underground railway was opened between this site and the Head District Sorting Office six miles away in Paddington. It enabled the Post Office to move letters across the capital more efficiently than using lorries, but it was expensive to run and finally mothballed in 2003.

Continue on to see the ❻ **Blind Beggar pub**. This is infamous for being where Ronnie Kray shot and killed George Cornell in 1966. He later helped his brother Reggie kill Jack 'the Hat' McVitie and both brothers were jailed in 1969. The Krays grew up just around the corner from here on Vallance Road (number 178) and owned a number of establishments in the vicinity.

An inn was established here before 1654, but the current building dates from 1895. Back in 1904 a member of the Blind Beggar Gang – a group of pick-pockets – stabbed another man in the eye with an umbrella and killed him. In 2011 a group of Asian men attacked the pub in the mistaken belief that members of the far-right English Defence League were inside. Two of the men were jailed for the attack.

Whitechapel & Bow Walk

7

8

Continue east, crossing over Cambridge Heath Road to enter Mile End Road and pause for a few moments by the trees. This area is known as **7 Mile End Waste**. The road leading south of here is Sidney Street, where the siege of 1911 took place, although the house at number 100 no longer exists.

On this walk you will follow old London roads such as Whitechapel Road, Mile End Road and Bow Road, that for centuries have connected the capital to Essex – all now part of the A11. The districts along the way (from west to east) – Whitechapel, Stepney, Mile End and Bow – were, until the 18th century, mainly small hamlets that lay along these roads.

However, over time as London spread out, these villages began to merge into each other. During the 19th century in particular, the fields in between were built over for residential streets, factories and railways. The old districts were incorporated into new boroughs, making it harder for them to maintain their original identities.

As the population of London swelled in the 19th century, the parish authorities struggled to keep up with their traditional duties, particularly looking after the poor. By 1900 various Metropolitan Boroughs were created that incorporated these historic districts. For example the Metropolitan Borough of Stepney covered Mile End Old Town (where you are now), Mile End New Town (east of Spitalfields), Spitalfields and Wapping. The Borough of Poplar covered traditionally distinct districts such as Poplar, Bromley-By-Bow (formerly Bromley-St-Leonard) and the Isle of Dogs.

In turn, these Metropolitan Boroughs were folded into the new London Borough of Tower Hamlets in 1965 – making it even harder today to identify where one old district ends and another begins. However it is generally held that the true East End lies within the boundaries of the borough of Tower Hamlets.

As you stand in Mile End Waste you are in the district of Stepney. The narrow strip of trees is all that is left of the common ground that lay on either side of the road. Mile End Waste has historically been a gathering place for Londoners – for troops in Tudor times and later on for people wishing to make speeches or stage marches.

Look out for two memorials to **William Booth** (1829-1912) – a bust and also a statue depicting him preaching. Trained as a pawnbroker, Booth became a Methodist preacher and chose this spot in July 1865 to begin preaching to the locals. He also used to favour a spot outside the Blind Beggar, lecturing those inside on their moral failings.

Perhaps unsurprisingly, Booth and his growing band of supporters frequently encountered violence and intimidation from locals, some of whom were funded by local brewers to fight any visible sign of the temperance movement that became a significant force in Victorian London. Booth went on to found the Salvation Army, which today operates in around 125 countries. The massive

Whitechapel & Bow Walk

Booth House on Whitechapel Road (number 153-175) provided food and shelter to the homeless in the area for many years before its closure in 2018.

In July 1888 the striking Match Girls of the Bryant & May factory in Bow held a public meeting on Mile End Waste attracting thousands of supporters. Their strike went on to change the history of industrial relations in this country and you will find out more about them later on in the walk.

Walk along the north side of Mile End Waste to reach the **9 Trinity Almshouses** (look out for the model ships). These were built in 1695 and (according to London lore) were designed by Christopher Wren. The funding for their construction came from Captain Mudd of Ratcliff who left a legacy to provide accommodation for 28 'decayed' ship masters or their widows.

While immigration is a key theme on this walk, these almshouses remind us that the history of the East End is also closely connected to London's historical status as one of the greatest ports in the world – a position it retained well into the 20th century. Many sailors lived in Stepney between sea-voyages, attracted (prior to the 19th century) by its semi-rural setting that was nevertheless close to the wharves, quays and later, docks on the Thames. Thousands of Irish immigrants also arrived in the East End to help build the docks (such as St Katherine's Dock, London Docks and West India Docks) and many stayed on to work there as dockers when the docks were completed.

The Trinity Almshouses were saved in the 1890s thanks to a campaign led by Victorian luminaries such as Walter Besant, Octavia Hill and William Morris. Today the houses are largely privately owned. The impressive Edwardian building to the left was home of the Albion Brewery engineer and dates from 1905.

On the right-hand side of the almshouses is the ⑩ **Tower Hamlets Mission** – a Christian charity that helps the homeless suffering from addiction. It was founded by Frederick Charrington (1850-1936), a member of the Charrington dynasty who once owned a huge brewery nearby.

Frederick was due to join the family business, but his life changed after seeing a poor woman being battered by her drunken husband after he left the Rising Sun – a Charrington pub on Cambridge Heath Road. Shocked at the effect alcohol was having on the poor, he devoted the rest of his life to campaigning against brewers, pubs, brothels and their corrupting influence.

Charrington would spend his days noting down any illicit activities he could see taking place in his black book, and directing the police to shut down hundreds of illegal drinking dens and brothels. While Charrington received numerous beatings from angry local pimps, he was clearly no pushover, and was once sued for kicking a brothel worker in the stomach. His attentions were so feared that one local madam is said to have died from a heart attack after learning Charrington was on his way to confront her.

Charrington founded a Great Assembly Hall just here (beside the almshouses), and established the Tower Hamlets Mission in 1870. The Great Assembly Hall could hold 5,000 people and provided various activities to attract the poor including a 'coffee tavern' and bookshop. Notable people associated with the old hall include Karl Marx's daughter Eleanor Marx-Aveling and William Morris, who spoke at a meeting here in 1890 against the Russian persecution of Jews.

Whitechapel & Bow Walk

The Great Hall was bombed during the Blitz in 1941; however Charrington's Tower Hamlets Mission survives to this day. Today, it runs a three stage residential drug and alcohol service for men who are suffering from addiction. As well as working in the East End, Charrington also purchased Osea Island – off the Essex coast – and set up a retreat for those suffering from addictions. The ominous causeway leading up to the Island featured heavily in the 2012 horror film *The Woman in Black* starring *Harry Potter* star Daniel Radcliffe.

On Mile End Waste (outside 39 Mile End Road) look out for another ⓫ **bust to Edward VII** – the inscription reads 'erected by a few freemasons of the Eastern District of London 1911'.

Cross over now to the south side of Mile End Road. Stepney is first recorded as Stybbanhythe in around c.1000 AD and is thought to refer to the landing place of a man named Stybba. It was the only place in the East End to be named in the Doomsday survey of the late 11th century, and the Manor of Stepney was owned by the Bishop of London. Once seen as the capital of the East End, Stepney now straddles the streets between Mile End Road and Commercial Road with the parish church of St Dunstan's at its centre.

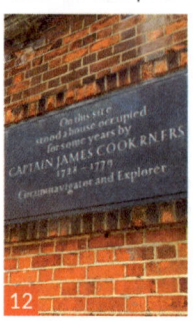

Like other adjoining districts, Stepney was still semi-rural for much of the 18th century. However industrialisation and the growth of London's population, meant the area was fully urbanised by 1900. This population growth was fuelled by the arrival of the Huguenots (from the 17th century), the Irish in the 18th and 19th centuries, and the Ashkenazi Jews from the 1880s.

Look out for a large memorial on the front of number 88 which remembers ⓬ **Captain James Cook** (1728-1779) – the most

Whitechapel & Bow Walk

famous of the many sea captains who lived around here in the 17th and 18th centuries. He occupied a house here (now demolished) with his wife. It must have been strange for him to adjust to life back in Stepney after returning from his epic voyages.

Continue westwards on the same side of Mile End Road. Shortly after the Cook memorial you will see number 102 that was until recently the ⑬ **Ocean Somali Community Centre**, a convenient reminder of immigrant communities who are shaping East End life in the early 21st century. The centre has moved further east but continues to provide assistance to the Somali community many of whom live at the Ocean Estate nearby.

Continue on and look over to the north side of Mile End Road. You will see a small building wedged in beside two much larger constructions that look like they should have been joined together. These main structures were once occupied by the ⑭ **Wickham's department store**. The store was opened in 1927 and named after a draper named William Wickham who opened the first shop on this site in 1850. From the very start, the Wickham family had to deal with the Spielgelhalters – a Christian Moravian family who had arrived from Germany in the 1820s and who opened their jewellery shop right in the middle of the road.

The department store developers could not persuade the Spielgelhalters to sell and so had to build their new department store around them. Wickham's becoming known as the Harrods of the East End. However by 1969 it was no longer profitable and closed down. The Spielgelhalters had the last laugh as they managed to stick it out until the 1980s.

Next door is a small cinema called **Genesis** which was host to one of the most iconic moments in East End gangster history when on February 27th 1963 the musical film *Sparrers Can't Sing* was premiered here. Filmed locally and starring Barbara Windsor, the Kray twins had a fleeting role in the film. They helped host the premiere, attended by celebrities including Lord Snowdon – although his wife Princess Margaret decided not to come, no doubt conscious of the publicity had she had been seen associating with criminals. The film itself is definitely worth watching for a glimpse of the East End in the early 60s.

These were the glory years for the Krays, and years later Windsor recalled how she had 'arrived in a Roller... There were thousands of people lining the Mile End Road, cheering and waving flags. Evidently Ronnie and Reggie had turned them all out of their houses... Stanley Baker and Roger Moore stayed for dinner. Then we had a drink at the Krays' club, The Kentucky, across the road from the cinema'.

A pub and early music hall known as the Eagle was built on this site in 1848. It was later replaced by the much larger Paragon Theatre of Varieties in 1885, featuring performers such as Charlie Chaplin. By the First World War, the age of the music hall was being challenged and Paragon was converted into a cinema – the current structure dates from 1939.

Continue westwards on the south side of Mile End Road, passing a mix of attractive buildings dating from the 18th and 19th centuries, alongside drab flats and uninspiring office blocks that were mostly built on bomb sites after the Second World War.

In a few minutes head right down **Stepney Green**, the centre of a conservation area and one of the prettiest streets in the district. It connects Mile End Road to the parish church of St Dunstan's to the south – the historic centre of Stepney. On the right side look out for the ghost advertisement for **Daren Bread**

– 'best for health'. Daren bread was a brown loaf that was produced at Walton's store in Market Lavington and was particularly popular in the first half of the 20th century.

The name Stepney Green was actually a 19th-century invention and the street was originally called Mile End Green. In the 17th and 18th centuries many fine houses were built on this road, which was at that time surrounded by fields and favoured by sea captains and merchants who wanted to be near central London, while benefiting from the clean rural air. Even today you notice the sound of traffic from Mile End Road slowly fades and you feel as if you are in another part of London altogether.

As you walk down Stepney Green you see a strip of green lined by trees – this is ⑱ **Stepney Green Gardens**, created in the 1870s out of the last remnant of Mile End Green. Bear left and walk around the eastern side.

You will see a number of fine old houses on the eastern side, and in particular look out for ⑲ **number 37** which dates from the 1690s. In 1714 the house was bought by the widow of the East India Company's governor of Bombay, a sign that this area was still a place for the well-to-do. As Jewish immigration increased, the property became a Jewish old people's home in the 1890s. A Jewish hospital was also located beside number 37 in the early 20th century.

Continue south down from number 37. Shortly on the left you will see the large red-brick complex that originally housed the **20** **Stepney Jewish School** – look out for the monogram SJS which is still visible on the iron gates that date from 1906. The school later moved to Ilford – part of general movement of the Jewish community away from the East End after World War II. But when the school was built some 125,000 Jews lived in the area.

By the second half of the 19th century Stepney was blighted by overcrowded slums. In the decades before state or local council-built estates, the only alternative to the slums were housing developments funded by a number of philanthropic organisations that sprung up in London from the 1870s.

Continue south to see an example – **21** **Stepney Green Court**. This was built in 1896 by the 4% Industrial Dwellings Company – a Jewish philanthropic organisation chaired by Edward VII's great friend, Nathaniel Rothschild (1840-1915). Rothschild was open-minded enough to also act as a trustee of the London Mosque Fund. This began in 1910 and operated for several decades to provide prayer facilities – and eventually a mosque – for Muslims in London. It is unlikely Rothschild could have imagined that within 100 years nearly all the Jewish synagogues in the East End would have closed.

From here cross over Stepney Green Road to the west side and walk back towards Mile End Road. On the left-hand side look out for the red-brick and ivy covered **22** **Dunstan Houses**. These were built by the Christian-influenced East End Dwellings Company in 1899. This company was founded in the early 1880s to 'house the very poor while realizing some profit' and by 1906 had built around 15 housing blocks. One of its founders was the clergyman and reformer Samuel Augustus Barnett (1844-1913) – also responsible for Tonybee Hall in nearby Spitalfields.

21 Stepney Green Court

Whitechapel & Bow Walk

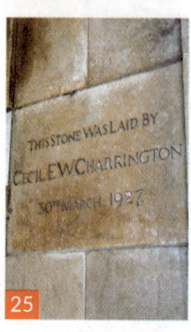

Although a little far away to include on this walk (unless you have time), St Dunstan's – the 1000 year old parish church of Stepney – can be found about half a mile away from here if you continue down Stepney Green. However, on this walk we re-trace our steps north up Stepney Green to reach Mile End Road. When you get there, cross over to ㉓ **Anchor Retail Park** on the other side.

This occupies the site of the former Anchor Brewery, which was owned by Charrington family mentioned earlier. Not much is left of the old brewery buildings, but if you continue down Mile End Road you will see the remains of firstly the ㉔ **former Adams House office block** and beside it, as you turn the corner into Cephas Avenue, ㉕ **Charrington House**. At the doorway to Charrington House you will see a foundation stone recalling it was laid by Cecil Charrington in 1927.

The original brewery was founded in 1738 and moved here in 1757. In the following decade John Charrington purchased an interest in the business, later taking it over completely. By the early 19th century this was the second biggest brewery in London and during its heyday the Charrington family took over another forty breweries in London. Two of its most famous brands were Anchor Stout and Toby Ales. The Charrington family became one of the wealthiest families in the district, and also a major employer, notwithstanding Frederick's efforts to turn the local populace away from alcohol. In 1967 the brewery merged with Bass to become Bass Charrington and production here ceased in 1975.

Continue eastward and on your left you will shortly come across ㉖ **Malplaquet House**, a beautifully restored 1741 mansion that was once home to brewer Henry Charrington. For decades the house lay hidden behind old shop fronts. Owned by the Spitalfields Trust and uninhabited for over a century, it was sold to Tim Knox, the former director of the Sir John Soane's Museum and landscape gardener Todd Longstaffe-Gowan. They spent 5 years carefully restoring the house to its former glory.

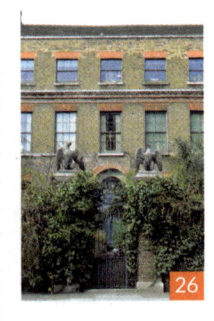

Mile End was once a rural hamlet first recorded in 1288, its name signifying that it was one mile from Aldgate. In 1381, 60,000 rebels from Essex camped here during the Peasants' Revolt, and a young Richard II rode out to Mile End to discuss their grievances. As houses began to form along the road, the area became known for a while as Mile End Old Town – a name that distinguished it from Mile End New Town, the area directly east of Brick Lane.

As you continue on the north side you reach ㉗ **Stepney Green underground station**, which dates from 1902. The extension of the transport system encouraged even more people to settle here as commuting became easier.

As you continue along the north side of Mile End Road, you cross over Globe Road. This was probably named after a tavern that stood in the vicinity in the 18th century or even earlier, and the road leads up to an area east of Bethnal Green known as Globe Town. This district was originally developed as residential streets in the early 1800s – the developers were targeting artisans and the growing number of silk weavers then living in Bethnal Green.

28 Mile End Place

Whitechapel & Bow Walk

After you pass Globe Road, look out for a small street on the left (between numbers 241 and 245) that leads into ㉘ **Mile End Place**. This contains a number of pretty 19th-century workers cottages and – like Stepney Green – feels a world away from the traffic and fast food outlets that dominate this part of the A11. David Bailey's photographs of these cottages were included in his 2012 exhibition of East End photographs – Bailey being famously from this area.

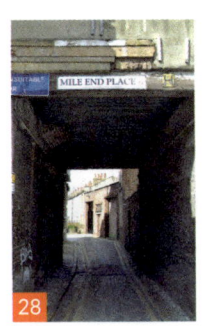

Behind the wall at the end of the street, and just to the east (behind Albert Stern House) lie two of the most historic Jewish cemeteries in the country. Their foundation can be traced back to the 1650s when Oliver Cromwell permitted the Jews to return to England – a historic moment following the expulsion of all Jews from the country in 1290. Members of the Sephardi community (Jews of Spanish and Portuguese origin) were among the first to settle in London. They founded a synagogue and naturally also needed somewhere to bury their dead. The authorities permitted them to use a few acres out of the way in Mile End, then still largely open fields. This cemetery – known as the ㉙ **Betahayim Velho** or old cemetery – opened in 1657 and closed in 1742. Initially Jews from the Eastern European tradition – known as the Ashkenazi community – were also buried there. However, they decided to open their own neighbouring cemetery in 1696 which continued to operate until 1852. The entrance door to the cemetery can be found on Alderney Road just to the north of Mile End Place, but access to the cemetery is by appointment only.

Return to the Mile End Road and continue in the same direction. Look out on the left for ㉚ **Albert Stern House** (at number 253). Now part of Queen Mary College, this used to be a home for elderly Sephardi Jews. It is named after Lt Col Sir Albert Gerald Stern (1878-1966), who helped develop Britain's first tank in World War I and was a member of the Stern banking dynasty. The building dates from 1913.

Follow the map to head left up Bancroft Road, the entrance of which is through the College's Faculty of Engineering (see left). Shortly you pass ③① **Mile End Hospital** – walk into the entrance and bear right towards the imposing red brick building. This was originally a ③② **workhouse** that opened in 1859. It replaced an earlier workhouse that was opened in 1803 and stood just to the north of the Jewish cemeteries. If you look closely you can see the foundation stone which records that it was laid in 1858 by Spencer Charrington, chairman of the workhouse's Board of Guardians, and in later decades an MP for the area. His involvement with the workhouse is perhaps ironic given that many poor people drank away their paltry earnings in the Charrington family's public houses.

To protect children born here from the stigma of being born in a workhouse, their birth certificates gave their address as simply The Lodge, Bancroft Road. Despite many in the wealthier classes despairing that workhouses created a dependency culture, the reality was that the poor dreaded ending up there. It meant families being split up, mandatory labour more akin to a prison, and often abysmal living conditions that resulted in high sickness and mortality rates. In 1908, 11 serving and former members of the Board of Guardians of this workhouse were imprisoned after being convicted of taking bribes from a local builder in return for construction contracts. In 1930, the site was taken over by London County Council and became part of Mile End Hospital.

Continue up Bancroft Road and after a couple of minutes on the right you will see behind some railings (opposite a row of shops) another small ㉝ **Ashkenazi Jewish cemetery** that was connected to the Maiden Lane Synagogue in Covent Garden which closed in the 19th century.

Retrace your steps, passing both the hospital and the ㉞ **Tower Hamlets local history library**. The latter contains a large number of historic East End archives and is worth a visit.

Continue south to rejoin Mile End Road and turn left to see the main building of Queen Mary College. The college stands on the site of Bancroft's hospital, school and almshouses, which were founded in 1737 and made possible because of a generous bequest provided the decade before by a wealthy City draper,

Francis Bancroft. His tomb can be seen in the church of St Helen's, Bishopsgate. The school was run by the Drapers' Company – one of the 12 great City Livery companies. The school eventually moved out of London in the 1880s to Woodford Green in Essex; however, the Drapers' Company still provides scholarships and funding for pupils from Bancroft's original bequest.

The school site was sold and used to build the People's Palace – a philanthropic venture aimed at bringing education and respectable entertainments to the local residents. The People's Palace was opened by Queen Victoria in 1887 and became known as 'The Albert Hall of East London'. It offered recreational and educational facilities including swimming baths, library, technical school, winter gardens, gymnasium, art school, lecture rooms and rooms for various social activities.

The original Great Hall of the People's Palace was enormous, but was destroyed by fire in 1931. It was rebuilt in the course of the next few years and during this period the educational part of the complex was split off into the East London College, later becoming today's Queen Mary College. The People's Palace continued as a place of entertainment until 1954, when it was acquired by Queen Mary's and incorporated into the current campus. The University recently re-opened the People's Palace after a major renovation programme and it hosts regulator orchestra performances and other entertainments. Notable former students include Bruce Dickinson, lead singer with Iron Maiden, although on a more serious note five Nobel laureates have either been students or academic staff at the college.

On your left you will shortly see the ㉟ **Great Hall**. As mentioned earlier, this was built in the 1930s after the original was destroyed in a fire. It was opened in 1937 by King George VI and Queen Mary (after whom the college was named).

The elegant art deco exterior is most notable for its relief sculptures depicting Drama, Music, Dance, Brotherhood and Sport sculpted by Eric Gill (1882-1940). Gill was also a designer of typefaces (his most famous is Gill Sans), a printmaker and a member of the influential Arts and Crafts movement. His work also adorns the exterior of the BBC's Broadcasting House in Great Portland Street. A complex man, Gill's reputation has suffered in recent years after his diaries revealed abuse of his children, the family dog, and an incestuous affair with his sister.

Next to the Great Hall is the ㊱ **clock tower and drinking fountain**. It was erected in 1890

Whitechapel & Bow Walk

by the Jewish financier and philanthropist Herbert Stern (1851-1919) in memory of his father – a Portuguese banker. Herbert inherited £2 million from his father, and among his many philanthropic acts was the contribution of funds to purchase works of art for the National Gallery. During World War I he also bought the Hotel Astoria in Paris solely as a place for injured British troops to be treated. When the tower was built it stood alongside the original People's Palace, and you can see reference to this institution on the inscription.

Following the map, continue eastwards until you reach the main campus entrance on your left. To the right of the gates is a campus map with directions to the ㊲ **Betahayim Nuevo – or 'new' Sephardi cemetery**. In the past this cemetery has been difficult to see but the university has recently made this historic place more accessible by installing a viewing platform. It was first opened in 1725 after the old cemetery became too crowded. Although many

㊲ Betahayim Nuevo or 'new' Sephardi cemetery

graves were moved when the college was extended, it remains a dramatic sight to see the flat tombstones laid out in the middle of the busy campus. It is a Sephardi tradition to lay the gravestones in this fashion, symbolising that we are all equal in death.

Walk just a little further past the Jewish cemetery toward the university library and you will find the very fine monument of ㊳ **Clement Attlee** by Frank Forster. In a recent poll of British academics Attlee was voted the greatest Prime Minister of the 20th century and so it seems rather strange that his likeness should be sited in a quiet courtyard of an east London university rather than the central locations of Churchill, Gladstone and Disreali. Attlee's monument originally stood outside Limehouse Library, but when this shut his figure was boarded up and left for several years. This new location is at least an improvement on the situation and is perhaps fitting considering Attlee's early career as a social worker based at Toynbee Hall in the east end.

Just around the corner from the Attlee monument, high on the wall, is a plaque to another east end legend, bare-knuckle boxer ㊴ **Daniel Mendoza**. A blue plaque to the Jewish pugilist is featured in the Bethnal Green & Hackney Wick Walk (see page 342 for more details).

Leaving the university grounds, look to your right to see in the distance the sprawling ㊵ **Ocean Estate** – typical of the post-war housing estates erected by local authorities to replace decrepit slums and the large number of residential buildings flattened during the Blitz. The drive for better housing, a welfare state and the establishment of the NHS were all the work of the Labour government under the leadership of Clement Attlee between 1945 and 51.

Continue east on the northside of Mile End Road. Soon you cross over the ㊶ **Regent's Canal**, which stretches from the Paddington arm of the Grand Union Canal to Limehouse Basin by the Thames. It is over eight miles long, and was completed in the 1820s. It linked the Port

Whitechapel & Bow Walk

of London to the rest of the national canal system and, in the era before a developed railway network and modern roads, many Victorian industrialists decided to take advantage of the canal and build their factories in this part of London.

Almost immediately after the canal you pass under the 80 acre ㊷ **Mile End Park**. This was planned in the late 1940s and has been extended several times over the last few decades. The park occupies former industrial and residential areas, but in the 1840s and 50s a park had been established in the area called The New Globe Tavern Gardens. The gardens were the idea of Thomas Gardner who owned the tavern. At the garden's height thousands of people would flock to see concerts, fireworks, light shows and even hot-air balloons. The success of the gardens proved short lived and was probably not helped by the establishment of Victoria Park, just a mile from here. By 1860 Gardner had sold the tavern and its garden for redevelopment. The new park is a welcome continuation of the pleasure garden tradition and is well worth a visit.

Shortly you will see on your left the imposing ㊸ **Roman Catholic Church of the Guardian Angels** that was first opened in 1868 (the current building dates from 1903). Until 1791 the Penal Laws made it illegal to celebrate Catholic Mass in England, but once these were repealed new Catholic missions targeted the East End – popular particularly among the Irish immigrant population.

Continuing on, walk under the award winning 🟠 **Green Bridge**. This was designed by CZWG Architects and opened in 2000. As you pass under, be sure to walk up the steps along the side and climb up to the top – it offers a fantastic view over this part of London and in particular towards Canary Wharf.

The Blitz had a devastating effect on this part of London, destroying over a third of homes in Stepney alone. This forced thousands of Eastenders to move away, and many never returned. Mile End was hit by the first V-1 flying bomb to strike London on 13 June 1944 – it exploded by the railway bridge on Grove Road killing eight people and injuring 30 more.

As you continue eastwards after the Green Bridge look out for Grove Road running to the north. The artist Rachel Whiteread famously made a cast – entitled *House* – of the inside of a condemned Victorian terraced house at number 193 on this road. *House* won the Turner Prize in 1993 but was itself demolished by Tower Hamlets Council in 1994, to accommodate an extension to Mile End Park. Critics were divided on its merits, although the *Independent* at the time described it as 'one of the most extraordinary and imaginative sculptures created by an English artist this century'.

Continue on past Mile End underground station on the north side. In 1902, the writer Jack London (1876-1916) spent several weeks in the East End, among some of the 500,000 people then estimated to be living in poverty in London. He turned this experience into the seminal study of London entitled *The People of the Abyss* (1903). In the book, he recalls walking with two poverty-striken men on the way to Poplar Workhouse along Mile End Road – 'a wide thoroughfare, cutting the heart of East London, and there were tens of thousands of people abroad on it'. He notices his companions keep stooping down, and eventually he realises with shock what is happening, 'From the slimy, spittle-drenched, sidewalk, they were picking up bits of orange peel, apple skin, and grape stems, and, they were eating them... And this, between six and seven o'clock in the evening of August 20, year of our Lord 1902, in the heart of the greatest, wealthiest, and most powerful empire the world has ever seen.'

As you continue along on the north side you pass on the left the unusual looking ㊺ **Onyx House**, dating from 1986, and just beside that a Territorial Army building. This stands on the site of Deaconess House, which was opened in 1879 by Dr Barnardo (1845-1905) – the famous social reformer who created a number of homes to look after destitute children.

While not on the walk route, the excellent Ragged School Museum lies on the south-west corner of Mile End Park on Copperfield Road. The museum building was originally used by Barnardo to educate poor children between 1877 and 1908 and is definitely worth a visit if you want to find out more about the awful social conditions that so troubled Booth, Barnardo, Charrington and Jack London.

46 Tredegar Square

Whitechapel & Bow Walk

In 1870s Charrington and the Reverend George Reynolds spread rumours that Barnardo had had an affair with his landlady – who was a prostitute – during his days as a student at the London Hospital. The men also suggested Barnardo was secretly lining his own pockets with money raised ostensibly to fund his charitable work – one of a number of allegations that dogged Barnardo for the rest of his life.

Follow the map to reach the magnificent **46 Tredegar Square**. Built in 1828, this square is regarded as the grandest in the East End. It was built on land owned by Sir Charles Morgan, Baron of Tredegar, whose ancestral home was in Newport in Wales which explains why a number of streets around here have Welsh names. The nearby Tredegar Estate was largely developed between 1820 and 1860.

In 1875 the square was at the centre of a sensational murder case. A wealthy brush manufacturer named Henry Wainwright lived with his family at **47 number 40**. He lived a secret life, conducting many affairs, but when one turned sour he killed his mistress and buried her body under the floor of his factory in Whitechapel. Later when the factory was sold, he had to move the body and was caught red-handed with the dismembered and rotting body-parts badly wrapped in parcel-paper. He was tried and publicly hanged, still protesting his innocence.

Follow the map on the north side of the square along Morgan Street. At the corner with Coborn Road is the impressive looking **48 Morgan Arms**, which was founded in 1892 and is now a respected gastropub. It is an excellent place to stop for lunch and symbolic of how this part of the East End continues to have pockets of significant wealth.

Whitechapel & Bow Walk

From the pub turn south down Coborn Road and almost immediately on the right, about six feet up on the wall, you will see a ㊽ **boundary stone** from 1885 inscribed 'M.E.O.T' – this refers to Mile End Old Town.

Cross over Coborn Road and down Coborn Street, which bends round to the right. A plaque outside number 30 (opposite the school) marks ㊾ **Dr Barnardo's first lodgings** in London. There is also a plaque on the school exterior that remembers a superstar of the music hall named ㊿ **Charles Coborn** (1853-1945). His real name was Charles Whitton McCallum, however he decided to take his stage name from the place he was living in. Coborn became most famous for his rendition of the songs *The Man Who Broke the Bank of Monte Carlo* and *Two Lovely Black Eyes*.

Continue down Coborn Street to reach Mile End Road again. Cross over and head slightly westwards stopping outside the colourful former entrance to the now closed ❺ **St Clements's Hospital**. For much of the 19th century part of the area to the south was occupied by the Merchant Seamen's Orphan Asylum and a workhouse. Another link with the area's maritime past, the Asylum was founded in 1827 to look after the orphans of people lost at sea while serving in the merchant navy. It moved out of London in 1862 and today – now known as Bearwood College – is based in Berkshire.

The adjoining workhouse was originally built in the late 1840s for the Board of Guardians of the City of London Union.

Whitechapel & Bow Walk

In the 1870s the workhouse became a medical infirmary and then, in 1936, a psychiatric unit named St Clements. In 1968 this unit became part of the London Hospital and was eventually closed in 2005. The huge former hospital building has recently been redeveloped for community housing.

Follow the map down Brokesley Street. Ahead you will see the green urban woodland of ㊾ **Tower Hamlets Cemetery**. Turn right at the end of Brokesley Street and walk until you reach the main entrance to the cemetery on the corner with Southern Grove.

This atmospheric 27 acre site was opened in 1841 and was used for burials until 1966. By then around 350,000 Eastenders had been laid to rest here. It was founded in an era when London's growing population meant the old churchyards had become too full for new burials. A change in the law permitted companies to found larger cemeteries further away from the centre of the capital and this place was one of London's 'Magnificent Seven' – the others being the cemeteries at Highgate, Nunhead, West Norwood, Kensal Green, Brompton and Abney Park.

During the Victorian era between 60-80% of all burials here were in public graves, usually indicating that the family of the deceased could not afford a funeral. Some of these public graves were 40 feet deep and could hold up to 30 bodies.

Today the cemetery has been transformed into a tranquil nature reserve. People buried here include Dr Rees Ralph Llewellyn, who performed the autopsy on Jack the Ripper victim Mary Ann Nichols. A number of victims of the 1943 Bethnal Green Disaster are also buried here. A memorial to the disaster has recently been erected outside the underground station where 173 people lost their lives in the worst British civilian disaster of World War II (see page 341).

When you have finished looking around the cemetery, exit through one of the gates on the north side and walk up British Street turning left at Merchant Street to reach Mile End Road again. This is also the start of Bow Road which is the next section of the A11 running eastwards.

Cross over to the other (north) side of Bow Road to the ❺❹ **Central Foundation School**. It was originally known as Coborn School for Girls, its origins dating back to 1701 when Prisca Coborn – the widow of a wealthy brewer – bequeathed money in her will to establish a free school for 50 poor children. The school was originally near Bow Church but moved here in the 1890s.

Continue east on the north side and stop at the junction with Harley Grove. There is a memorial here to the MP and Poplar Mayor ❺❺ **George Lansbury** (1859-1940). Lansbury was one of the best known radical politicians of his day and was at the forefront of several progressive campaigns. He was elected as a local MP but in 1911 resigned his seat to fight (and lose) a by-election on a 'Votes For Women' ticket. He was also twice elected Mayor of Poplar. During the first half of the 20th century, Poplar became famous for pursuing an aggressive programme of social reform – so radical at times that it gave rise to the term 'Poplarism'.

53 Tower Hamlets Cemetery

Whitechapel & Bow Walk

In 1921, when Lansbury was mayor, the Poplar council defied the government and refused to levy high rates on the poor. The 30 councillors were ordered to appear before a judge, and they marched to the court in a grand procession of 2,000 supporters. The councillors were jailed for six weeks for contempt of court. Lansbury went on to become leader of the Labour Party (1931-35) and he lived very near this memorial, although his family house was destroyed during the Blitz. His granddaughter was the actress Angela Lansbury (1925-2022), who a few years ago erected a memorial to him at Bow Church (seen later in the walk).

Following the map up Harley Grove you will see a **56 Sikh Gurdwara** (or place of worship). A testament to the changing social framework of the East End, this was originally founded as a Congregationalist Chapel in 1836. It became a synagogue in 1927 and then a Gurdwara in 1979.

Follow the map down Benworth Street, and look out on the right for **57 Byas House**, which dates from 1932. The central part of the entrance contains the coat of arms of Lansbury's radical Poplar Borough Council – a reminder of the kind of decent social housing erected before World War II in this district.

Continue eastwards then turn right on Alfred Street to rejoin Bow Road. At the junction look up to see a **58 green and gold clock** dedicated to Minnie Lansbury. She was George's daughter-in-law – herself a committed political activist and suffragette who served time in prison for the rates rebellion. One of the 30 jailed councillors, she contracted pneumonia in Holloway Prison and died six weeks after her release aged only 32. On the wall beneath the clock are two plaques also remembering her.

Whitechapel & Bow Walk

Near the clock and facing Bow Road is an easily overlooked but rare example of a ⑤⑨ **London mile post** which dates from 1807. It tells us the distance from St Mary's Whitechapel is two miles and that it is a further one and a half miles from Stratford.

Cross over to ⑥⓪ **Bow underground station** on the southside, which was opened in 1902. The area of Bow received its name from the bow-shaped bridge built here in the 12th century after Queen Mathilda – King Henry I's wife – almost drowned trying to cross the River Lea. The area was originally part of Stratford and was later recorded as Stratford atte Bow (or Stratford at the arched bridge) in around 1279. This was almost certainly designed to help distinguish it – being located in Middlesex – from the Stratford found on the other side of the bridge in Essex. Eventually Stratford was dropped from the area's name and it just became known as Bow.

Continue past Bow underground station, looking out for the ⑥① **police station** on the north side which dates from 1903 and was designed by John Dixon Butler, who designed 200 police stations and courts as architect and surveyor to the Metropolitan Police. The station still has stables at the rear and held suffragette Sylvia Pankhurst (1882-1960) in 1913 after she was arrested for breaking windows.

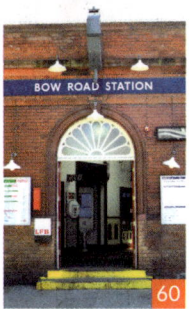

Bow became the heartland of a radical splinter group of the suffragette movement after 1912 when Sylvia Pankhurst – daughter of the suffragette leader Emmeline – based her activities here. She rented a shop at 198 Bow Road (now demolished but located opposite Bow church) and painted a sign outside that read 'Votes for Women'. She established a campaign office there for the Women's Social and Political Union, and also various other facilities nearby – such as a Women's Hall (not far from here on Old Ford Road to the north).

When the First World War broke out, Sylvia disagreed with her mother's support for the war effort, and took a more radical path. She organised cheap restaurants to feed the hungry, as well as a toy factory to provide work for unemployed women. She also worked with George Lansbury when he ran on a 'Votes for Women' ticket as described above. Sylvia had an extraordinary life and when she died in Ethiopia she was given a state funeral by Emperor Haile Selassie.

Continue along Bow Road looking out for the Victorian 62 **Bow Bells pub** on the right. It is worth a visit to see the photographs on the walls of how the area used to look, including the pub's football team in early 20th century. There are also a few newspaper clippings that report how in past years the pub was haunted by a ghost who liked to flush the toilet whilst ladies were sitting on the seat. A séance was held to try and flush the ghost out but was unsuccessful – you have been warned.

Follow the map to the junction with Fairfield Road. On the opposite corner is an Art Deco style business centre that was constructed in 1937 and was originally the site of 63 **Poplar Town Hall**. Cross over to the north side of Bow Road to take a closer look. You can see the representations of artisans who built this town hall

Whitechapel & Bow Walk

including an architect, stonemason, navvy, carpenter and welder. There is also a large mosaic depicting a map of the Thames the activities taking place in the docks.

Facing the former town hall on the corner is an office block originally occupied by the ⑥④ **Stratford Co-Operative & Industrial Society**, which was built in 1919. If you look up you can see the beehive that was the symbol of workers co-operating. The co-operative movement was popular in inner-city areas such as Bow.

Walk up Fairfield Road. It is named after an annual fair that used to be held near here in a location behind the town hall, known as Fair Field. The fair itself had originally been held in Mayfair (hence that area's name) but had moved to Bow in 1764 after local residents in Mayfair complained about the boisterous behaviour taking place among the revellers. The fair continued here until 1823 when it too fell victim to increasing urbanisation and opposition from local residents.

Shortly on the right you pass a sign to Grove Hall Park and shortly after that a large bus station. These both stand on or near the site of the Grove Hall Lunatic Asylum – an establishment built in the 1820s by the Byas family within an existing mansion house. Many of the inmates were ex-servicemen and the gardens featured in Charles Dickens's *Nicholas Nickelby* (1839). The asylum was later closed and demolished in 1909. Part of the grounds were purchased for the public and form today's park. During the Whitechapel Murders of 1888, a mentally unstable Swiss immigrant and butcher named Jacob Isenschmidt came under suspicion. However as Isenschmidt had been committed to Grove Hall Aslyum at the time when further women were murdered by Jack the Ripper, the police turned their attention to other suspects.

331

Whitechapel & Bow Walk

Continuing ahead you pass an old transport building dating from 1910, then under the bridge to reach a large red-brick building on your right that was once occupied by the 65 **Bryant and May match factory**. William Bryant and Francis May were Quaker businessmen who helped revolutionise the manufacture of safety matches in the 1860s.

Timber for the matches arrived on the nearby waterway, and around 1,200 women and girls then dipped the match sticks into a white phosphorous mix before they were boxed up. This exposure to the white phosphorous caused health problems for the workers and many developed 'phossy jaw' – a horrible condition that caused their jaws to become deformed and even glow in the dark. The terrible working conditions came to the attention of social reformers such as Annie Besant (1847-1933). The factory owners tried to counter the poor publicity by asking their workers to sign a statement refuting the allegations but they refused. Some were sacked, but this galvanised the whole workforce to strike. Besant – somewhat reluctantly at first – was persuaded to become their organiser.

The strike achieved huge publicity and support and the factory owners quickly backed down, agreeing to improve factory conditions. The match girls – who could have faced starvation or the workhouse if they had lost their jobs – were incredibly brave to take such action and their strike became seen as an important milestone in both the trade union and early women's rights movements. The factory was rebuilt in 1911 and production of matches ceased there in 1979. The building has now been converted into high-end apartments.

In 1891 Booth's Salvation Army opened up its own match factory in Bow, using the less dangerous red phosphorus and paying better wages than Bryant & May. However the result was more expensive matches that did not sell well and the factory closed in 1900 – ironically it was taken over by Bryant & May. The use of white phosphorus for matches was only banned in Britain after 1910.

Return down Fairfield Road and walk through 66 **Grove Hall Park**, exit on the south side and follow the map down Bow Arts Lane. On the right you will pass 67 **the Nunnery** – an excellent little local gallery with a café run by Bow Arts organisation. It is housed in a 19th century nunnery.

Continue south to reach Bow Road again. To your left – you will see the monstrous Bow flyover, which was constructed in the 1960s and which stands on the site of the original Bow bridge. Legend has it that the Krays buried some of their victims' bodies in the foundations of the flyover.

Ahead, and marooned on an island in the middle of Bow Road, is the famous 68 **St Mary's Church of Bow**. According to London lore, a true cockney must be born within the sound of the Bow bells – whether it meant this church or St Mary le Bow on Cheapside is a debate never likely to be concluded. The church was built upon a small chapel of ease that dated from 1311. Such chapels were designed for locals who found it difficult during periods of bad weather to reach their main parish church – in this case St Dunstan's in Stepney.

The main structure you see today dates from 1719 when St Mary's became a parish church in its own right. Prisca Coborn – founder of the girl's school seen earlier – was buried here in 1701, and the font dates from the 14th century.

In 1556, during the tyrannical reign of Mary I, religious prisoners were brought here by cart from Newgate and burned at the stake beside the church. This included 13 men and women who were burned on June 27 of that year and became known as the Stratford Martyrs.

Whitechapel & Bow Walk

Turn right and walk east along Bow Road. On your left you will see a statue of **(69) Prime Minister William Gladstone** erected in 1882 by Theodore Bryant, of the infamous match factory. Legend has it that the match girls of the time cut themselves and smeared their blood on the statue in protest against their employers having deducted its cost from their wages.

The real story is that years before the Match Strike of 1888, the government of the day had tried to impose a tax on matches. After much protest the government backed down and to commemorate the victory Bryant erected a drinking fountain, deducting a shilling from the match girls to pay for it and so causing much dissatisfaction (the fountain was demolished in 1953). The red hand of Gladstone more likely refers to his indifference to the plight of the match girls and his support for Theodore Bryant.

From here you can retrace your steps to Bow Road underground station and the end of this walk. ●

VISIT...

The Nunnery (see p.233)
181 Bow Rd, E3 2SJ
www.bowarts.org/nunnery

Tower Hamlets Cemetery
(see p.326)
Southern Grove, E3 4PX
www.fothcp.org

EAT, DRINK....

The Blind Beggar (see p.297)
337 Whitechapel Rd, E1 1BU
www.theblindbeggar.com

Bow Bells (see p.330)
116 Bow Road, E3 3AA

Nunnery Café (see p.333)
181 Bow Rd, E3 2SJ

Morgan Arms (see p.323)
43 Morgan St, E3 5AA
www.morganarmsbow.com

Hackney Wick

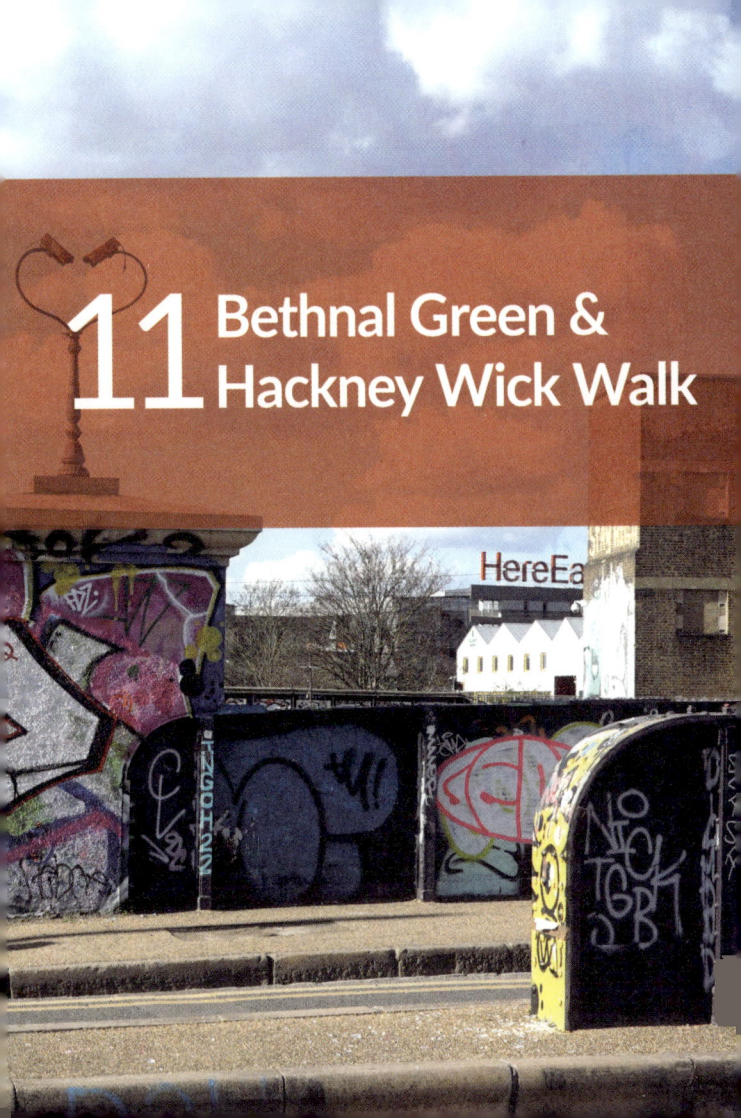

11 Bethnal Green & Hackney Wick Walk

Bethnal Green & Hackney Wick Walk

1. Bethnal Green Memorial
2. Bethnal Green Library
3. St John's Church
4. Daniel Mendoza (plaque)
5. Salmon & Ball public house
6. Alice Denman Fountain
7. Young V&A
8. Museum Passage
9. 17 Victoria Park Square
10. Netteswell House
11. Priory of the Assumptionist Fathers
12. York Hall
13. Raines Secondary School
14. Former London Chest Hospital
15. Stone column

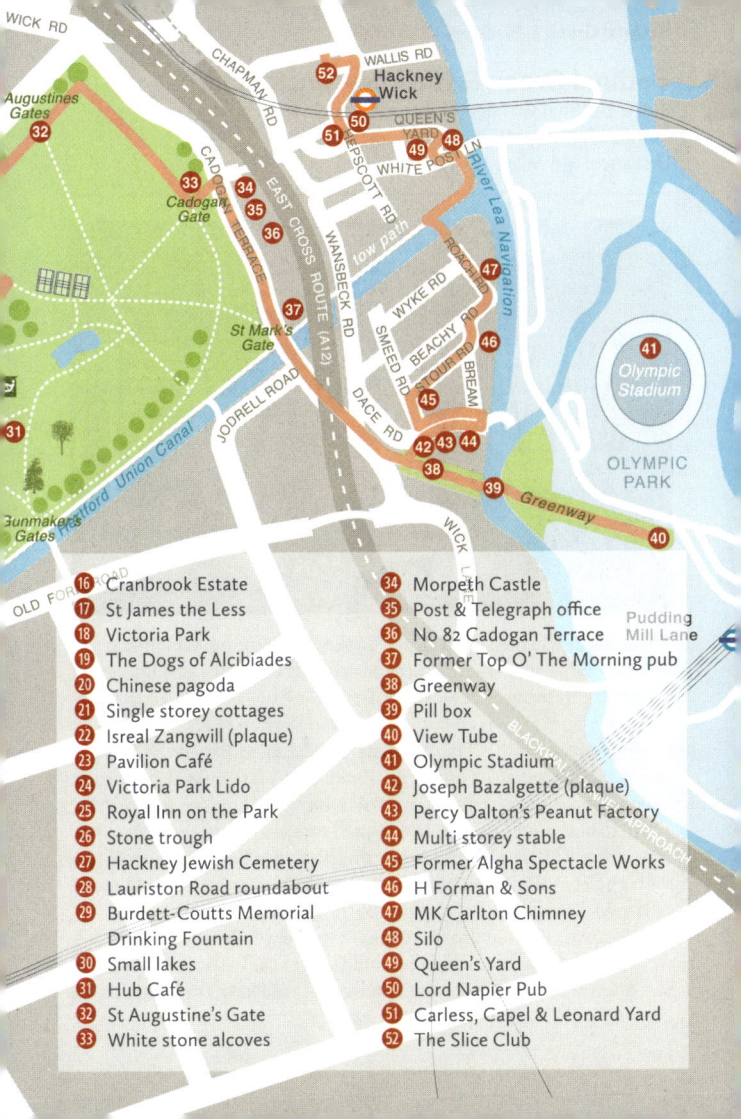

- 16 Cranbrook Estate
- 17 St James the Less
- 18 Victoria Park
- 19 The Dogs of Alcibiades
- 20 Chinese pagoda
- 21 Single storey cottages
- 22 Isreal Zangwill (plaque)
- 23 Pavilion Café
- 24 Victoria Park Lido
- 25 Royal Inn on the Park
- 26 Stone trough
- 27 Hackney Jewish Cemetery
- 28 Lauriston Road roundabout
- 29 Burdett-Coutts Memorial Drinking Fountain
- 30 Small lakes
- 31 Hub Café
- 32 St Augustine's Gate
- 33 White stone alcoves
- 34 Morpeth Castle
- 35 Post & Telegraph office
- 36 No 82 Cadogan Terrace
- 37 Former Top O' The Morning pub
- 38 Greenway
- 39 Pill box
- 40 View Tube
- 41 Olympic Stadium
- 42 Joseph Bazalgette (plaque)
- 43 Percy Dalton's Peanut Factory
- 44 Multi storey stable
- 45 Former Algha Spectacle Works
- 46 H Forman & Sons
- 47 MK Carlton Chimney
- 48 Silo
- 49 Queen's Yard
- 50 Lord Napier Pub
- 51 Carless, Capel & Leonard Yard
- 52 The Slice Club

Bethnal Green & Hackney Wick Walk

Start: Bethnal Green underground station
Finish: Hackney Wick overground station
Distance: 4.6 miles

Museum Gardens

This walk starts outside Bethnal Green tube station, which is in the heart of what was once a rural parish in the county of Middlesex. The name Bethnal Green derives from the Anglo-Saxon 'Blithehale' or 'happy corner', which in time became Bethan Hall Green and so to its present form. The folk tale of *The Blind Beggar of Bethnal Green* was popular in medieval times and was revived in Percy's *Reliques of Ancient English Poetry*, which was published in 1765. The expansion of London and improvements in transport brought the area within the confines of London and it became part of the metropolis in 1855. The blind beggar was used in the Common Seal of the Metropolitan Borough of Bethnal Green.

    Bethnal Green prospered as a place of light industry, silk weaving and market gardening and further on in the walk you will see one of the industrial areas where an unlikely combination of plastics, petrol and sweets were made.

Bethnal Green & Hackney Wick Walk

When leaving the tube station be sure to take the south-east exit to your left – following signs for Bethnal Green Library. Above the exit is a plaque commemorating the Bethnal Green Tube disaster which has recently been joined by the ❶ **Bethnal Green Memorial** directly to your right. The memorial is the result of a long campaign to commemorate the 173 Londoners who died on March 3rd 1943 in a crush as people tried to enter the station, which was being used as an air raid shelter. The tragedy was hushed up at the time for fear of damaging morale and partly because the panic was triggered by the noise of an anti-aircraft battery launched close to Victoria Park. The perseverance of the bereaved has resulted in this impressive monument, which lists the names and ages of those that died and explains the course of events with quotes from survivors. The monument was unveiled 70 years after that terrible night and is a reminder of the tragedy of war.

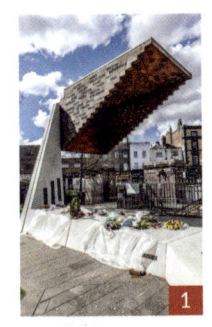

The area to the east of Cambridge Heath Road where you stand was formerly called the Poor's Land. In 1678 wealthy local property owners purchased 15 acres of 'Bethnal Green' to preserve the views from their fine houses; the land was then placed under the management of a charitable trust to help the poor. The municipal park behind the monument contains ❷ **Bethnal Green Library**, which is the last surviving part of the once notorious lunatic asylum which stood here for over 200 years – the park is still referred to as 'Barmy Park', by some locals. The library is a Grade II listed building and has medallions depicting Karl Marx, Richard Wagner, Charles Darwin and William Morris as well as Bethnal Green's famous blind beggar.

Just opposite the park on the other side of Roman Road is ❸ **St John's Church**. The church was designed by Sir John Soane and completed in 1828 and having survived fire and the Blitz is now Grade I listed. The exterior looks a little the worse for wear but the interior contains a vestibule and staircase that are fine examples of Soane's restrained style. The church is also home to 14 *Stations of the Cross* by Chris Gollon, a site specific commission installed in March 2009.

Just opposite the church is a well-preserved terrace of Georgian houses called Paradise Row. One house has a blue plaque commemorating the great boxer ❹ **Daniel Mendoza** (1764-1836), who billed himself 'Mendoza the Jew' and lived here when writing his book *The Art of Boxing*. Mendoza was a popular champion who stood only 5ft 7in but fought all-comers to become champion. Unlike the brawling fighters of the time, Mendoza employed defensive techniques that he later taught at his school to fee-paying gentlemen after his retirement. His popularity declined when he was employed to suppress the Old Price Riots of 1809. The riots were a popular response to the increase in prices at the theatres of Covent Garden. A cartoon by Cruikshank depicting the brutality of Mendoza and his cohorts furthered the popular idea that Mendoza was a thug for hire by the rich. In a rough and tumble world Daniel Mendoza was one of the toughest and he confessed in his memoirs to engaging in three fights on his way to see a fight.

Another sporting connection to this area is not commemorated in any way but is still vivid in the memory of local men of a certain age who remember drinking at ❺ **The Salmon and Ball** pub in the 1970s. At that time it was called Moro's and was owned by football legend Bobby Moore. Sadly Moore's success on the pitch did not extend behind the bar and the pub soon closed.

The pub also has a more gruesome past, for it was here on 6th December 1769 that two weavers called John Doyle and John Valine (of Irish and French extraction respectively) were hanged following the Spitalfields Riots. The riots were caused by the decline in the piece rates for weavers and the importation of cheap French silk. The conflict began in 1765 as local weavers campaigned to maintain their wages and vandalised the cheap imported fabric by cutting it, and so became known as 'cutters'. Both men protested their innocence on the scaffold, and it was known at the time that they were convicted on perjured evidence. Later we will encounter the famous Muller case, which, almost 100 years later, also ended with the execution of a poor textile worker.

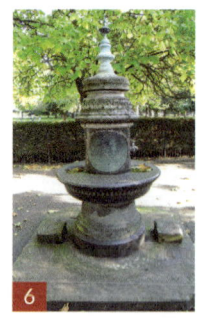

Follow the map to retrace your steps past the tube station until you come to the gates of Museum Gardens. Here you will find the ❻ **Alice Denman Fountain** which was erected by public subscription to commemorate Ms Denman and a passerby called Peter Regelous. The pair lost their lives trying to save others from a fire in a building that stood on this site in April 1902. The ground floor of the building was occupied by a company of ticket writers, who were the graphic artists of their day, writing small posters and cards for shops and other businesses.

Exit the park and walk along Cambridge Heath Road until you come to the ❼ **Young V&A**, that for many years was the Museum of Childhood (see p.367 for visiting details). The building looks like a converted railway station but its design is in fact based on a wrought iron frame originally erected in Kensington, where the V&A now stands. The frame was moved here and a building designed around it by architect James William Wild who was involved in the Kensington works. Wild spent the last years of his life as curator of the Sir John Soane Museum and would no doubt be pleased that his work stands just a few hundred metres from Soane's church. The museum has recently undergone another major refurbishment to reopen under the V&A brand with new interactive displays and a representation of the original collection.

Follow the map down ❽ **Museum Passage**, which runs between the museum and it's gardens.

Bethnal Green & Hackney Wick Walk

At the end of which can be seen a large red brick house which is ❾ **17 Victoria Park Square**. This was the home of Brigadier General Sir Wyndham Henry Deedes (1883-1956) who lived here between the world wars. He was involved in the administration of Palestine after World War I and was sympathetic to the plight of the Jews. Deedes went on to become a social worker in the East End. There is a plaque on the side of the chapel commemorating him.

Earlier in the walk mention was made of the grand properties that once occupied this area and here you can see the last of these houses still standing. ❿ **Netteswell House** is on the corner of Old Ford Road and is easily missed with large trees and high walls surrounding it. The gabled roof can be seen just to the right of the Museum of Childhood. In 1547 Bishop Bonner leased the site to former Lord Mayor, Sir Ralph Warren and he built his grand house on the site. Parts of the basement still date from this time although the house was later remodelled in 1705 and 1862.

Just opposite Netteswell House is the
⑪ Priory of the Assumptionist Fathers.
Originally a French religious order, the Assumptionists were effectively expelled from France having been dissolved by law in 1900. Their newspaper *La Croix* was virulently anti-Semitic. They established themselves here in 1901 and built this Jacobean-style red brick building with stucco bands and window dressings in 1912, using money from the bequest of Florence Cottrell-Dormer in memory of her husband.

Walking past the house you arrive at the junction with Old Ford Road. Opposite and just to your left is ⑫ **York Hall** which was built in 1929 and has become part of Bethnal Green folklore as a boxing venue where many great pugilistic battles have run their bloody course. The hall is now a leisure centre with Turkish baths, a gym and swimming pool, but is still a venue for boxing.

Proceed along Old Ford Road. The road continues for over a mile to the River Lea. It used to ford the river and continue even further but since 1967 it has been truncated by the A12 dual carriageway, which we will encounter later in the walk. Take a left onto a pleasant tree-lined avenue called Approach Road and you will soon see on your right ⑬ **Raines Secondary School**. The name of the school derives from devout Christian, Henry Raine, who made his fortune as an alcohol merchant and sought to alleviate his guilt by opening a free school in Wapping in 1719. Raine's school moved several times before taking over this site in 1985, following the departure of Parmiter's School, which was another school founded by a local businessman (silk merchant Thomas Parmiter).

Just after the school is the mini roundabout where you meet Bonner Road. Edmund Bonner (1500-69) was the Bishop of

12 York Hall

London who owned a large swathe of Bethnal Green. He prospered during Henry VIII's schism with Rome and subscribed to the *Six Articles*. Bonner appears to have had a supple conscience which allowed him to become a driving force behind the persecution of Protestants under Mary I, and he became known as 'Bloody Bonner' for the enthusiasm with which he made Protestant martyrs. Bonner was too closely associated with Mary's reign and he ended his days imprisoned by Elizabeth I at the Marshalsea Prison in Southwark.

Turn right down Bonner Road; on the left is the site of the former ⑭ **Former London Chest Hospital**. The foundation stone was laid by Prince Albert in 1851 and his patronage helped raise £30,000 to complete the building. The need for a cardiopulmonary hospital was caused by the prevalence of tuberculosis, which was so contagious that most hospitals would not admit sufferers. The site was sold to a housing association in September 2015 and has been left derelict and surrounded by wooden hoardings for many years while disputes continue over the future nature of the proposed development.

Within the grounds of the abandoned hospital is a ⑮ **stone column** commemorating the 60th year of Queen Victoria's reign in 1897. The stone was present by Sir M M Bhownaggree who at the time was the Conservative MP for Bethnal Green North East and only the second MP of Indian origin. Mancherjee Bhownaggree was the son of a merchant and head of the Bombay State Agency in India before moving to England in 1882 at the age of 42. Unlike his Asian predecessor in parliament, Dadabhai Naoroji, Bhownaggree was a supporter of British rule in India and this monument describes Queen Victoria as 'Empress of India'.

Bethnal Green & Hackney Wick Walk

Continue along Bonner Road with the hospital to the left. There is a well preserved Victorian terrace facing the hospital, but you will soon notice that the road ends with a vista of modern streets and the vast ❻ **Cranbrook Estate**, designed by Berthold Lubetkin, in the distance. The contrast in housing can be explained by the Blitz and the public housing drive that transformed the area in the 1960s. Turning left up St James's Avenue, there is a fine example of this dichotomy between old and new – ❼ **St James the Less** with its Victorian tower designed by Lewis Vulliamy and the rest of the church dating from 1960. The modern building arose from the ruins after a direct hit from a bomb in 1944. The join can be seen between the old and new brick, but the overall effect is pleasing.

Continue along St James's Avenue to the grand wrought iron gates of ❽ **Victoria Park**. Before you explore the park it is worth taking note that you are now crossing the Regent's Canal and the bridge offers great views of the water way. To your right the canal extends towards Limehouse and the Thames, while to your left it leads to Islington. The canal opened in 1820 and a watercolour by T H Shepherd painted in 1828 shows the Limehouse Basin teeming with heavily laden barges entering the canal system. The commercial use of the barges ended in 1969 but the growing number of narrow boats seen from the bridge shows how some Londoners have turned the canal into their floating home.

349

It is at this gate that you can see the statues of two mythical dogs – ⑲ **The Dogs of Alcibiades**. The original sculpture was Greek but came to these shores as a 2nd century Roman copy. The sculpture is also known as the Jennings Dog, after its first modern owner (Henry Constantine Jennings) and is on display at the British Museum.

The name of Alcibiades became associated with the sculpture as the dog's tail is docked: in Plutarch's account of the life of Alcibiades, the statesman is said to have cut off the tail of his handsome dog in order to invoke pity and distract from his misdeeds. This was a trick that Richard Nixon was to employ to some effect with the use of his dog Checkers in his speech of 1952 following an expenses scandal. Checkers died in 1964 and was not on hand to lend canine support when the Watergate scandal engulfed his master.

You are now entering one of London's finest parks. The radical politician Joseph Hume was one of the driving forces behind the creation of a vast public park to help improve

Regent Canal

Bethnal Green & Hackney Wick Walk

conditions in East London. In 1842 York House in St James's was sold to purchase the 290 acres, which included Bonner's Fields where the eponymous Bishop of London had burned heretics in the 16th century. The park was designed by James Pennethorne – a street nearby still bears his name. In 1848 Victoria Park was the venue for one of the largest Chartist demonstrations. Chartism was a popular movement demanding an extension of the franchise and other freedoms and rights for the working man. Over 1500 police were mobilised in case of disturbance but the essentially peaceful nature of the crowds and a passing thunderstorm helped prevent disorder.

As you walk through the park you will notice a ⓴ **Chinese pagoda** that is a recent addition following the park's redevelopment in preparation for the 2012 Olympics. There had been a pagoda here for many years, but it fell into disrepair. This modern structure, and the newly landscaped area around it, is a welcome improvement to the park.

Walking along the main thoroughfare, after 200 metres you will see a small path leading to the canal and some ㉑ **single storey cottages**. These lock keepers' cottages and stables are remnants of the canal's industrial past and used to provide feed and rest for the horses that worked on the canal. Return to the park and continue around the lake and you will see a row of terraced houses that are on part of Old Ford Road, encountered earlier in the walk.

Bethnal Green & Hackney Wick Walk

Lauriston Road

At number 288 is a **㉒ blue plaque to Israel Zangwill**, the Jewish author and philanthropist, who wrote *Children of the Ghetto*. Walking around the small lake with its fountain you will encounter the **㉓ Pavilion Café**, which serves good coffee if you want a break.

Continue around the lake and you will notice a road that cuts through the park. This is Grove Road and just on the other side, where cars now park, was once **㉔ Victoria Park Lido**. The lido was opened in May 1936 and remained a popular Hackney attraction for over 50 years. During the heat wave of 1976 there was a riot when the doors were closed due to overcrowding and 900 people forced entry and swam for free, forcing the pool's closure for two days for repairs. The anarchic 1970s ushered in the authoritarian '80s when the closure of the GLC in 1986 and tightening of public purse strings saw the closure of the lido and its demolition in 1990. The lido at London Fields (about a mile from here) has greatly improved the situation for East London swimmers since being restored and reopened in 2006.

As you make your way along the path and pass the newly refurbished children's playground, veer to the right and take the exit onto Grove Road. Just opposite is the **㉕ Royal Inn on the Park**. In June 1993, when the pub was called the Royal Hotel, the notorious bank robber and criminal enforcer Jimmy Moody was gunned down inside by an unknown assassin. The pub is now a very different place with life drawing classes and a well chosen wine list. Just opposite the Inn on the Park is the Bagel on the Park, which is a great place to get a freshly-filled bagel if the weather is fine.

Another relic of the Victorian effort to provide clean drinking water can be seen just a little further along on Lauriston Road on a small traffic island. This **㉖ stone trough** has the words Metropolitan Drinking Fountain & Cattle Trough Association inscribed upon it. The association was established in

London by Samuel Gurney MP and barrister Edward T Wakefield in 1859 to provide clean drinking water for man and beast alike. This was a matter of great public concern at the time following the cholera epidemic of 1854 and the pioneering work of Dr John Snow, which proved that dirty drinking water was the cause. The association performed an essential task and although the remaining fountains and troughs are now dried up relics like this one, at its height 300,000 thirsty Londoners used the fountains daily.

On the other side of this broad road can be seen some grand wrought iron gates marking the site of the **27 Hackney Jewish Cemetery.** They are a testament to this area's long link with the Jewish community. The cemetery was purchased by the Hambro Synagogue in 1788 and closed its gates to new admissions almost 100 years later in 1886. The Hambro Synagogue was in disagreement with the more established synagogues in the City and this explains why many of those buried here have City addresses. The disputes were resolved in 1870 when the three synagogues of London combined to form the United Synagogue. Many of the tomb stones are inscribed in Hebrew, but are not of the simple flat stone design found in many Jewish cemeteries. Vandalism has necessitated closure of the cemetery to the public, but the wrought iron gates give a good view of this atmospheric place.

Just ahead is the small but surprisingly lush **28 Lauriston Road roundabout** which was originally brought to life by local potter – Caroline Bousfield Gregory. The project started as guerrilla gardening, but has since gained the support of the council and won several awards over the years.

Retrace your steps and enter Victoria Park at the main gates next to the Royal

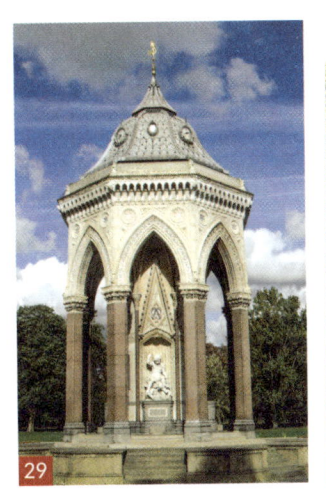

Inn on the Park. Follow the map to reach the ㉙ **Burdett-Coutts Memorial Drinking Fountain** which was finished in 1862, designed by architect H A Darbishire and cost the then incredible sum of £6,000. Angela Burdett-Coutts was one of the major philanthropists of her day and was also responsible for the indoor market that stood on Columbia Road in East London, which proved an expensive failure. This grand fountain was a useful source of fresh water for Londoners but became redundant with the widespread provision of drinking water in the late 19th century. The fountain remained an abandoned relic for many years and an ugly fence was put around it to prevent vandalism. The build-up to the 2012 Olympics witnessed a huge investment in the park and the fountain has now been fully restored and a landscape of small water features has been built around the original structure.

Follow the path past the system of ㉚ **small lakes** that were formerly used for bathing. The bathing lakes existed in Victoria Park from 1876 to 1933. Domestic plumbing was a rarity at this time and the lakes were an important facility of the park. The

Bethnal Green & Hackney Wick Walk

lakes were built to discourage bathing in the canals, which had previously been the favoured way of keeping clean. The lakes soon became dirty and efforts were made to increase the water flow and so improve the quality of the water. The lakes are relatively modest now and the only bathers are wildfowl, but at their height there were concrete terraces and diving boards with 25,000 people bathing in the morning. In 1904 a women's lake was introduced and a further children's lake, where up to 5,000 children would bathe in the afternoon.

If you want some refreshment – on your right is the ㉛ **Hub Café**. Both the café and skatepark next to it are the newest editions to this historic park.

Follow the map to make the long walk across the park to ㉜ **St Augustine's Gate**, which is named after a Victorian church that once stood here. There is still a stone in the ground by the Park's entrance marking the location of the alter, and the trees still define the church's outline. The church was damaged during World War II and demolished in 1953. Victoria Park certainly played its part in the war effort and this area was used to house Italian and German prisoners of war who were put to work on the allotments which were created as recreation gave way to food production. On the other side of the park and alongside the Grand Union Canal stood the anti-aircraft rockets whose noise contributed to the disaster at Bethnal Green featured at the start of the walk.

Bethnal Green & Hackney Wick Walk

This part of the park is now a regular venue for open air rock concerts and none have proved more famous than the Rock Against Racism event held here in the spring of 1978. The movement was a response to a drunken racist rant made by Eric Clapton in 1976 and the rise in popularity of Enoch Powell and the National Front. The Clash stole the show and footage of their performance shows the three residential tower blocks in the distance that stand here today. The park now hosts music festivals every summer.

From this corner you can cut across to reach the park's eastern boundary with some very fine housing looking out over the park from Cadogan Terrace. You will soon see ❸❸ **two white stone alcoves** facing towards the park, which were part of the old London Bridge. The alcoves were moved here after the bridge's demolition in 1831 and belong to the refurbishment of the bridge that was undertaken in 1760. The insignia of the Bridge Association can be seen inside the alcoves.

From this point you can look beyond the park and see

Victoria Park looking towards Cadogan Terrace & Olympic Park

Bethnal Green & Hackney Wick Walk

to your right an unusual curved building that was for many years a pub called the ③④ **Morpeth Castle**. The building was designed by A E Sewell and thankfully his work has been preserved despite the pub's closure in 1990. The Truman brewery insignia can still be seen above what was the pub's entrance.

Next door is the former ③⑤ **Post & Telegraph office** with its original signage still in place. The existence of these enterprises on such a quiet terrace is explained by the closed-off road that gives an open vista onto the roaring A12 East Cross Route. Until building work began in 1967 as part of the M11 road link system, this small road led directly to Hackney Wick, with the North London Railway line crossing on a bridge above. Earlier you briefly encountered the Old Ford Road, which was also truncated by the arrival of the dual carriageway.

If you are feeling tired at this stage and want to end your walk early, then this is a good point to head home. Exit the park by the Cadogan Gate and walk over the pedestrian bridge that crosses the dual carriageway, and leads directly to the ultimate destination of this walk, Hackney Wick station. If your legs are fresh and your heart willing, then continue walking along Cadogan Terrace.

The houses along this terrace are some of the finest in Hackney. Probably the most impressive house on the terrace is ③⑥ **number 82**, which is an imposing four storey Georgian building that formerly belonged to fashion designer Alexander McQueen.

At the far end of Cadogan Terrace are modern luxury flats that were until 2015 the ③⑦ **Top O' The Morning pub**. The plaque explaining the pub's link with a notorious Victorian murder is still there. On the night of 9th July 1864 a 69 year old banker by the name of Thomas Briggs was found bloody and beaten on the railway embankment of the North London Railway line which passed just behind the pub. The badly injured man was taken from the pub to his home in Clapton where he died the following night. The railway carriage in which Briggs had been travelling was found to be covered in blood and his gold watch, glasses and hat had been taken and another hat left in its place.

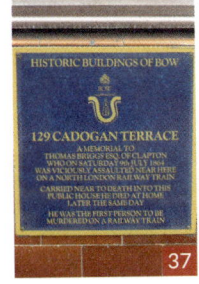

The murder attracted a great deal of attention from the press and public and was the first murder to have been committed on a railway train. A large reward was offered and a cab driver named Jonathan Matthews came forward to identify a 24 year old German tailor by the name of Franz Müller who had been a lodger at Matthews' house and was engaged to his daughter.

Briggs' watch chain was tracked down to a Cheapside jeweller with the appropriate name of John Death, and he identified Franz Müller as the seller. The hunt began for the young German who had left the country via a sailing ship heading for New York. Detective Richard Tanner and two witnesses embarked on a faster steam ship and Müller arrived in New York on 25th August to find a reception party and large crowds gathering to witness his arrest.

There was some sympathy for Müller among the considerable German community of London and money raised for his defence. Even King Wilhelm I of Prussia made an appeal for clemency on Müller's behalf. The efforts were in vain as the evidence was overwhelming and he was found guilty. Müller was one of the last people to be publicly executed on 14th November 1864 before a raucous crowd of over 50,000 people.

The famous Müller Case led to changes in the design of railway carriages, which had been enclosed, and the introduction of communication cords for longer journeys. Behind the lurid headlines, the court transcripts tell a sad tale of urban poverty, with Müller and his acquaintances struggling in desperate circumstances and all leading to a violent and brutal murder.

Bethnal Green & Hackney Wick Walk

Now proceed to the underpass that carries the A12 and continue along Wick Lane towards the large chimney that towers above you. At the top of the incline on your left is the start of the ❸❽ **Greenway** which leads to the View Tube offering views over the vast Olympic site.

You will later take the steps on your left down to the street level of the old industrial area known as Hackney Wick, but for the meantime proceed along the Greenway until you come to a concrete ❸❾ **pill box**, the remnant of an anti-tank position from World War II. Throughout the walk there have been signs of the impact of the Blitz on the East End and these emplacements give some idea of the strategic importance of the waterways and light industry to the war effort. From here look north to see the Old Ford Lock Cottage from where Channel 4's Big Breakfast show was broadcast for nearly ten years.

Walking along the raised Greenway you will soon reach the ❹⓿ **View Tube** with its fabulous café and garden. To your left can be seen the main ❹❶ **Olympic Stadium**, the Aquatic Centre and the bold red looping form of Anish Kapoor's observation tower. Officially called the ArcelorMittal Orbit but nicknamed the 'Helter Skelter', it is Britain's largest piece of public artwork but has received mixed reviews with one critic describing it as a 'catastrophic collision between two cranes!'

On the other side of the path is a huge expanse of wasteland with factory buildings

40 View of River Lea from pill box

Bethnal Green & Hackney Wick Walk

41

41

43

Bethnal Green & Hackney Wick Walk

in the distance including the Bryant and May red-brick matchbox factory the story of which is mentioned in the Whitechapel to Bow Walk (see p.290-335).

At this stage double back, return to the start of the Greenway and take the steps that lead down onto Dace Road and the part of Hackney Wick called 'Fish Island'. Descending the steps you will see a plaque on the right identifying this as part of the the main sewer system constructed by **42 Joseph Bazalgette** in the mid-19th century. Earlier in the walk the problems of water supply and the spread of cholera were mentioned in relation to the drinking fountains found along the way, but it was Bazalgette's vast modern sewer system that was to solve the problem. The Greenway you have just walked is raised above street level because it sits upon Bazalgette's outflow pipe, which leads to the Abbey Mills Pumping Station to the east.

The steps lead down to the street level of Fish Island. This area was developed in 1876 for industry and commerce and it is from here that many famous British products originate. Just to the right on Dace Street is the old **43 Percy Dalton's Peanut Factory**. Percy Dalton started out as a fruit seller at Spitalfields Market. His business took off when he began selling roasted peanuts at sporting events and he soon made his fortune. It is tempting at this stage to use the metaphor of a small nut becoming a mighty tree, but peanuts are in fact a form of legume grown in the soil. The company moved to Suffolk in the 1990s and although the Percy Dalton signs are still visible, the building is now used by a mixed assortment of artists, designers, filmmakers and other creative types who have helped make this one of London's most fashionable areas.

Bethnal Green & Hackney Wick Walk

Follow the map along Dace Road – you will notice what a strange area Hackney Wick has become with its mix of workshops, industrial buildings and new housing developments sitting cheek by jowl with the art community. At the far end of Dace Road is a building called the Iron Works with an unusual redbrick building to the right, which was built as a vast ㊹ **multi storey stable** when horses were the main engine of haulage in the area. Just a bit further along is the Lock Keepers Cottage we saw earlier from the Greenway.

Walk back until you come to Smeed Street and take a right to find the ㊺ **former Algha Spectacle Works**. Founded by Max Wiseman in 1898, the company produced the famous gold-rimmed glasses worn by Mahatma Gandhi and John Lennon. At its height this factory employed 200 people but had dwindled to only 15 staff by 2016. The company has since moved production to Italy and the building is destined for redevelopment.

Take a right along Stour Road and you will soon reach the new building of ㊻ H

Bethnal Green & Hackney Wick Walk

Forman & Sons who have been smoking salmon on Fish Island since 1905. Their old factory stood where the Olympic Stadium now stands. They used the compensation received to create this handsome new building designed by Phil Hudson and painted salmon pink.

Follow the map onto Roach Road and a little way along, surrounded by modern flats, is the ❼ **M K Carlton Chimney**, the last remnant of the eponymous shoe factory. The chimney dates from 1893 when Hackney Wick was an area dedicated to industry where thousands of people would work. The arrival of the Olympic Park and changes in manufacturing have largely brought an end to this tradition, leaving just a few such remnants as a reminder.

There is now a short trek which takes you across the pedestrian footbridge over the Grand Union Canal. After crossing the bridge, take a right and head around the corner following the towpath on the bank of the River Lea. You will soon walk up a pedestrian footpath onto White Post Lane, which is one of the main entrances to the Olympic Park and was formerly a through road leading to Stratford.

At this stage you are at a nexus with the following walk – Lea Valley to Olympic Park Walk (see p.368-383). If you wish to, you can head east over the bridge and into the Queen Elizabeth Olympic Park but on this walk we head west along White Post Lane to explore more of the ever changing Hackney Wick.

On your right is ㊽ **Silo**. Once a print works, it is now an upmarket restaurant that prides itself on a zero waste policy. The building also houses the **Crate Brewery and Pizzeria** which makes its own award winning beers and stone baked pizzas. With its vast seating area overlooking the canal – it's a great place to enjoy an artisan beer and a bite to eat.

Enter ㊾ **Queen's Yard** either through the White Building or by taking the first right on White Post Lane. This is another place to stop for refreshments with a host of bars and eateries occupying what were once industrial units, but be warned the crowd here is largely young and the music always loud. Follow the map through Queen's Yard, back onto White Post Lane and continue along – you can now see Hackney Wick station just a little ahead, which is your final destination.

At the junction with Hepscott Road is the ㊾ **Lord Napier Pub**, which was closed for many years, but has been revamped and is now one of London's busiest pubs, although catering for a different crowd than in its former incarnation. Just opposite are modern flats called The Bagel Factory that were once the site of ㊾ **Carless, Capel and Leonard Yard.** This was where distilled crude oil was distributed, initially as a solvent from 1859. Following an agreement with Daimler cars they began to sell a product which was termed 'Petrol' to distinguish it from other forms of gasoline.

Bethnal Green & Hackney Wick Walk

Follow the map to the junction with Wallis Road where you will find a branch of Sainsbury's. This was once the site of Alexander Parkes' factory that manufactured one of the first forms of plastic. There was a plaque commemorating this fact but it has since been removed by the developers. From here you can see the **52 The Slice Club,** just opposite, that is dedicated to offering beer and pizza and has outdoor seating. From here you can get a train at Hackney Wick Station or catch a bus from Chapman Road. ●

VISIT...

Young V&A (see p.344)
Cambridge Heath Rd, E2 9PA
www.vam.ac.uk/moc

View Tube (see p.360)
The Greenway, E15 2PJ
www.theviewtube.co.uk

EAT, DRINK...

Crate Brewery & Pizzeria
(see p.366)
Silo Building,
Queen's Yard, E9 5EN
www.cratebrewery.com

The Slice Club (see p.367)
11 Prince Edward Rd, E9 5LX
www.thehackneypearl.com

Hub Café (see p.356)
The Hub Building,
Victoria Park East, E9 5HD

Pavilion Café (see p.353)
Victoria Park, E9 7DE

Royal Inn on the Park (see p.353)
111 Lauriston Rd, E9 7HJ
www.royalinnonthepark.com

View Tube Café (see p.360)
The Greenway, E15 2PJ
www.theviewtube.co.uk

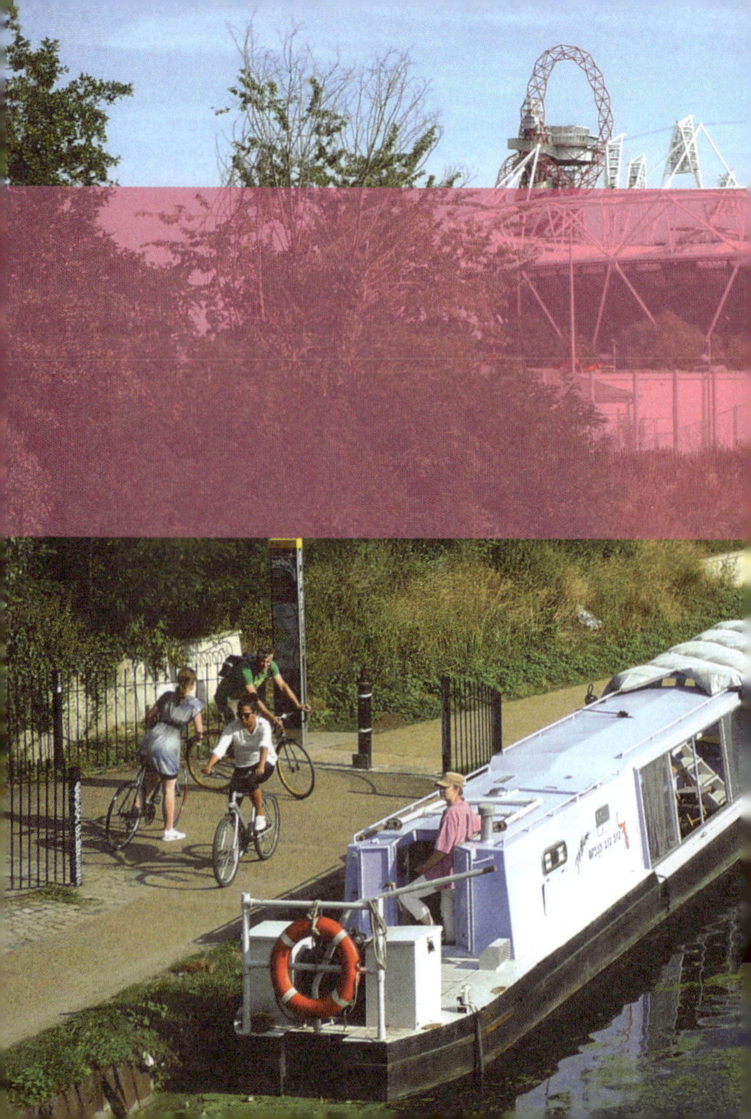

Lee Valley & Queen Elizabeth Olympic Park Walk

View from bridge on White Post Lane, see p.380

Lee Valley & Queen Elizabeth Olympic Park Walk

1. Tottenham Lock
2. Tow path
3. Markfield Park
4. Warwick Reservoir West & East
5. Lea Rowing Club
6. Springfield Park
7. Springfield Marina
8. Walthamstow Marshes
9. A.V. Roe (blue plaque)
10. tree-lined path
11. Waterworks Nature Reserve & Middlesex Filter Beds
12. Bridge
13. New Spitalfields Market
14. Matchmakers Wharf
15. Lee Valley Park Wick Community Woodland
16. Whitepost Lane bridge
17. Silo Building
18. Queen Elizabeth Olympic Park
19. The Copper Box Arena
20. Tumbling Bay Playground
21. Timber Lodge Café
22. North parklands
23. South parklands

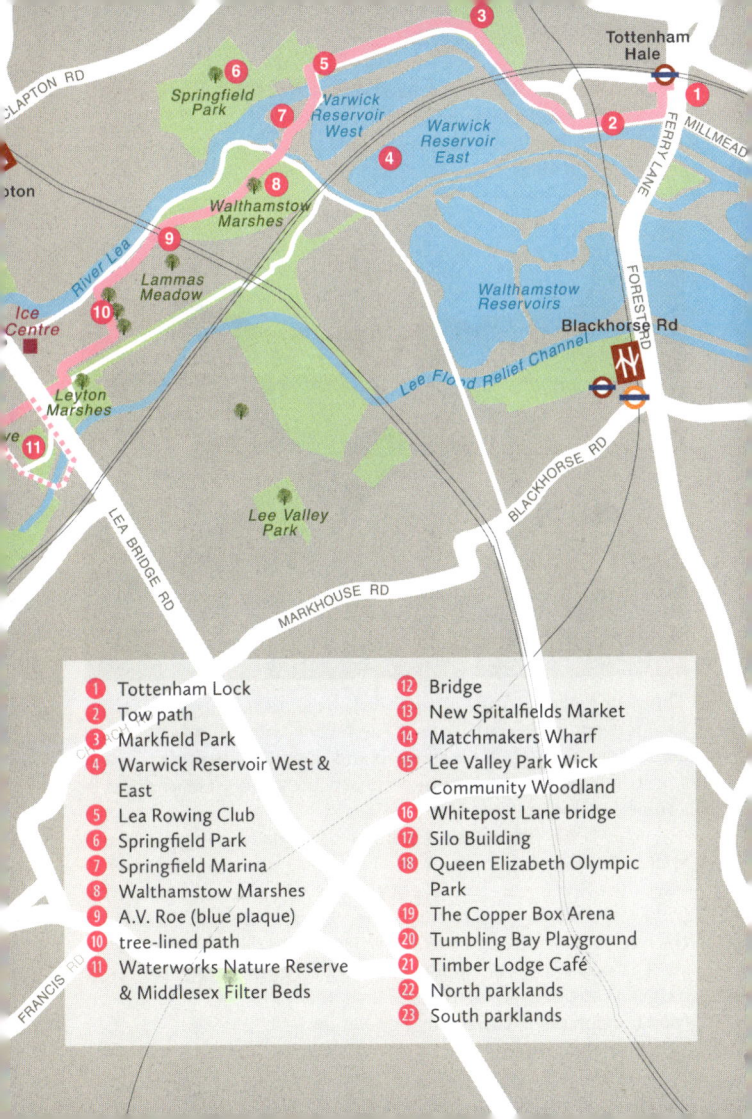

Lee Valley & Olympic Park Walk

Lee Valley & Queen Elizabeth Olympic Park Walk
Start: Tottenham Hale underground station
Finish: Stratford International rail and DLR station
Distance: 5.8 miles

This walk begins at Tottenham Hale tube station. From the station turn left and walk up hill along Ferry Lane through a fairly urban landscape. Cross Mill Mead Road and shortly on the left you will see a lock and waterway underneath the road. Head down a cobbled pathway to the lock itself.

This is ❶ **Tottenham Lock**, built originally in 1776, and the 17th lock along the route of the Lee Navigation, a canal formed out of the River Lea. The River Lea rises near Luton and then runs from Hertford to the Thames. The Vikings once sailed north up the river from the Thames to attack Hertford and in later centuries the Lea was known as the Barge River due to the large number of barges that travelled along its course, many transporting grain to feed London's ever expanding population.

Lee Valley & Olympic Park Walk

The increasing amount of commercial traffic on the river led to work being undertaken from the 14th century to improve the river's navigability. However these changes prompted bitter conflicts between the barge owners, who welcomed the improvements, and mill owners who wanted any available water to be used for their mills by the river edge rather than diverted along newly cut channels.

The River Lea Act 1766 began the first proper canalisation of the river, which remains the only London waterway that is a canalised river rather than a purpose built canal. The uncanalised River Lea limps alongside, however it is the poor cousin of the Navigation, often ignored and for much of its course going through a concrete tunnel. The original locks were single gate 'flash' locks which required a build-up of water and a sudden release that allowed boats to pass through. Subsequently the 'pound' lock was introduced in the 18th and 19th centuries – the type you see today – which have gates at each end, waste less water and are easier to navigate.

Turn right (southwards) and walk along the ❷ **tow path** with the water to your left. You will probably begin to see some of the wildlife that makes this walk so interesting, including large numbers of swans. You pass under a railway bridge, and just after this point you will see the Lee Navigation converge with the River Lea itself.

Walk under a second railway bridge and pause by the ❸ **Markfield Park** on the right. This is not a particularly interesting

Lee Valley & Olympic Park Walk

park except for the fact it contains a rare Victorian survivor, the Markfield Beam Engine. This was used to pump sewage from late Victorian times and is housed in the original Tottenham sewage treatment works and pumping station which were operational for over 100 years until 1964. The engine itself was first used in 1888 and is an incredible example of Victorian engineering. The Grade II listed Engine House is open to the public on occasional Sundays (see p.383 for visiting information), but the engine can be seen through the windows of the building when closed.

Continue south with ❹ **Warwick Reservoir West and East** to your left, each covering around 40 acres, although it is hard to see these expanses of water due to the bank running alongside. You will now start to see narrow boats moored along the river bank. This part of London is peppered with vast reservoirs known as the Lee Valley Reservoir Chain. This comprises 13 reservoirs which are crucial for London as they supply much of its drinking water, however surprisingly few residents of the capital are aware of their existence.

View from bridge

Lee Valley & Olympic Park Walk

After some distance on the right you pass ❺ **Lea Rowing Club** and its pleasant café. To the west is ❻ **Springfield Park** which dates from 1905 and covers nearly 40 acres. It was formed out of the gardens of three large private residences. Today only one of these still exists – Springfield House (known now as The White Lodge) at the top of the park by the main entrance. This contains a good café (Springfield Park Café, see p.383) and the higher ground of the park offers great views over London.

Cross over the bridge – just past the Lea Rowing Club – and walk by ❼ **Springfield Marina**. Continue along the path until you reach a junction – bear right down and then follow any of the narrow paths which lead after a few minutes into the wide open space of Walthamstow Marshes. Follow the map walking diagonally towards the green bridge in the distance – the Lee Navigation should be a few hundred yards to your right. You should converge again with the canal towpath just under a railway bridge that crosses over the canal.

Lee Valley & Olympic Park Walk

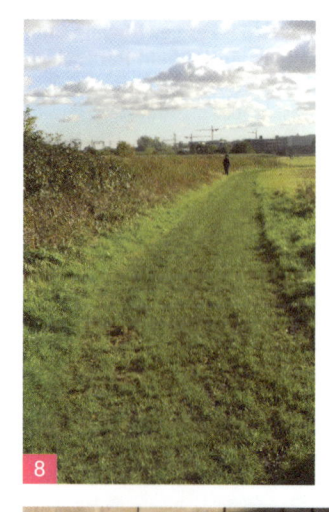

8

9 WALTHAM FOREST HERITAGE
A.V. ROE 1877 - 1958
UNDER THESE ARCHES ALLIOTT VERDON ROE
ASSEMBLED HIS AVRO No1. TRIPLANE.
IN JULY 1909 HE MADE THE FIRST
ALL BRITISH POWERED FLIGHT FROM
WALTHAMSTOW MARSH.

11

Lee Valley & Olympic Park Walk

❽ **Walthamstow Marshes** would have been a treacherous place to cross in medieval times however drainage was slowly improved from the 16th century. For many centuries these were Lammas Lands where locals had rights to graze their livestock for parts of the year. While many of the factories, railway and water companies that based themselves here during the 19th century bought out these grazing rights, they continued to exist until the local council took over control of the land in the 1930s.

Although part of the marshes have been turned into reservoirs to the north, 100 acres have been preserved for public use and have been designated a nature reserve and site of special scientific interest. The marshes are home to rare plant species such as creeping marshwort and brookweed, and birds including reed buntings, and willow warblers.

In 1909 Alliott Verdon Roe (1877-1958) made the first all-British powered flight across the marsh in a Roe I triplane. A ❾ **blue plaque** records his achievement under a railway arch near the canal, the location of his workshop.

Carry on for a few more minutes then walk left down a ❿ **tree-lined path**. After passing the last tree take a right and walk along the path on the edge of the marsh – you should see the curved roof of the Lee Valley Ice Centre on your right. At the end of the path take a left (away from the Ice Centre) and cross a small wooden bridge before taking an immediate right that leads to a tunnel under Lee Bridge Road.

After the tunnel there are signs for the ⓫ **Lee Valley Waterworks Nature Reserve and Middlesex Filter Beds**. This was once home to the East London Waterworks

377

Lee Valley & Olympic Park Walk

Company. From the mid-19th century the Company's filter beds helped tackle the problem of cholera by providing clean drinking water to the nearby boroughs. Now 150 years old, the site is home to over 500 species of plants and 25 types of birds. The Nature Reserve is open on most days, but the café and information centre has much more restrictive hours (see www.visitleevalley.org.uk for more details).

If you want to visit the Nature Reserve follow the map to the Visitor Centre. Otherwise continue ahead along the winding path for a few minutes before crossing over a bridge. Ahead is the vast expanse of Hackney Marshes which has the River Lea running along the east side and the Hackney Cut – a section of the Lee Navigation – on the west side.

Hackney Marsh covers nearly 340 acres and is home to a famous amateur football tradition – its 82 pitches host nearly 100 games on a typical Sunday. Continue along the eastern side (bearing left as you cross the bridge). There is a good path along the edge of the River Lea and a smaller path closer the water if you want to take that.

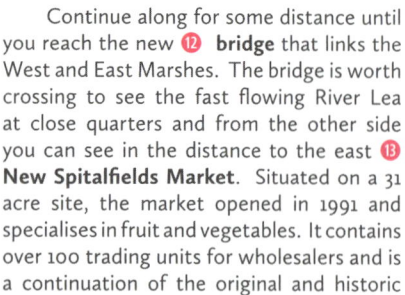

Continue along for some distance until you reach the new ⑫ **bridge** that links the West and East Marshes. The bridge is worth crossing to see the fast flowing River Lea at close quarters and from the other side you can see in the distance to the east ⑬ **New Spitalfields Market**. Situated on a 31 acre site, the market opened in 1991 and specialises in fruit and vegetables. It contains over 100 trading units for wholesalers and is a continuation of the original and historic Spitalfields Market east of the City that began in 1638 and was finally closed in 1991 when the market site was controversially re-developed. If you are eager to explore the Olympic site and want to shorten this walk follow the path to the right which will lead to a bridge into the Queen Elizabeth Olympic Park – just head towards the curved roof of the Velodrome in the distance.

Lee Valley & Olympic Park Walk

Those with fresh legs can retrace their steps across the bridge. After WWII the cleared rubble of buildings destroyed in London by enemy bombing was brought to Hackney Marshes to raise their height and reduce the risk of flooding. You can occasionally still see some remnants of this rubble alongside the bank of the River Lea as you cross the bridge.

From the other side of the bridge cross diagonally over the main part of Hackney Marshes. The best way to navigate across the fields is to head towards the multi-coloured flats on the other side of the fields. Until 2010 you would have set your sights on the famous **Lesney Matchbox Factory** which had its name proudly emblazoned on the outside of its 1960s concrete factory complex. The company was founded after the war by John 'Jack' Odell and flourished in the 1950s and 60s, becoming one of Hackney's largest employers. The small die-cast toys manufactured here are a cherished memory for children of that era and Matchbox toys are now very collectable. Sadly the company declined in the 1970s and went into liquidation in 1982. The factory continued to function, producing parts for domestic appliances, but was closed for many years before its demolition in 2010. The complex of smart flats that now occupy the site is called ⑭ **Matchmakers Wharf** in memory of the famous toys.

Cross over Homerton Road and before the bridge take the path down to the canal towpath. On your left is ⑮ **Lee Valley Park Wick Community Woodland** – a pleasant triangle of land that is worth a look around and a possible stopping point for an inner city picnic. The woodland also offers an alternative tree lined path that runs parallel to the canal.

Lee Valley & Olympic Park Walk

Whether you use the towpath or walk through the woods, the two paths converge at the concrete bridge which you pass under with the busy Eastway dual carriageway rumbling overhead. In the distance is the stadium built for the 2012 Olympic Games. The Olympic site covers some 560 acres and transformed a mixed industrial site that was previously famous for its enormous car boot sale on the site of an abandoned dog track, and the old Eastway Cycle Circuit which stood on the site of the Lee Valley Velopark.

Follow the map until you reach another bridge and after passing under it take the steps up onto Whitepost Lane. Standing on the ⑯ **bridge** crossing over the canal, you are on the boundary of two very different visions of the same area. Walk over the bridge – you are now in Hackney Wick.

This area became industrialised in the Victorian era but declined in the mid 20th century; it has recently experienced a rejuvenation thanks in part to the Olympic effect and its location as home to many East London artists. This transformation is well demonstrated in ⑰ **Silo Building**. Once an old print works, it now houses the Crate Brewery which makes its own beers and stone baked pizzas and is an excellent place to stop for a bite to eat. This area is explored in more detail in the Bethnal Green to Hackney Wick Walk, see p.336-367.

Return across the bridge and follow the map down the hill. Take the first left – Clarnico Lane – which brings you up to the same raised level as the Olympic Park.

18 Queen Elizabeth Olympic Park

Lee Valley & Olympic Park Walk

You are now entering ⑱ **Queen Elizabeth Olympic Park** – the largest new urban park in the capital since the Victorian era. After temporary closure for post-Games redevelopment much of the park and it's facilities are now open to the public.

⑲ **The Copper Box Arena**, one of the Olympic venues and now a leisure centre and home to the London Lions basketball team will be to your left. There is a massive mirrored word RUN in front of the complex, but as you have now walked around five miles you may wish to ignore the suggestion.

From here you can cross Waterden Road and follow the broad pedestrian avenue which lead to the ⑳ **Tumbling Bay Playground** and ㉑ **Timber Lodge Café**. The surrounding ㉒ **north parklands** have wonderful landscaped wild flower beds and a series of ponds which are fed from the River Lea. Visitors can now explore the Lee Valley VeloPark which includes the Velodrome, road cycle circuit, BMX track and 8km of mountain bike trails.

The now established ㉓ **south parklands** was landscaped by James Corner Field Operations the designer of the High Line in New York. Visitors can explore the Aquatics Centre and ascend the ArcelorMittal Orbit – the UK's tallest sculpture designed by Sir Anish Kapoor and Cecil Balmond.

The modernity of the landscaped Olympic Park is a fitting place to finish this walk. From here follow signs to Stratford International and underground stations. ●

VISIT...

Markfield Beam Engine & Museum (see p.374)
Markfield Rd, N15 4RB
www.mbeam.org

Olympic Park
Copper Box Arena, The Orbit, Aquatics Cntr, Velopark, E20 2ST
www.queenelizabetholympicpark.co.uk

Waterworks Nature Reserve & Middlesex Filter Beds
Lammas Road, E10 7NU
www.visitleevalley.org.uk

EAT, DRINK...

Crate Brewery & Pizza (see p.380)
Silo Building,
Queen's Yard, E9 5EN
www.cratebrewery.com

Lea Rowing Club Café (see p.375)
The Boathouse, Spring Hill, E5 9BL
www.learc.org.uk

Springfield Park & Café (see p.375)
E5 9BL
www.springfieldparkcafe.co.uk

Timber Lodge Café (see p.382)
Timber Lodge,
Queen Elizabeth Olympic Park,
E20 1DY

North parklands

Index

A
Achilles 32
Adams, Douglas 92
Alexander Fleming Museum 127
Algha Spectacle Works 339, 364
Almeida 62
Angel Studios 62
Angerstein, John Julius 271
Anne of Denmark 248, 250
Antelope public house 15
Antonioni, Michelangelo 272
Archbishops House & Cathedral House 194, 202
Arlington Square 68
Arnold, Matthew 7
Ashkenazi Jewish cemetery 293, 313
Astey's Row Rock Gardens 64
Attlee, Clement 293, 317, 318

B
Bacon, Sir Francis 65, 81, 84
Bailey, David 311
Bainbridge, Beryl 92
Baldwin, Stanley 7, 22
Barnardo, Dr 293, 321, 324
Barnard Park 53, 54, 55
Barnett, Samuel Augustus 306
Barry, Sir Charles 59
Bazalgette, Joseph 132, 339, 363
Bazoft, Farzad 92
Beatles 16, 19, 27, 150, 155
Bedford House 131, 144, 147
Bell, Vanessa 64
Berners, de 53, 64
Besant, Annie 332
Betahayim Nuevo cemetery 293, 316

Betahayim Velho cemetery 293, 311
Bethnal Green Memorial 338, 341
Betjeman, Sir John 74, 80, 82, 87
Bevan, Aneurin 42
Bevin, Ernest 50
Bevin Court 37, 49, 50, 51
Blair, Tony 55, 63, 117
Blind Beggar 292, 297, 299, 335, 340
Boleyn, Anne 240, 248
Bolivar, Simon 7, 27
Bonner, Edmund 346
Boogaloo pub 77
Booth, William 48, 292, 299
Boothby, Lord 7, 22
Bow Bells 94, 293, 330, 335
Bowie, David 163, 191
Braganza, Catherine of 137
Branson, Richard 101, 118, 120, 124
Brick Lane Music Hall 265, 282, 283, 289
Brixton Village 163, 185, 187, 191
Brockwell Hall 162, 177, 178, 179, 180, 191
Brockwell Lido 162, 179
Brockwell Park 5, 161, 162, 163, 164, 177, 179, 181, 191
Brown, Gordon 63
Browning, Robert 103
Brunel, Isambard Kingdom 127
Bryant & May 293, 300, 332, 333, 335, 363
Budd, Henry 162, 170
Burdett-Coutts 88, 91, 339, 355
Burgess, Guy 7, 19
Buzzcocks, The 61
Byron, Lord 86, 103, 235

C
Cabmen's Shelter 100
Calligrapher Edward Johnston 131
Canonbury Square 64, 71

Index

Canonbury Tower 65
Captain James Cook 238, 292, 302
Carlyle, Thomas 84
Carnegie, Andrew 228
Cato Street Conspiracy 98, 112
Chamberlain, Neville 7, 22
Chambers, Ephraim 65
Champion, Harry 41
Chapel Market 37, 52, 71
Charlie Chaplin 1, 194, 206, 211, 212, 213, 218, 304
Charles I 94
Charles II 135, 137, 144, 146, 238, 248
Charles Rowan House 45
Charrington, Frederick 292, 301, 302, 308, 309, 312, 321, 323
Chaucer, Geoffrey 24, 219
Chiswick House 131, 144, 148, 149, 150, 159
Cholmeley, Sir Richard 79
Chopin, Frederic 24
Church House 82, 83
Churchil, Lord Randolph 98, 119
Church of St Alfege 224, 257
Church of St John the Evangelist 37, 71
Church of St Peter 7, 22
Cinema Museum 194, 211, 221
Clash, The 61, 104, 110, 172, 189, 357
Cloudesley, Richard 59
Coade, Eleanor 110
Coborn, Charles 293, 324
Coleridge, Samuel Taylor 74, 81-86
Colthurst, Edmund 43
Columbus, Christopher 7, 27
Cons, Emma 200, 201
Copperfield, David 78, 82, 85
Corbusier, Le 78
Corpus Christi
 Catholic Church 162, 172

Coutts, Thomas 88, 91, 355
Coward, Noel 7, 14, 16
Cromwell, Oliver 146, 153, 154, 311
Cromwell Carpenter, Richard 57
Crosfield, Sir Arthur 87
Cruft, Charles 92
Cruikshank, George 37, 49, 50, 343
Thomas Cubitt 9, 13, 19, 21, 24, 26
Nicholas Culpeper 53
Thomas Cundy 13, 19
Cutty Sark 224, 246, 254, 255, 256, 261

D

Dalton, Percy 339, 363
Day-Lewis, Daniel 224, 242, 258
Darbishire, Henry Astley 66, 88, 91, 355
Dead Comics Society 77
Defoe, Daniel 253
Denman, Alice 338, 344
Dickens, Charles 38, 50, 74, 78, 79, 80, 85, 88, 91, 94 217, 221, 235, 243, 246, 331
Dissolution of the Monasteries 40
Doherty, Pete 77
Donne, John 106
Doyle, Arthur Conan 108
Drapers Arms 57, 71
Duke of Wellington 7, 33, 88
Duke of Wellington pub 15, 32
Duncan, Admiral 71

E

Edward VI 248
Edward VII 149, 292, 295, 302, 306
Electric Cinema 37, 60, 66

385

Index

Elephant and Castle 195, 209, 211, 212, 213, 214
Eliot, George 92
Eliot, TS 80
Elizabeth I 79, 84, 94, 226, 240, 248, 348
English National Opera 41
Epstein, Brian 7, 27
Estorick Collection 37, 65, 71

F

Fan Museum 224, 258
Faraday, Michael 92, 209, 214, 215
Faraday Memorial 195, 214, 215
Fields, Gracie 37, 61
Filthy MacNasty's 37, 47
Finsbury Health Centre 42, 78
Flamsteed, John 236
Flamsteed House 224, 236
Flask, The 85, 86, 95
Fleming, Sir Alexander 105, 126, 127
Fleming, Ian 14, 216
Fleming Court 98, 105
Foot, Paul 92
Fuller's Griffin Brewery 131, 143
Furnivall, Frederick James 134

G

Gainsborough Studios 68
Garrud, Edith Margaret 37, 56
Garvey, Marcus 162, 182
Gatehouse public house 80, 95
Gaunt, John of 24
General Wolfe 224, 232, 235, 240, 258
George II 13, 232, 250
George III 13, 157, 203, 278
Gibson, Thomas Milner 59
Gill, Eric 315
Gillman 81, 82, 84, 86
Ginsberg, Allen 19, 47

Gladstone, William 246, 293, 335
Globe Town 309
Goldfinger, Erno 216
Gormley, Antony 269
Gort, Field Marshal Viscount 7, 27
Grand Union Canal 70, 97, 101, 102, 318, 356, 365
Granita 62
Grant, Duncan 64
Grant, Eddy 189
Great Fire 8
Greenwich Foot Tunnel 224, 256
Greenwich Hospital 241, 248, 249, 250, 252, 253
Greenwich Market 224, 256, 261
Greenwich Palace 227, 246, 248
Greenwich Park 224, 230, 232, 235, 242, 250, 261
Greenwich Peninsula Ecology Park 269
Grenadier public house 4, 30, 31, 34
Grimaldi, Joseph 40
Grossmith, Weedon 65
Grosvenor family 8, 14, 15, 16, 24, 23, 28
Grosvenor, Sir Robert 7, 28
Guillermin, John 157
Gwyn, Nell 94, 135

H

Hackney Jewish Cemetery 339, 354
Halley, Edmund 236, 289
Halliwell, Kenneth 70
Hammersmith Terrace 131, 140, 159
Harrison, George 19
Harrison, John 238, 242
Hawksmoor, Nicholas 249, 252, 258

Index

Hazlitt, William 84
Hendrix, Jimi 116, 231
Henry V 221, 227
Henry VI 227
Henry VII 68, 227, 248
Henry VIII 40, 65, 68, 107, 217, 235, 240, 248, 258, 275, 278, 348
Henry Wood Hall 195, 217
H Forman & Sons 339, 365, 367
Highgate Cemetery 74, 91, 92, 95
Highgate Literary & Scientific Institution 74, 82, 95
Highgate School 79
Highgate West Cemetery 78
Hitchcock 68, 173
Hitler, Adolf 76
Hogarth, William 86, 106, 131, 146, 147
Hogarth House 131, 144, 147, 149, 159
Holford Gardens 49
Holly Lodge Estate 88, 91
Holly Village 88, 89, 91
Holmes, Andy 131, 137
Holmes, Sherlock 92
Holy Trinity Church 37, 59, 217
Houndsditch Murders 296
Houseman, AE 74, 79

I

Imperial War Museum 194, 203, 204, 221
IRA 24, 29, 133, 176
Iron Duke 15, 33

J

Jack the Ripper 144, 177, 212, 294, 295, 325, 331
James I 43, 85, 235, 248, 250, 251
James II 12, 248
Johnston, Edward 131, 141

Jones, Claudia 92
Jones, Inigo 149, 250, 251
Jonson, Ben 85

K

Kapoor, Anish 360
Kashket & Partners 99, 121, 127
Kelmscott House 131, 136, 137, 159
Kew Bridge 131, 132, 153, 156, 158, 159
Kew Bridge Steam Museum 131, 158, 159
Kew Railway Bridge 131, 154
King George III 203
King George IV 234
King Henry IV 227
King's Head pub 62
King's Head Theatre 71
Krays, The 22, 297, 304, 333

L

Lamb, Charles 84
Langtry, Lillie 7, 30
Lansbury, George 293, 326, 330
Lansbury, Minnie 328
Lauderdale House 74, 94, 95
Lawns, The 84
Lee Valley 5, 369, 370, 371, 372, 374, 377, 379
Leigh, Vivien 7, 22
Lenin, Vladimir 37, 48
Lennon, John 98, 116, 118, 364
Little Angel Theatre 37, 63, 71
Little Venice 97-98, 102-104, 127
Litvinenko, Alexander 92
Lloyd, Marie 41
Lloyd Webber, Andrew 23
Loach, Ken 67
London, Jack 321
London County Council 41, 178, 244, 272, 274, 313
London Zoo 42, 78, 127

387

Index

Lord, Thomas 54
Lord Napier 339, 366
Loutherbourg, Philip James de 131, 146
Lubetkin, Berthold 41, 42, 49, 78, 349
Lord Lucan 21

M

Macartney House 224, 232, 234
MacGowan, Shane 47, 77
Macmillan, Harold 7, 19
Major, John 167, 171, 183
Malplaquet House 292, 309
Mann Crossman & Paulin's Albion Brewery 296
Marquess of Westminster 9, 14, 28, 30
Marshalsea Prison 195, 220-221, 348
Marx, Karl 86, 92, 301, 342
Maryon Park 264, 265, 272, 274
McCartney, Paul 28, 116
McLaren, Malcolm 92
Mellon, Harriot 88
Mendoza, Daniel 293, 318, 338, 342, 343
Merrick, Joseph 295
Metropolitan Water Board 37, 44
Metternich, Prince 7, 22
Mile End Park 293, 319, 320, 321
Miliband, Ralph 92
Mill, John Stuart 84
Millennium Dome 236, 266, 269
Millennium Mills 265, 285
Moore, Roger 23, 304
Moreton House 74, 82, 86
Morley College 200, 201, 202
Morris, William 135, 136, 141, 301, 342
Mosley, Oswald 14
Moss, Kate 77, 86

Mountbatten, Earl 7, 29
Mozart, Wolfgang Amadeus 7, 11, 12, 13
Mullins, Dougie 224, 229
Myddelton, Sir Hugh 43, 44, 45, 60
Mylne, William Chadwell 44, 45, 47, 48

N

Nag's Head public house 30
Narrow Boat public house 70, 71
National Maritime Museum 121, 224, 249, 254, 261
Nelson, Lord 122, 252
Newlands, J.A.R. 194, 206
New River 43, 44, 45, 48, 52, 60, 63, 64, 65, 71
Nicolson, Harold 7, 13

O

Old Hall, The 84
Old Royal Naval College 222, 246, 248, 253, 261
Oliver's Island 131, 154, 155
Olympic Stadium 339, 360, 365, 380
Orange public house 13
Orton, Joe 70
Orwell, George 64, 259

P

Packington, Dame Ann 68
Paddington Basin 70, 99, 101, 102, 103, 104, 124, 125, 126
Painted Hall 224, 252, 261
Pankhurst, Emmeline 56
Pankhurst, Sylvia 329
Pantechnicon building 29
Peabody, George 7, 11, 22, 37, 66, 91
Peabody Trust 11, 23, 66

Index

Peace Garden 194, 205
Pennethorne, James 351
Penton, Henry 52
Percy Dalton 339, 363
People's Palace 314, 316
Pepys, Samuel 201, 232
Pink Floyd 1, 67, 68
Plumber's Arms 19, 33
Pogues, The 47, 77
Poplar Town Hall 293, 330
Priestley, JB 86
Prime meridian 239
Primrose, Archibald 41
Prince Albert 115, 348
Princess Caroline 224, 234
Princess Christian 115
Princess Margaret 42, 304
Pugin, Augustus 194, 202-203

Q

Queen Mary 250, 252, 312, 313, 314, 315, 318, 344
Queen's House 224, 248, 250, 251, 261
Queens Wood Café 95
Queen Victoria 14, 26, 87, 88, 115, 218, 280, 314, 348

R

Raleigh, Walter 248
Ranger's House 224, 232, 233, 235, 261
Ravilious, Eric 131, 138
Richard II 24, 309
Richardson, Sir Ralph 92
Richmond Crescent 55, 67
Ringo Starr 80, 116
Ritzy Cinema 162, 167
Rock Against Racism 357
Rosebery, 5th Earl of 41

Rossetti, Christina 91
Rossetti, Dante Gabriel 84, 91, 136
Rothschild, Baron Nathaniel 295
Rothschild 295, 306
Roupell, John 199
Rowan, Sir Charles 45
Royal London Hospital 292, 294
Royal Observatory 224, 235, 236, 238, 240, 244, 261
Royal Opera House 41
Royal Victoria Dock 265, 286, 287, 288
Russell, Lord John 7, 22

S

Sackville-West, Vita 7, 13
Sadler, Thomas 40
Sadler's Wells Theatre 37, 39, 40, 41, 71
St Michael's church 85
Salter, Dr Alfred 224, 260
Sargant, Dr William 196
Sayers, Tom 92
Screen on the Green cinema 61
Sellers Peter 74, 77
Sex Pistols 61
Shaftesbury, Lord 100
Shakespeare 41, 82, 200, 203, 209, 213, 248
Shelley, Mary 7, 19
Siddons, Sarah 98, 106
Siege of Sidney Street 296
Silver, Samuel Winkworth 280
Smirke, Sir Robert 114
Smithfield Market 80
Dr John Snow 354
Lord Snowdon 304
Southwyck House 163, 184
Spa Green Estate 37, 41, 45, 78
Springer, Jerry 77
SS Robin 265, 288

389

Index

St Andrew's Church 56
St Andrew's Church (Islington) 37, 56
St Clements's Hospital 293, 324
St David's Welsh church 98, 105
Stepney Jewish School 292, 306
Stern, Albert Gerald 312
Stern, Herbert 316
St George's Catholic Cathedral 194, 203
St George the Martyr 195, 219
St James's Church 67
St James's Church (Islington) 37, 67
St John's Church 99, 124, 338, 342
St John the Evangelist Church (islington) 71
St John The Evangelist Church 194, 197, 198
St Katherine's Dock 26, 300
St Mark's Church 45, 46, 47
St Mary's Bourne Street 10
St Mary's Church (Paddington) 37, 62, 98, 105, 293, 334
St Mary's Hospital 99, 106, 126, 127
St Mary's (Islington) 39, 62, 63
St Matthew's 170
St Matthew's Church 162
St Michael's Church 7, 19
St Michael's church (Highgate) 74, 85
St Nicholas Chiswick 131, 142, 145
St Paul's Church 131, 150
Strummer, Joe 98, 110
Suffrage 56

T

Tate, Henry 162, 168, 281
Tate & Lyle 168, 264, 265, 272, 274, 281, 282
Tempest, Sir Henry 88

Thackeray, William Makepeace 24, 99, 121, 144
Thames Barrier 153, 246, 264, 265, 271, 272, 273, 285, 289
Thames Barrier Park 265, 285, 289
Thatcher, Margaret 7, 19
Thomas, Dylan 15, 157
Thomson, James 135
Thornhill 55, 56
Thornhill Square 55
Thornycroft, John Isaac 145
Tibberton Baths 66
Tierney Clarke 132
Tottenham Lock 371, 372
Tower Hamlets Cemetery 293, 325, 327, 335
Tredegar Square 293, 322, 323
Trinity Almshouses 292, 300, 301
Trinity Church Square 195, 217
Trinity Hospital 224, 245
Truman's Brewery 274
Turpin, Dick 86, 147
Tyburn Convent 99, 120
Tyburn gallows 98, 119

V

Vanbrugh, John 224, 241, 249
Vanbrugh Castle 224, 241
Victoria Cross 27
Victoria Park 178, 319, 336, 338, 339, 341, 345, 349, 351, 353, 354, 355, 356, 357, 367
Vigar-Harris, Henry 60, 61

W

Walker, Sir Emery 131, 141
Wall, Julian 163, 183
Walpole, Robert 144
Walpole House 131, 144, 146
Walthamstow Marshes 371, 375, 377

Waterloo Station 194, 196
Waterlow Park 74, 92, 93, 95
Waugh, Benjamin 259
Waugh, Evelyn 64
Wellington Duke of 15, 32, 33, 88
Wernher Collection 232
West Library 56
Westminster, Duke of 8, 14, 28
Westway 98, 104, 105
White Building 366, 380
White Conduit Club 54
Whiteread, Rachel 320
Whittington, Dick 94
Whittington Stone 74, 94
Wilberforce, William 33
Wilkes, John 203
William the Conqueror 8, 120
Wilton Arms 30, 33
Wilton Arms public house 30
Windrush Square 162, 164, 165, 167, 168, 170
Witanhurst 74, 86
Woolwich Foot Tunnel 265, 278
Woolwich Free Ferry 265, 276, 279
Wordsworth, William 84
World War I 27, 106, 182, 230, 278, 312, 316, 345
World War II 14, 26, 27, 50, 76, 77, 79, 105, 120, 135, 138, 150, 155, 167, 168, 170, 231, 240, 258, 260, 306, 326, 328, 356, 360
Worth, Adam 92
Wren, Christopher 238, 241, 248, 250, 251, 252, 258, 300

Y

York Hall 338, 346, 347
Young V&A 338, 344, 345, 367

Z

Zachary House 131, 157, 158
Zoffany, Johann 157

About us:

Based in London, Metro is a small independent publishing company with a reputation for producing well-researched and beautifully-designed guides.

London's Hidden Walks Series

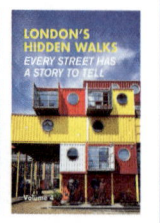

A wonderful way to explore this sometimes secretive city." Robert Elms, BBC London 94.9FM

To find out more about Metro and order our guides, take a look at our website:

www.metropublications.com

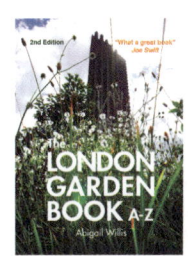

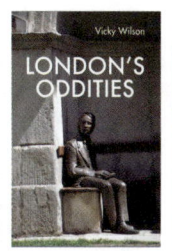

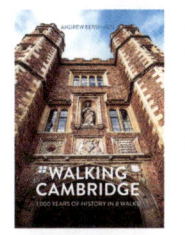

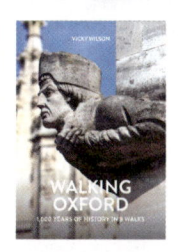

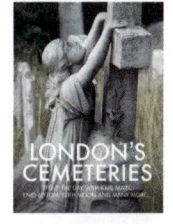

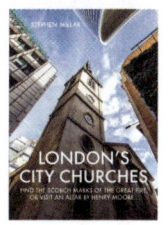

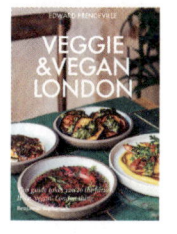

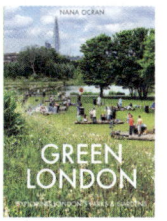

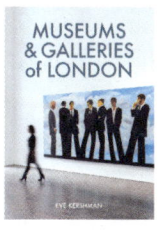

- The London Garden Book A–Z (2nd Edition) — Abigail Willis
- London's Oddities — Vicky Wilson
- London Architecture — Suzanne Butler
- Walking Cambridge — Andrew Kershman
- Walking Brighton & Hove — Andrew Kershman
- Walking Oxford — Vicky Wilson
- London's Cemeteries
- London's City Churches — Stephen Millar
- Veggie & Vegan London — Edward Prendeville
- London's Houses: From workhouse to royal palace, come in, close the door and step back in time
- Green London — Nana Ocran
- Museums & Galleries of London — Eve Kershman